D0529325

Confronting the Weakest Link

Aiding Political Parties in New Democracies

THOMAS CAROTHERS

Confronting the
Weakest Link

Other books by the Democracy and Rule of Law Project
of the Carnegie Endowment for International Peace

Promoting the Rule of Law Abroad: The Problem of Knowledge
Thomas Carothers

Uncharted Journey: Democracy Promotion in the Middle East
Thomas Carothers and Marina Ottaway, Editors

Critical Mission: Essays on Democracy Promotion
Thomas Carothers

Aiding Democracy Abroad: The Learning Curve
Thomas Carothers

Democracy Challenged: The Rise of Semi-Authoritarianism
Marina Ottaway

Open Networks, Closed Regimes: The Impact of the Internet
on Authoritarian Rule
Shanthi Kalathil and Taylor C. Boas

Funding Virtue: Civil Society Aid and Democracy Promotion
Marina Ottaway and Thomas Carothers, Editors

The Third Force: The Rise of Transnational Civil Society
Ann M. Florini, Editor

Assessing Democracy Assistance: The Case of Romania
Thomas Carothers

To read excerpts and to find more information on these and other publications
from the Carnegie Endowment, visit **www.CarnegieEndowment.org/ pubs.**

Confronting the Weakest Link

AIDING POLITICAL PARTIES IN NEW DEMOCRACIES

THOMAS CAROTHERS

CARNEGIE ENDOWMENT FOR INTERNATIONAL PEACE

WASHINGTON, D.C.

© 2006 Carnegie Endowment for International Peace. All rights reserved.

No part of this publication may be reproduced or transmitted in any form or by any means without permission in writing from the Carnegie Endowment.

Carnegie Endowment for International Peace
1779 Massachusetts Avenue, N.W., Washington, D.C. 20036
202-483-7600, Fax 202-483-1840
www.CarnegieEndowment.org

The Carnegie Endowment for International Peace normally does not take institutional positions on public policy issues; the views and recommendations presented in this publication do not necessarily represent the views of the Carnegie Endowment, its officers, staff, or trustees.

To order, contact:
Hopkins Fulfillment Service
P.O. Box 50370, Baltimore, MD 21211-4370
1-800-537-5487 or 1-410-516-6956
Fax 1-410-516-6998

Library of Congress Cataloging-in-Publication data
    Carothers, Thomas, 1956-
    Confronting the weakest link : aiding political parties in new democracies / Thomas Carothers.
      p. cm.
    Published in the Democracy and Rule of Law Program of the Carnegie Endowment for International Peace.
    Includes bibliographical references and index.
    ISBN-13: 978-0-87003-225-7
    ISBN-13: 978-0-87003-224-0
    1. Political parties--Developing countries. 2. Democratization--Developing countries. 3. Political corruption--Developing countries. 4. Developing countries--Politics and government. I. Title.

    JF60.C38 2006
    324.209172'4--dc22   2006025891

11 10 09 08 07 06   1 2 3 4 5   1st Printing 2006

Composition by Oakland Street Publishing
Printed by United Book Press

Contents

Foreword

Democracy faces daunting challenges everywhere that it is being pursued, but especially in the approximately 100 countries that have made up democracy's "Third Wave." Ethnic, religious, and other sectarian conflicts, illiberal leaders elected by citizenries angry about corruption and insecurity, resurgent authoritarian structures that were never fully dismantled in abrupt transitions, windfall oil and gas revenues emboldening strongmen leaders—the threats to democracy only seem to grow. Diverse though it is, the global landscape of attempted democratization is marked by a ubiquitous institutional deficiency: troubled political parties that command scant respect from their citizens due to the strong perception that they are corrupt, self-interested, unprincipled, ideologically incoherent, and focused only on near-term electoral goals. Given that political parties are supposed to play key functions in democracy, their debilitated state in most new democracies is a sign of serious trouble. Some major questions stand out in this regard. Above all, why are political parties so problematic in countries attempting democratization and why are their problems so strikingly similar in such different regional and national contexts?

The worrisome state of political parties around the world has not escaped the attention of the international democracy promotion community. An ever-growing number of Western party foundations and institutes as well as multilateral organizations are actively engaged in trying to help strengthen and reform parties around the world. Although these efforts date back for decades and are carried out in the open, they have until now been the subject of remarkably little study. As a result, major questions abound here as well. For example, does aid for political parties really help and what is being learned about how to make it more effective?

In this pathbreaking book, Thomas Carothers, director of the Carnegie Endowment's remarkably successful Democracy and Rule of Law Project, and vice president for international politics and governance, answers these and other fundamental questions both about the state of political parties in the world and the effectiveness of international aid for parties. Artfully combining extensive field research in aid-receiving countries with numerous interviews in donor capitals and serious study of the scholarly literature on comparative political party development, Carothers paints a nuanced but clear portrait of this complex landscape. He identifies the key causal factors underlying the common shortcomings of parties in new democracies and shows how the best intentions of aid providers are often frustrated in the face of hard-to-change structural conditions. Although his analysis is cautionary, he identifies areas of innovation in party aid and argues that a second, strengthened generation of party aid is potentially emerging in the wake of a first, weaker one.

Confronting the Weakest Link is a vital contribution to the extraordinary body of work on democracy promotion that Carothers has produced in the past fifteen years, writings that have effectively defined a field of study where none existed before. As with all of his work, this book will spark heated debates, provoke policy actors to ask basic questions about what they do, and prompt further studies that take up the many leads he opens up. In short this book will do precisely what first-rate policy analysis should do. It represents the essence of what the Carnegie Endowment seeks to offer the international policy community through its work in the United States and, increasingly, around the world.

Jessica T. Mathews
President
Carnegie Endowment for International Peace

Acknowledgments

I have accumulated many debts of gratitude in researching and writing this book. First and foremost I benefited enormously from the willingness of hundreds of people in my case study countries as well as in various Western capitals—politicians, party activists, party aid representatives, diplomats, political analysts, scholars, journalists, and others—to take time out of their busy schedules to talk with me and answer my endless questions about political parties and political party assistance. I received help with the logistical arrangements for my field research from many people but especially from the following: César Micheo and Eduardo Nuñez in Guatemala; Stephanie Flynn, Tom Garrett, Mareska Mantik, Paul Rowland, and Benny Subianto in Indonesia; Sarah Johnson, Gérard Latulippe, and Kenza Aquertit Mzibri in Morocco; Sharon Carter and Jan Nico van Overbeeke in Mozambique; Cristian Ghinea and Alina Mungiu-Pippidi in Romania; and Lilia Shevtsova in Russia.

Many people within organizations working on party aid were very helpful in sharing information about their organization's activities. I cannot thank them all here but I wish especially to thank Shari Bryan, Lorne Craner, Brian Dean, Ivan Doherty, David French, Anna-Klara Granstrand, Steven Griner, Roger Hällhag, Erik Jennische, Laura Jewett, Nelson Ledsky, Linda Maguire, Peter Manikas, Maryam Montague, Alvaro Pinto, Isabella Rozenbawn, Kristen Sample, Helene Schroyen, Chris Sands, David Timberman, Jan Tuit, Kenneth Wollack, Jeroen de Zeeuw, and Daniel Zovatto.

Christopher Sabatini, Vicky Randall, and George Perkovich read all or parts of a draft of the book and gave me highly useful comments. Former Carnegie Junior Fellows Hania Kronfol, Jeffrey Krutz, Bethany Lacina, Meredith Riley, and Geoffrey Swenson all provided outstanding research assistance and good company at different stages of the project. Patricia Mallan did heroic, indispensable work helping prepare the manuscript and taking care of countless other administrative matters. Past and present members of Carnegie's publications department, Phyllis Jask, Emily Hancock, Carrie Mullen, and Ilonka Oszvald, were a pleasure to work with and did a wonderful job bringing the book to life. Carnegie's irreplaceable librarians Kathleen Higgs and Chris Henley were always there to supply me the necessary books, articles, and other materials.

Early financial support from the Swedish International Development Cooperation Agency was invaluable to getting the research under way. I am deeply indebted to Helena Bjuremalm of that organization for her interest and backing. The Netherlands Institute for Multiparty Democracy, the Ford Foundation, and the John D. and Catherine T. MacArthur Foundation also provided valuable financial support. The views and opinions contained in this book are of course entirely my own; none of the funding organizations is in any way responsible for or necessarily in agreement with them.

The Carnegie Endowment continues to be an ideal home for my work on democracy promotion. I am deeply grateful to Carnegie president Jessica Mathews and vice presidents Paul Balaran and George Perkovich for creating such a supportive, stimulating work environment. Last but certainly not least, I thank Laura Bocalandro, my wife, and Christopher and Vera Carothers, my children, for their constant love and support.

Parties and Organizations

ANC   African National Congress (South Africa)
        Alfred Mozer Foundation
APRA   Alianza Popular Revolucionaria Americana (Peru)
        Alliance of Liberties (Morocco)
        Austrian Social Democratic Party
BJP   Bharatiya Janata Party (Indian People's Party)
        Botswana Democratic Party
        British Conservative Party
        British Labour Party
        Centrist Democrat International
        Charter 77 (Czechoslovakia)
        Christian Democratic Party (Chile)
        Christian Democratic Party (El Salvador)
COPEI   Christian Democratic Party (Venezuela)
        Colorado Party (Paraguay)
        Demos (Finland)
AD   Democratic Action (Venezuela)
        Democratic Convention (Romania)
        Democratic Progressive Party (Taiwan)
PRD   Democratic Revolutionary Party (Mexico)
AWEPA   European Parliamentarians for Africa
FMLN   Farabundo Martí Liberation Front (El Salvador)
        Fidesz (Hungary)
        Freedom Party (Austria)
        Frelimo (Mozambican Liberation Front)
        French Socialist Party
        Friedrich Ebert Stiftung
        Friedrich Naumann Stiftung
        Greater Romania Party

Guatemalan Christian Democratic Party
URNG Guatemalan National Revolutionary Unity
Hanns Seidel Stiftung
Heinrich Böll Stiftung
Hungarian Democratic Forum
IFES (formerly the International Foundation for Election Systems)
Indian National Congress
Inkatha Party (South Africa)
PRI Institutional Revolutionary Party (Mexico)
IDB Inter-American Development Bank
IDU International Democrat Union
IRI International Republican Institute (United States)
PJD Justice and Development Party (Morocco)
Konrad Adenauer Stiftung
KMT Kuomintang (Taiwan)
Lavalas (Haiti)
Liberal Democratic Party (Russia)
Liberal International
MMD Movement for Multiparty Democracy (Zambia)
PAN National Action Party (Mexico)
PAN National Advancement Party (Guatemala)
NDI National Democratic Institute for International Affairs (United States)
National Democratic Party (Egypt)
National Front (France)
National Peasant Party (Romania)
ARENA National Republican Alliance (El Salvador)
National Salvation Front (Romania)
NED National Endowment for Democracy (United States)
NIMD Netherlands Institute for Multiparty Democracy
Norwegian Centre for Democracy Support
Olof Palme International Center
OAS Organization of American States
OECD Organization for Economic Cooperation and Development
OSCE Organization for Security and Co-operation in Europe
Justicialist (Peronist) Party (Argentina)
Portuguese Socialist Party
Radical Civic Union (Argentina)
Renamo (Mozambique)
CCM Revolutionary Party of Tanzania
Russia's Choice
Sandinista National Liberation Front (Nicaragua)
PSD Social Democratic Party (Romania)
Socialist International
USFP Socialist Union of Populist Forces (Morocco)
Solidarity (Poland)
SWAPO South-West African People's Organisation (Namibia)
SIDA Swedish International Development Cooperation Agency

	Social Democratic Labor Party (Sweden)
UDF	United Democratic Forces (Bulgaria)
SPS	Union of Right Forces (Russia)
UNDP	United Nations Development Programme
	Unity (Russia)
WFD	Westminster Foundation for Democracy
	Workers' Party (Brazil)
	Yabloko (Russia)

PART ONE

Introduction

CHAPTER ONE

The Standard Lament

In the global democratic trend that flourished in the last quarter of the twentieth century, approximately one hundred countries in the developing world and the former Soviet bloc experienced at least some movement away from authoritarian or totalitarian rule toward political openness. The outcomes of many of these attempted democratic transitions are still very much in question. It is unfortunately evident that many of the heady hopes for a better political future that soared around the world in the peak years of what Samuel Huntington labeled democracy's "Third Wave" will be disappointed.[1] Nevertheless the world has experienced a tremendous increase in the amount of political pluralism and competition, including a remarkable growth in the number and seriousness of multiparty elections.

With those changes has come an enormous surge in the number and range of political parties in many parts of the developing and postcommunist worlds. Parties mushroomed when elections were first held after the fall of authoritarian regimes, sometimes numbering more than a hundred. Usually the very high number of parties fell as successive elections were held, but parties have remained numerous and active in most Third Wave societies, or what I call new or struggling democracies. Throughout these countries, political activists have devoted enormous amounts of time and energy during the past few decades to building political parties. Hundreds of millions of citizens in these countries have familiarized themselves with the often bewilderingly dense new array of parties, making choices among them, and sometimes investing hope in them.

Although political parties are becoming much more numerous and active in the developing and postcommunist worlds, this is by no means their golden age. In fact this period of remarkable growth in political parties around the world has an enormous, dark underside: Throughout the developing and postcommunist worlds, political parties are held in extremely low regard; in most of these countries they are the least respected or trusted of any public institution.[2]

In my research on democratization and democracy promotion in recent years I have encountered this low regard for political parties firsthand everywhere I go. I have been very struck not only by the ubiquity and intensity of the negative views that people hold vis-à-vis their political parties but also by the similarity of these views across drastically different political contexts. When one asks people almost anywhere in Asia, Central and Eastern Europe, East and Southeast Asia, Latin America, the Middle East, South Asia, the former Soviet Union, and sub-Saharan Africa about their political parties, one is almost always answered with harsh statements of disgust and disrespect. People come forward with scathing criticisms about parties that sound almost uncannily similar wherever one is. The main elements of this critique, which upon repeated hearing I have come to call "the standard lament" about parties, are the following:

- Parties are corrupt, self-interested organizations dominated by power-hungry elites who only pursue their own interests or those of their rich financial backers, not those of ordinary citizens.
- Parties do not stand for anything; there are no real differences among them. Their ideologies are symbolic at best and their platforms vague or insubstantial.
- Parties waste too much time and energy squabbling with each other over petty issues for the sake of meaningless political advantages rather than trying to solve the country's problems in a constructive, cooperative way.
- Parties only become active at election time when they come looking for your vote; the rest of the time you never hear from them.
- Parties are ill-prepared for governing the country and do a bad job of it when they do manage to take power or gain places in the national legislature.

In different countries one sometimes hears additional points of indictment about their parties, emphasizing issues that may be particular to that political scene, such as a party leader known for especially flagrant misbehavior, collusion between the opposition and the ruling party, or cheating by the ruling party in the last election. The standard lament is a common core narrative in almost all new or struggling democracies, but not necessarily always the full story of the public's unhappiness with parties.

Are Parties Really So Troubled?

Confronted with the rising tide of discontent about political parties in new and struggling democracies, some political observers are unalarmed. It is natural for citizens in a democracy to be disgruntled with their parties, they assert, and parties in established democracies have themselves been suffering an erosion of respect and loyalty over the past several decades. In fact, they argue, the rabid dislike of parties in new or struggling democracies may actually be a positive sign. It shows that citizens are avoiding any blind faith in their politicians and instead expecting tangible performance from them and punishing them when they do not deliver.

Appealing though this point of view may be, it risks passing too quickly by the very real, serious problems that parties in many new or struggling democracies have. It settles too easily for a facile equivalence between the skepticism or cynicism that citizens of established democracies often feel toward their parties, and the harsh, bitter disregard for political parties that has become common in new or struggling democracies.

It appears to be true that many citizens new to the messy realities of multiparty politics have a hard time distinguishing between, on the one hand, those negative elements of politics that although regrettable are essentially inevitable, and, on the other hand, those that are signs of serious political dysfunction. For example, they are horrified that politicians competing for power turn out to be self-serving and relentlessly ambitious. They are shocked by the unprincipled, hypocritical nature of so much of the behavior and rhetoric of politicians. They are disillusioned that parties reflexively fight over every little thing, turning even trivial issues into partisan skirmishes. They are angry that money plays such an important role in political campaigns. In short, there is a distinct "welcome to democracy" quality to some of the standard lament about political parties, as citizens confront the often disappointing realities of multiparty competition.

The devastating unpopularity of political parties in so many countries grappling with democratization also appears to be partly due to citizens blaming parties for many things that are not, strictly speaking, the parties' fault, or at least are not attributable to the deficient nature of parties as organizations.

Most of these countries, for example, have chronically weak, ineffective states that deliver poor services and lack the capacity to design and implement effective policies. They often have poorly performing economies or, even if growth is achieved, high levels of inequality and persistent poverty. Citizens of these countries naturally tend to become frustrated and angry about the poor services, harsh economic conditions, and other difficult elements of their lives that are related to the weakness of the states. They tend to cast a wide net of blame against the government and "the politicians" for such problems. Political parties, being closely wrapped up with the governing powers, often are blamed as well, even though the things about parties that irritate citizens, such as their corruption or self-interestedness, are not necessarily primary causes of the country's poorly functioning economy or state. In other words, because the political parties of a country are the institutions that formally run the country, they will tend to be blamed for whatever goes wrong, no matter what the larger set of causes are for the country's ills. And given that life for many citizens of countries attempting democratization is riddled with serious hardships and aggravations, it is not surprising that political parties, as a group, are an unpopular institution.

Undoubtedly many citizens new to pluralistic politics are having trouble sorting out which of the negative features of parties and politicians are unavoidable elements of democracy and which are really signs of serious trouble. They are blaming parties for many things that are not necessarily the result of shortcomings in the parties per se. Nevertheless, it is clear that political parties in many new or struggling democracies are indeed highly problematic organizations from the point of view of democratic development.

Most are what might be called political cabals or clubs—highly personalistic, leader-centric organizations in which an assertive, ambitious, often charismatic party leader, together with a set of close followers and associates, pursues political power through elections. Such parties tend to have weak organizations with few paid staff and often only a skeletal presence outside the capital. In extreme cases they are miniscule organizations, nicknamed "briefcase parties" in some societies (or "Toyota parties" in Peru, based on the idea that all their members can fit into a Toyota), that consist of no more than a self-appointed leader and a few followers. What party organization does exist is run in a command fashion by the party leader no matter what formal management structures and procedures have been established. The parties are usually financed by small numbers of wealthy backers, sometimes including the party leaders themselves. The identities of the parties' main financial backers are usually kept secret and the party finances are controlled by the party leaders and managed in a nontransparent fashion. These parties are primarily oriented toward campaigning. They swell in size and activity during electoral periods and diminish substantially outside them. They usually have little capacity for analyzing and formulating policies and their electoral platforms are collections of generic policy positions lacking any well-defined ideological orientation.

A small number of parties in new or struggling democracies—although often the more important of the parties in any one country—are somewhat more organizationally developed than the other, more common type. In some cases these larger parties have developed a substantial organization through slow growth over a long period of time with periods in power that have allowed them to make use of patronage and state resources to build up the party. Some of the older South American parties, such as those in Argentina, Chile, Colombia, and Uruguay, are of this type, as well as some of the older parties in South and Southeast Asia. In other cases, the larger parties are successors to precedent organizations from which they have been able to inherit resources, personnel, and institutional structures. These predecessor organizations may be former ruling parties in single-party systems, as in the former communist countries and some African countries, or liberation or other armed movements, as in parts of southern Africa and Central America.

Although these parties have more substantial organizations than the very personalistic parties described previously, and have often passed through several or even many party leaders, they nevertheless also usually remain quite centralized, top-down organizations in which the party leader and those immediately around the leader wield extensive power in all matters institutional. Party financing is often more extensive than in the less organizationally developed parties but still usually dependent on a limited set of behind-the-scenes backers (and state resources if the party is in power), and is handled from the top in nontransparent ways.

These more organizationally developed parties are also highly electorally oriented. They often have a stronger relationship to a defined constituency and membership that they attempt to service and protect, usually through patronage networks. They may have a certain ideological tradition, often based on the political ideas that were most popular in the developing world in the 1950s and 1960s, such as socialism or decolonization and nationalism. Yet their ideology has typically faded over time and has little connection with the policies they actually pursue, which are largely opportunistic or pragmatic.

Obviously this initial description of parties in new or struggling democracies is extremely broad-brush and leaves out many particularities and variants, which are considered in subsequent chapters. The point for now is that very generally speaking, political parties in these countries exhibit certain consistent features. Although they can be divided into categories of less and more organizationally developed, almost all display a tendency toward leader-centrism, top-down organizational management, nontransparent and often highly personalistic financing, relentless electoralism, and ideological vagueness. In short, the standard lament that so many citizens in new or struggling democracies have about their parties does indeed have roots in the reality of their parties, even taking into account the often excessively high expectations that citizens of these countries have at the start of the attempted democratic transitions.

The systems that are made up by the troubled parties of new or struggling democracies are, not surprisingly, fraught with problems as well. In chapter 3, I consider one framework for analyzing the different types of party systems in these countries. Here I highlight two of the principal problems that their party systems tend to exhibit. First, some of the party systems are unstable and volatile. New parties rise and fall quickly. Only a small number of parties last more than a few elections and in some cases none lasts more than a generation. Parties lack defined constituencies. Voters cycle through the choices on offer, embracing sudden enthusiasms and dropping them just as quickly after the initial thrill is gone. Not being able to count on a stable base, and facing extinction if they fail to score in elections, many parties in such systems have to work increasingly hard to try to win votes. This fuels their need for money to finance their campaigns, which pushes parties to multiply certain behaviors, such as corrupt financing and selling places on the party lists to the highest bidders, that only vitiate their credibility with citizens, thereby deepening the problems of unstable bases and aggravating the boom and bust cycle. Guatemala, Peru, the Philippines, Poland, Thailand, and Venezuela are all examples of countries with party systems that have shown high levels of instability in the past fifteen years.

Second, other party systems in new or struggling democracies have the opposite problem from instability. They are systems in which one or two parties, usually parties of the latter type described above—parties with substantial party organizations but a high degree of centralization, corruption, and other problematic features—have a virtual lock on the system. New political entrants are unable to gain a place in the system. A small closed circle of elites accumulates a large amount of power and the main parties are able to resist any pressure for reform due to their predominant position. Many countries in South America, sub-Saharan Africa, and the former Soviet Union have systems of this sort. If the system stays closed while performing poorly for the majority of citizens over a sustained period, pressure on it will accumulate. If the pressure is not relieved through reforms it may lead to the rise of a strong antiparty challenger to the system, such as occurred in Venezuela in the 1990s with the rise of Hugo Chávez and Bulgaria in a milder form in the late 1990s, culminating in the coming to power in 2001 of a new political movement led by former King Simeon Saxe-Coburg-Gotha. Or the system may face sharp disjunctive change in which striving political actors or movements overwhelm the decayed or brittle established ones, as in Georgia in 2003 and Kyrgyzstan in 2005.

The Inevitability of Parties

Given the depth and pervasiveness of problems with parties, it is natural to ask whether it might not make sense just to give up on them, to look for other ways to institutionalize democratic politics. Perhaps, it can be asked, the widespread weaknesses of and unhappiness with parties is a sign of some deeper evolution in global politics away from parties altogether, one that should be embraced rather than resisted.

The idea of moving beyond political parties—simply jettisoning them with all their accumulated deficiencies—certainly holds appeal to people all around the world exasperated to the point of despair with the parties they have. The problem, however (leaving aside the fact that at least some parties in many new or struggling democracies are deeply entrenched and are not going away anytime soon), is that it is not clear what institutions or processes might replace them and fulfill the core democratic functions that parties, at least in theory, are supposed to fulfill.[3] These functions are sometimes elaborated at great length by political scientists but basically boil down to several crucial things: in a well-functioning democracy, parties represent citizens' interests before the state (the terms *interest articulation* and *aggregation* are often used on this point), engage and involve citizens in democratic participation, structure the political choices that citizens have in elections, and form the governments and take responsibility for governing.

Perhaps the most common idea about possible "postparty" democracy is that a greatly strengthened civil society could take over from parties, redefining democratic politics as a complex set of disaggregated, pluralistic interactions between highly empowered citizens and that state. The presumed virtuous nature of many civil society organizations would replace the swamplike nature of party politics.

It is difficult to envisage such a scenario actually occurring in any new or struggling democracies in the foreseeable future. It is true that in many countries civil society organizations have multiplied rapidly, thanks in no small part to donor funding. The civil society boom consists in most cases of the proliferation of a narrow range of groups, mostly advocacy and service non-governmental organizations (NGOs), that have serious limits of their own as a new form of interest representation. Many of these groups have surprisingly weak ties to the citizenry. They are self-appointed representatives of an assumed public interest, following the rather particularist agenda of a cir-cumscribed set of activists (and often their foreign funders). Even if these NGO leaders were widely and fairly representative, it is not clear how a polit-ical system could function effectively with the very disaggregated nature of such representation, in which no organizations attempt to aggregate a broader pool of interests and issues. In those societies, such as the United States, where specialized interest groups are unusually strong, democracy does not seem to be transforming into a new and better form. Instead, polit-ical analysts usually lament the paralyzing and distorting effects of hyper-trophic interest-group politics.

Visions of a civil society–based, nonparty democracy also fall short regard-ing the structuring of political choices and the organization of governance. For democracy to be meaningful, citizens must have some real choices between alternative sets of both people and policies. If parties do not exist to structure choices and run the government, some other organizations would have to fulfill that role. If the political choices presented to citizens were merely a scattering of individuals not organized in groups, it is hard to imagine how a government made up of such nonassociated individuals would function coherently. If the political choices were ordered in groups, it is hard to see how these groups would not quickly take on the characteristics of parties once they started competing for power, including the various familiar negative attributes, such as self-interest, corruption, and combative rivalries. Stated differently, if civil society organizations did become the organizing bodies for political competition and governance they would quickly lose whatever vir-tuous qualities they had once they were subjected to all the competitive pres-sures that make parties so problematic.

In short, although democracy is of course an evolving corpus of political ideas and practices that will take on new forms over time, it is difficult now to envisage a genuine democracy—with real political alternatives open to cit-izens and broad-based representation of citizens' interests—without political parties or some organizations very much like them. The fact that parties are falling so glaringly short in new or struggling democracies does not point to a path of doing without them. Although it is very hard to live with parties, if one wants to make a serious attempt at democracy it remains necessary for now to live with them.

Consequences of Party Problems

Political parties are hardly the only problematic institutions in new or struggling democracies. Most of the major political institutions in these countries, whether executive branch ministries, legislatures, judiciaries, or local governments, are beset with serious shortcomings. Nevertheless, given the crucial democratic functions that political parties are expected to play, the consequences of troubled political party development are especially harmful.

Attempting to identify these consequences is complicated by the general difficulty of sorting out causes and effects when it comes to broad political phenomena. Is widespread political apathy in a country, for example, a result of the failings of the country's political parties or one of the factors that contributes to the difficulty of building effective parties? Should the existence of entrenched, corrupt patronage networks in a state bureaucracy be understood as a result of patronage-oriented parties or an impediment to the development of parties not rooted in patronage? The political fabric of any society cannot be separated into neat piles of causes and consequences. Interactive and sometimes circular relationships exist at every level.

Probably the most obvious and possibly the most serious negative consequence of the problematic party development common to so many new or struggling democracies is the inadequate representation of citizens' interests. Leader-centric parties with weak organizations, low policy capacity, and vague ideologies are poor at articulating and aggregating the interests of citizens. They usually fail to develop close, regular ties to a defined constituency. They concentrate on serving their own immediate interests, which are often the direct interests of their leaders or of the small circle of financial backers of the party. Even those parties that have managed to develop substantial organizations and roots in a defined constituency usually fall badly short on representation because their relationship to their constituency is based on patronage ties.

Inadequate representation of interests appears as one of the central problems facing new or struggling democracies. In Latin America, for example, the much-discussed crisis of democracy that the region faces is often cast in the region precisely as a dual crisis of representation and crisis of parties. All around the world in countries that have moved away from authoritarianism, citizens are very frustrated with their governments and their frustration is rooted in the sense that the government is not responding to their needs and interests. Political analysts often describe new or struggling democracies as facing the challenges of going beyond formal or electoral democracy to substantive democracy. It is the problem of representation—establishing governments that are not merely elected by the people but actually serve the people—that lies at the core of this overall attempted passage.

Although the troubled state of political parties is clearly a central cause of the problem of representation, it is not the only one. The effective representation of citizens' interests in a democracy requires an interconnected set of sociopolitical conditions and institutions, including a citizenry capable of expressing its interests and a state capable of doing something meaningful to respond to citizens' needs. Political parties are a critical connective mechanism between citizens on the one hand and the state and government on the other, but they cannot operate in a vacuum. The atomized nature of many post-authoritarian polities—the fragmentation, low levels of trust, and weak associational life—often undermines the ability of citizens to work together to express their interests. The high levels of poverty and socioeconomic marginalization in many new or struggling democracies also work against active, empowered citizenries. At the other end of the potential representational chain, the state weakness endemic in many of these countries also contributes significantly to the problem of representation.

At least two other major negative consequences for democratization of problematic political parties are also apparent. Parties often fall badly short in the domain of political education or socialization of citizens into the democratic process. They do little to help citizens understand the how and why of democratic participation beyond voting. Their own ideological incoherence confuses rather than clarifies the choices citizens might make about possible directions for their society. Their often insalubrious involvement in money politics of one type or another distorts the nature of contacts they have with citizens and the political values they embody.

Troubled parties also do damage to democratization through poor fulfillment of their governmental function. When parties come to power or at least participate in government, they tend to import their internal pathologies into government. Party elites used to working in hierarchical, personalistic, and untransparent organizations carry those habits into the governmental roles they assume. Parties dependent on powerful, behind-the-scenes financial backers bring those unhealthy ties into the center of power. Parties that sell places on their candidate lists to wealthy political actors create members of parliament who think they need to steal sizeable amounts of money to make up for what they spent to get into power.

In short, it is clear that the state of political parties in these countries spells trouble for democratization. Major functions of political representation, political socialization, and governance are poorly fulfilled by any parties, with manifold effects throughout the political systems. A closer look at different transitions could certainly identify still other political problems that parties are creating or contributing to. As discussed later in this book, it can be hard to agree at times on what optimal political party development might look like in any one place. The basic point should be clear: The troubled state of parties in new or struggling democracies constitutes a weak link, indeed often the weakest link, in their attempted democratization.

The Aid Response

There is an international response to the troubled state of political party development in countries attempting democratization—international political party aid. A large array of Western political parties, party foundations or institutes affiliated with parties, specialized aid organizations that work closely with political parties, as well as a growing number of multilateral organizations (such as the United Nations Development Programme, the Organization of American States, and the Organization for Security and Co-operation in Europe) carry out programs to bolster political party development all around the developing and postcommunist worlds.

The first phase of international political party aid was the work that the German *Stiftungen*, or party foundations, especially the Konrad Adenauer Stiftung, the Fredrich Ebert Stiftung, and the Friedrich Naumann Stiftung, did in Southern Europe and Latin America from the 1970s through the 1980s, the early years of democracy's Third Wave. They were joined in the mid-1980s by the two U.S. party institutes, the International Republican Institute (IRI) and the National Democratic Institute for International Affairs (NDI). As democracy spread in the late 1980s and across the 1990s, many European parties and party foundations, especially from France, Great Britain, the Netherlands, Portugal, Spain, and Sweden, joined the field. Party aid began reaching widely in Africa, Central and Eastern Europe, Latin America, and the former Soviet Union. In the current decade, the growing perception that political parties are doing poorly in many new or struggling democracies has prompted several Northern European countries, including Finland, the Netherlands, Norway, and Sweden, to get more deeply involved in political party aid, as well as some multilateral organizations, including the three mentioned above.

Party aid is one part of the larger domain of democracy aid, a field that has experienced enormous growth over the past several decades. Democracy aid has come to be made up of many specialized and often somewhat separate subfields. Aid for trade unions, for example, is carried out in fairly narrowly bounded programs by Western groups affiliated with trade unions. Media assistance is also its own domain, populated by media specialists working for Western media-affiliated organizations. Party aid also constitutes one of these subfields, with its own discrete programs carried out by its own set of specialized organizations, usually tied to Western political parties. Party aid is often even more separate than many other areas of democracy assistance. Quite a few parts of the democracy promotion community are wary of direct contact with parties. They perceive them as highly problematic potential partners, both because parties are openly political organizations and often have a reputation of being corrupt. Thus working with them carries a clear risk of being accused of engaging in partisan meddling or having corrupt counterparts. Simultaneously, many party aid groups cultivate a separation from other parts of the democracy aid domain, believing that they alone have the necessary expertise to work with parties and that the inherently political nature of party work naturally sets it apart from many of the other areas.

Analysis Missing

Although party aid has been going on for decades and has reached parties in probably close to one hundred countries, remarkably little has been written about it. Only a handful of articles or reports by policy analysts or scholars have been published on the subject.[4] Some evaluations of party programs exist, usually sponsored by funders of party aid or occasionally by party aid groups themselves. Most of these evaluations are focused on specific country programs.[5] They examine outputs of the programs, doing little to identify and assess basic assumptions and methods, judge the overall effects of such work, or attempt crossnational or crossregional comparisons. As new actors have joined the field in this decade they commonly ask what they should read to understand the state of the art. The answer they usually get is that there is little to read and that although some significant accumulated knowledge does exist about party aid, it is highly dispersed, being located largely in the minds of experienced individual practitioners.

This paucity of reflective, analytic assessments of past work and a corresponding dispersion of accumulated wisdom are not just characteristic of party aid but of democracy aid generally. I highlighted some of the reasons for this shortage in my 1999 book, *Aiding Democracy Abroad*, and the situation has only changed modestly since then. Democracy promoters tend not to reflect systematically on their work. They are action-oriented people and organizations, much more inclined to throw themselves into the next challenge than to take time to analyze carefully and critically what they did last. Funders of such work create few incentives for probing retrospection, pushing implementing organizations to deliver rapid results and rush from one assignment to the next. Democracy promoters are not only action-oriented, they are also often infused with a certain missionary spirit, a belief that their work is by nature valuable and good, which also inhibits critical self-reflection.

The scholarly community has been noticeably slow to take up the topic. Many of the issues presented by democracy aid are too applied to be of interest to scholars rewarded for advancing or attacking theoretical frameworks. Democracy aid falls in between academic disciplines, touching on international relations, comparative politics, law, and various others, but belonging squarely to none. Many scholars have not seen this domain as being especially significant, incorrectly dismissing it either as an area of little real import or just heavy-handed Cold War–style U.S. political interventionism revisited.

This lack of outside analysis and writing is starting to change, at least with respect to some parts of the democracy promotion field. Some useful writings on international efforts to promote free and fair elections, civil society development, and postconflict political construction, for example, have started to appear. Party aid, however, remains at the other end of the scale in terms of outside attention. To the extent it receives public attention, it comes as broadsides and pushback from certain autocratic governments accusing party aid actors of political meddling—attention that contributes some heat to the subject but not much light.

As a result, no extensive, up-to-date analytic treatment of party aid exists that answers basic questions about this vital, growing domain:

- What are the main characteristics of political parties in new or struggling democracies and what causes parties in such a varied set of countries to have a very similar set of problematic organizational and operational characteristics?
- Are the deficiencies of parties in new or struggling democracies basically similar to or different from the problems of parties in established democracies?
- What are the main contours and dimensions of the party aid response to the problems of political parties in new or struggling democracies—

who are the main actors, what are the principal types of activities, what methods are used, and what are the goals?

- What are the strengths and weaknesses of party aid, and what innovations are being tried?
- What political interests do party aid programs serve and, in particular, are they used to favor particular parties for the sake of influencing electoral outcomes?
- What effects does party aid have?
- What is the future of party aid? How can it be strengthened and what is reasonable to expect of it?

Aim, Structure, and Basis of the Book

This book aims to provide such an account. It offers an analytic overview of the state of political parties in new or struggling democracies and the world of political party aid, and at least preliminary answers to the aforementioned questions. It is not possible in this modest volume to attempt a comprehensive history or record of international party assistance, a history that would require an enormous amount of research to recover and tell (much of it not being written down anywhere and existing only in people's memories). The goal is to arrive at least at a stocktaking of where the field is and where it is likely going.

The book has a two-part structure. The first two chapters after this introduction set up the analysis of party aid by examining the state of political parties in new or struggling democracies. Chapter 2 provides a quick region-by-region tour of the evolution and state of parties in the developing and postcommunist worlds. Chapter 3 presents an explanation of why parties in new or struggling democracies are troubled and a framework for analyzing party systems in these countries. The remainder of the book concentrates on party aid. Chapter 4 is an overview of party aid—its principal actors, evolution, and method. Chapter 5 critically examines the standard method and identifies innovations that some organizations are attempting to make. Chapter 6 delves into the interests behind party aid and the issue of partisanship. Chapter 7 assesses the effects of party aid. Chapter 8 considers a new, rapidly growing part of the field—programs aimed at changing party systems rather than individual parties. Chapter 9 summarizes the main arguments of the earlier chapters and explores how party aid might go deeper through greater explicit attention to power and politics.

My analysis, both of the state of political parties and of party aid in new or struggling democracies, is based on several sources. First, in writing the book I carried out field research on parties and party aid in six country case studies, one each from the major regions of the developing and postcommunist worlds: Guatemala, Indonesia, Morocco, Mozambique, Romania, and Russia. No small set of case studies can be perfectly representative. I chose these countries not just for their geographic diversity but on the basis of two criteria: (1) in each of these countries the state of political parties has some important characteristics in common with the state of parties in other countries in the region (although party development is too varied in some regions to have what might be considered a typical regional pattern); and (2) party aid providers are active in each of these countries, and have been active for at least five years, allowing at least some temporal perspective on the work.

For each case study, I read extensive amounts of academic, policy-oriented, and journalistic writing about the country's current politics and political history, with a focus on the evolution of its political parties. Then in research trips to each country between late 2003 and mid-2005, I interviewed a total of approximately 150 persons involved in politics or in party aid—representatives of party aid groups and donor agencies, political party leaders, party cadres, and local branch activists, parliamentarians, journalists, lawyers, and scholars. In four of the countries (Guatemala, Morocco, Romania, and Russia), I had previously carried out research and writing on democracy aid and democratization, stretching back to the mid-1980s or early 1990s in some of those cases, and thus was building in the case study research on an existing foundation of at least some firsthand exposure and knowledge. I do not present the country case studies as separate chapters in the book. Rather, I integrate findings from them throughout the book.

To gain broader knowledge about party aid beyond the case studies, I also carried out in the same period approximately thirty interviews in the headquarters of various major U.S., European, and multilateral organizations involved in party aid and in the bilateral aid agencies or foreign ministries that fund them. I also drew on hundreds of formal interviews, informal meetings, and conversations I have had with both providers and recipients of party aid in my broader research and consulting work on democracy aid over the course of the last twenty years.

PART TWO

The Condition of Parties

CHAPTER TWO

A Quick Global Tour

B ehind the standard lament lies enormous variation in individual parties as well as in the overall patterns of party development in different countries. If we put aside the conventional Eurocentric lens for understanding parties and simply look at the realities of parties and their evolution in the developing and postcommunist worlds, a bewilderingly varied and unfamiliar landscape confronts us. The hundreds of parties in these regions (thousands if one counts small parties) differ markedly along many dimensions. Some parties are less than a year old, others more than a century old. Some are "briefcase" parties boasting no more than a leader and several followers, others are mass-based organizations with legions of cadres. Some represent the interests of just a few wealthy businessmen, others speak for millions of impoverished indigenous people. Some have little ideological basis beyond the vaguest commitment to generic prodemocratic principles, others hold to a strict program of religion-inspired positions. Some have origins as peace movements, others as armed insurgencies.

To provide a broad-brush overview of the state of parties in new or struggling democracies I start with a hurried global tour, briefly examining the evolution and current state of parties in each of the regions of concern in this book—Central and Eastern Europe, East and Southeast Asia, Latin America, the Middle East, South Asia, the former Soviet Union, and sub-Saharan Africa. Within each region considerable variation exists regarding parties. Nevertheless there are enough meaningful regional commonalities due to overlapping or shared histories and underlying structural conditions to make a region-by-region tour a plausible approach for an overview of the terrain.

Central and Eastern Europe

Of all the different regions that have been part of the Third Wave of democracy, it is in Central and Eastern Europe that political parties are developing most closely in line with what Western political experts usually consider "normal" parties, which is to say Western European-style parties.[1] This is hardly surprising given that the historical patterns of not only political but also economic, social, and cultural development in Central and Eastern Europe overlap in many substantial ways with those of Western Europe.

Central and Eastern Europe experienced significant political party development in the second half of the nineteenth century and first half of the twentieth century. It occurred as part of the spread of parliamentarianism throughout Europe, albeit in a more limited way in some places, especially those areas under Ottoman dominion such as Bulgaria and Romania. In the 1920s and 1930s, party development in Central and Eastern Europe was heavily marked by the nationalist aspirations and territorial struggles that World War I helped fuel, as well as by the rise of both fascist and Communist parties. Pluralistic party development was harshly interrupted in the late 1940s when communist regimes took over. All parties, except Communist parties and a scattering of closely controlled satellite parties, were banned. For forty years single-party systems ruled.

Thus when the countries of Central and Eastern Europe came out of communist rule at the end of the 1980s, their political, as well as economic, social, and cultural life had diverged significantly from Western Europe. Nevertheless, compared with most countries in regions taking part in democracy's Third Wave, most Central and Eastern European countries entered the post-1989 period with coherent states, differentiated, industrialized economies, high levels of education, low levels of inequality, and low levels of poverty. Although not necessarily determinative of a positive political outcome, these underlying socioeconomic conditions were a positive base on which new democratic processes and institutions could be built.

Political parties in Central and Eastern Europe exploded into life in the early 1990s, emerging by the dozens in every country. Initially almost all of these new parties were extremely weak, thin organizations, often little more than a few ambitious people and a small circle of followers trying to gain a place in the new political order. The exceptions were the small number of parties formed around dissident movements that existed in the previous decade or two, like Solidarity in Poland, or successor parties to the discredited Communist parties. Many of the civil society activists who had helped mount

challenges to the communist regimes in the 1980s shunned the idea of forming or participating in political parties once political life opened up. They
clung instead to an ideal of creating apolitical, ethically virtuous civil society
organizations. Party development was also slowed early on by the widespread
public skepticism about political parties. Many Central and Eastern Europeans were hopeful about what democracy might bring, but they were
strongly suspicious about and cynical toward the very idea of political parties
as a result of the many negative elements of their prior experience with parties, particularly with the Communist party.

Despite their initial weaknesses, parties gained a dominant place in the
new democratic systems of the region. Parties took advantage of the generally
high degree of political freedom and the regular national and local elections
to build their strength. New political entrepreneurs pushed ahead of the earlier civil society activists, creating substantial parties of the center and center-
right. Communist parties that had initially appeared to have been knocked
completely off the political stage demonstrated surprising success at reinvent-
ing themselves as center-left parties. In doing so they drew upon their political experience, managerial skills, and pre-existing institutional resources, as
well as the receptivity of substantial numbers of citizens to the idea of a more
cautious, socially protective approach to market reform.[2] The very large array
of parties competing in elections gradually shrank in number and in most
countries a compact set of major parties came to dominate the scene. Parties
that got into power on both sides of the political spectrum were able to use
their position to strengthen themselves, especially through control of
government-run media and political patronage.

In this decade, Central and Eastern European countries have arrived at
having what Paul Lewis, a leading expert on parties of the region, calls "proto
party systems," by which he means systems that share some though not all of
the main features of party systems in Western European countries.[3] In some
of the countries of the region the major parties have achieved a certain stability in terms of voter base and share of support (with some notable exceptions,
such as Poland, that have experienced persistent party instability). What in the
early 1990s appeared as "flattened" societies with few sharp socioeconomic
cleavages have become articulated polities in which many voters have developed a fairly settled attachment to a particular party or set of parties. None of
the countries has a dominant party that threatens to choke off space for others; most have somewhat regular alternation of power. The major parties have
become proficient at electoral campaigning and have some of the attributes
of what political scientists call "electoral professional" parties.

At the same time, most of the parties of the region suffer from serious shortcomings, at least compared with their Western European counterparts. On the whole they are institutionally thinner with less presence around the country and weaker ties to civil society. Many of the parties, especially those that have had at least one turn in power, are corrupt in various ways, often having ties to illicit financing and prone to overlooking or circumventing the law when it is in their interest to do so.

Although the parties have ideological identities, these identities are often quite shallow and the actual policy lines pursued by different parties once in power are not all that different on most major issues. The main parties are arrayed along a left-right spectrum with a marked tendency toward dualistic opposition of center-left versus center-right. The left-right spectrum in most Central and Eastern European countries is more complex and internally contradictory than the Western European one. On the right side of the spectrum are two very different political lines. One is support for a vigorous approach to market reforms; the other involves adherence to nationalist thinking, often of dubious democratic fidelity. Right-of-center parties thus are sometimes very different from one another, at least in their self-conception, and in general the center-right has failed to coalesce in some of the countries and is fraught with tension between the different impulses (a phenomenon that also exists in a few Western European countries including Austria, France, and the Netherlands). The left side is similarly bifurcated between a liberal, pro-Western intellectual left and political forces animated by an attachment to elements of the old socialist order, drawing support especially from unions, farmers, and pensioners. Although the major parties have achieved fairly stable voter bases (with some notable exceptions, such as the rout of the two main Bulgarian party groups in 2001 and the inability of Poland's center-right parties to cohere) they have not overcome the deep-seated antiparty attitudes of the postcommunist societies.[4] Distrust and disregard for parties is very high almost everywhere in the region.

The former Yugoslav republics represent a partial exception to these patterns due to their different political history and recent trajectories. As part of Yugoslavia they experienced a softer form of communism than their Warsaw Pact neighbors and no clear-cut 1989 democratic breakthrough. The 1990s brought the harsh, at times highly bloody, process of national breakup and the establishment of new states. Strongman rulers and ethnic nationalism dominated the politics of the area, often with tragic results. In this decade, peace has prevailed, political tensions have lessened, and multiparty systems are now in place in all of the former Yugoslav republics. Parties and party systems in these countries are somewhat more fragmented than in other parts of Central and Eastern Europe. They are less clearly divided along left-right lines, with both nationalist and ethnic attachments playing a major role.

The mixed picture of party development in Central and Eastern Europe—substantial progress combined with significant weakness—is consonant with the overall story of democratization in the region. Compared with most other participants in democracy's Third Wave, the countries of Central and Eastern Europe are doing fairly well in political terms. Compared, however, with the hopes and expectations of their citizens and with the (often idealized) model of Western Europe, they are still falling short. The mixed picture has encouraged divergent interpretations of the overall state of party development in the region: some observers lament what they view as very problematic parties whereas others argue that, broadly speaking, parties are making progress. The more pessimistic interpretations dominated in the 1990s. More recently, the "half full" as opposed to "half empty" view has gained ground, at least among political scientists who study the parties.

Former Soviet Union

The states of the former Soviet Union (with the exception of totalitarian Turkmenistan) are for the first time experiencing a period of multiparty political life, troubled though it is.[5] The wave of parliamentarianism and political liberalism that spread through much of both Western and Eastern Europe in the nineteenth century largely did not penetrate Russia and the other societies that now make up the former Soviet Union. Politics in Russia and its southern and eastern neighbors were locked in feudal, autocratic, and imperial modes until the Russian Revolution and the subsequent establishment of the Soviet Union. The subsequent seventy years of Soviet Communism were even more destructive of pluralism than the forty years of communism in Central and Eastern Europe, being much longer, more repressive, and grown from within (at least in Russia) rather than imposed from outside.

When Soviet Communism finally ended, it did so as a result of a failed top-down experiment in liberalizing reforms. Unlike in some of the Central and Eastern European countries, there was little stirring from below or bottom-up pressure for political change. As a result, only vague, unorganized constituencies for democratic change existed. The political pluralism that emerged in the successor states of the Soviet Union in the early 1990s was "pluralism by default," a temporary state of political dislocation and disorientation, a system in which elections continued to occur because no segment of the elite had the coordination and power to reestablish authoritarian control.[6]

Although the early pluralism proved to be short-lived in some places and shaky almost everywhere, it entailed at least some political openness and competition. In this new space many political parties were formed, numbering in the dozens in many of the former Soviet states. In Russia, for example, nineteen parties competed in the first post-Soviet national elections, the Duma elections of 1993, and forty-three in the 1995 Duma elections. Unlike in Central and Eastern Europe, however, this initial party proliferation did not turn into genuine processes of party development in most former Soviet republics. Large numbers of parties still exist in many states of the former Soviet Union but the overall condition of political parties is very weak and troubled. Except for a few cases, like Ukraine and Georgia, there is no identifiable positive momentum in terms of the development of democratically oriented multiparty life.

Although the idea of a common postcommunist political path may in the early 1990s have appeared a useful concept, by the mid-1990s it was already of doubtful utility and today it is completely inapplicable. The basic political configuration of most post-Soviet states is sharply different from that of the Central and Eastern European ones—highly centralized presidential systems with little alternation of power as opposed to parliamentary or mixed systems with fairly regular alternation of power. Some countries, including Belarus, Turkmenistan, and Uzbekistan, are of an outright authoritarian cast, with high levels of repression. A few, such as Georgia and Ukraine, have open systems that recently managed to get reformist leaders into power. Most of the others are semiauthoritarian systems in which strongman leaders maintain a tight grip on power yet allow a limited amount of political space to defuse pressure at home and win some credibility abroad. Some opposition parties and some independent civil society groups are allowed to operate in this space. The leaders hold regular elections as part of their legitimization strategy but they manipulate or undermine these elections as necessary to ensure that their hold on power is undisturbed.

In most former Soviet republics the personal wishes and actions of the president dominate political life, backed and carried out by the presidential "apparatus," which is made up of shadowy circles of people and groups around the president, including internal security services, personal cronies, co-opted business elites, and, in some cases, fellow clan members. The ministries do the president's bidding, the parliaments are weak, and the judiciaries are docile. Political party systems exist but are not central to the main exercise of political power and have a fundamentally different profile than in Central and Eastern Europe.

At the center of these party systems are the presidents' parties or, as they are often known in the region, the parties of power. These are parties created by or for the presidents. They have only the vaguest of ideologies; they are gray parties that vaguely espouse principles of national unity and strength. They are not reform-oriented former Communist parties, such as those that dominate the center-left in Central and Eastern Europe. They often draw upon structures and resources from the pre-1991 power system but are largely new, having been created from the top down to mobilize and channel votes for the president, solidify parliamentary blocs to support the president, and little else. In some Central Asian countries, such as Kazakhstan, Kyrgyzstan, and Tajikistan, presidents have used propresidential political "independents," more than parties of power, to dominate the parliament.

In almost all of the post-Soviet republics, at least a few opposition parties struggle against the ruling forces. They are led by the top members of whatever alternative sociopolitical elite has managed to survive outside the main circles of power. In some cases they are pro-Western reformers; in other cases, such as that of Russia's Communist Party, they are persons associated with the old regime who did not get included in the new circles of power when the transition occurred. Most of these opposition parties (Russia's Communist Party being something of an exception) are thinly institutionalized, personalistic, leader-driven organizations based in the capital city and lacking a strong presence in most other parts of the country. They are often divided among themselves, despite their common political foe, given to squabbling over political crumbs, and unable to work together effectively in coalitions or to unite. They are usually badly short of funds, reliant at best on a few wealthy businessmen who are willing to take on the ruling elite. They are ideologically indistinct other than somewhat proreformist with an implicit or occasionally explicit pro-Western orientation. They are continually weakened by the pressures and limitations exerted by the ruling forces. The limited powers of the institutions that are open to them—parliaments and provincial and local governments—further push the opposition parties to political marginality.

Scattered about the political scene, around the parties of power and the few principal opposition parties in most of the former Soviet states, are various very small parties. These are usually the personal enterprises of a few ambitious people trying to advance their own fortunes or fledgling efforts to build a party around a specific social group or issue—such as farmers' issues, women's rights, or environmentalism. Some are oppositional, others have been co-opted by the ruling powers or are creations of the ruling powers for the purposes of political distraction. Few play much of a role in political life and their often quixotic character only further undermines the public's belief in the idea of political parties.

Looking at the stunted development of political parties in the former Soviet Union, it is hard not to conclude that the post-Soviet political soil is unusually inhospitable to parties. Nowhere else in the world, except perhaps the Arab world, are parties so peripheral to the main conduct of political power. One could ascribe this fact to the highly centralized, often authoritarian nature of politics in most of the post-Soviet states. Clearly the repression and other forms of political constraint common in the region do great harm to party development. Yet in some other semiauthoritarian or even authoritarian countries, such as China and Malaysia, one or more political parties are central to how political power is organized and implemented. In contrast, in much of the former Soviet Union even where there is a party of power it is at most an instrument of underlying structures of power.

The unusually weak role of parties in most post-Soviet states is perhaps a result of the distinctive nature of the political transition that occurred when the Soviet Union ended: the Soviet Communist Party collapsed yet the bureaucratic structures of power survived (reinvented as specific national institutions in the process of state building in the various post-Soviet republics) as did many of the key local power figures (especially in Central Asia and the Caucasus). Thus there developed new states whose political systems had many characteristics of the old Soviet system, minus a pervasive, entrenched ruling party.

Adding to this picture is the profound cynicism of post-Soviet political culture. This is the same sort of inherent suspicion about the very enterprise of politics, mixed in with atomization and distrust of fractious pluralism, similar to that found in postcommunist Central and Eastern Europe. It is even stronger in the former Soviet Union given the harsher experience of Soviet rule. This does not mean that post-Soviet citizens are reflexively hostile to the idea of democracy. In some places a majority embrace it in theory. In a few countries, most notably Georgia and Ukraine, citizens have mobilized en masse around the idea. Citizens of most post-Soviet republics remain caught in a sociopolitical web of passivity and disorganization. Thus fledgling political parties seeking to gain a hold in these societies have to contend not only with overbearing presidential regimes crushing them from above, but a lack of organized constituencies and interest in parties from below.

Several other elements of the post-Soviet context contribute to the difficulties political parties face. The fact that the construction of new political systems in the former Soviet republics takes place not just as part of attempted economic and political transitions but also as part of the formation of national states complicates party development. The state-formation process in many post-Soviet countries, including Armenia, Azerbaijan, Georgia, Moldova, Russia, and Tajikistan has been plagued by ethnic-related conflicts. In such settings, power holders use appeals to national unity as a way of discouraging political pluralism, and many citizens become wary of party politics as a divisive game that may only lead to more conflict. With politics enmeshed in fundamental issues such as the boundaries and integrity of the state, it is inevitably a higher stakes game than the usual politics of democratic consolidation. As such it is more likely to be marked by extreme measures, including violence and intimidation, as well as intolerance of the very ideal of political opposition.

The presence in some former Soviet republics of powerful concentrations of economic resources and wealth, due to the existence of oil and gas and other mineral reserves, also negatively affects political parties. The existence of such resources, especially in contexts of attempted market reforms and the weak rule of law, creates powerful business actors with strong interests in influencing or even controlling the party process. This leads such actors to invest in political parties, both those in power and those that might be a vehicle for challenging power. Parties are thus at risk of becoming pawns of these oligarchic actors. In Ukraine, for example, party life across the 1990s was heavily corrupted by such actors and it became common to talk of some parties as being "owned" by particular business groups.

Finally, the existence of clans and clan politics complicates party development in some parts of the region, especially Central Asia and parts of the Caucasus. Clans are kinship networks, rooted in territorial areas, of a subethnic variety, not based on language or religion. They function as systems of loyalty and influence that can shape or sometimes even substitute for formal institutions of state of government. They impede party development in various ways.[7] Clan elders may determine or strongly influence the voting choices of the members of a clan network. In practice this influence often translates into a preference for so-called "independents" rather than parties, with the idea that independents can be more easily captured by a clan. Clans may monopolize the interest-aggregation role that parties or other organizations, such as unions, might otherwise fulfill, as well as patronage functions like the provision of services and jobs. In short, they are another element of the post-Soviet sociopolitical context that contributes to the hollowness of political parties.

Latin America

Latin America has a long, complex history of political party development.[8] Unlike in most other parts of the world that have been part of democracy's "Third Wave," Latin America's political transitions of the past few decades were not first-time or second-time efforts at democratization. Rather they were one further chapter in a very long story of alternating periods of democratic pluralism and repressive authoritarianism stretching back to the nineteenth century. Political parties have been part of that story all along the way.

Interestingly enough, while parties have a longer history in Latin America than in other regions also currently grappling with democratization, there is an even more acute sense in Latin America than elsewhere of parties having arrived at a state of crisis. The term "crisis of political parties" regularly arises in discussions and writings on Latin American politics and in regional meetings aimed at diagnosing Latin America's political ills. Latin American regional institutions, including both the Organization of American States and the Inter-American Development Bank, have launched initiatives to respond to the perceived crisis, such as the Inter-American Forum on Political Parties (see chapter 4).

The commonly cited symptoms of the troubled state of parties in the region include all the familiar elements of the standard lament, especially corruption, plus some larger-scale problems: the collapse of once well-established parties in some countries; a surge in leaders being forced out of office before the end of their term (which many Latin Americans blame on parties failing to produce effective leadership); the rise of alternative political figures whose appeal is based in some substantial part on their status as not being of the established parties; and an extremely low public regard, sometimes even active hatred, of the main existing parties.

The crisis of parties is a central element of the broader crisis of democratic performance in the region. On the whole, Latin America is more democratic today, and has been for the last twenty years, than at any earlier time in its history. Many Latin Americans, however, are deeply dissatisfied with how their political systems work in practice—what they see as rising corruption, endless political infighting, and persistent inefficiency. Many citizens also lament a lack of tangible socioeconomic benefits resulting from years of democratic rule. In short, the crisis of democratic performance is all about a widespread belief of a failure of democratic systems to represent citizens' interests. Political parties, as the institution assumed to be central to the process of political representation, are widely viewed as the locus of this failure of representation.

It is common in the region and among outside political observers to talk of the crisis of parties as a single, region-wide phenomenon. In fact very different patterns of party development are found in the region. Although it can be analytically perilous to try to reduce this heterogeneity into neat categories, two main paths of party development can be identified. In some Latin American countries, mainly in South America, including Argentina, Chile, Colombia, Uruguay, and Venezuela, although also in Costa Rica and Honduras, stable two- or three-party systems emerged across the course of the twentieth century. They followed something like the European pattern of party evolution, although with some significant differences. Small, elite-oriented parties in these countries initially emerged in the late nineteenth and early twentieth centuries out of the growing division in the ruling elite between conservatives and liberals. Elite conservatives were large landowners, who usually favored a privileged role for the Catholic Church in state affairs, centralized government, and protective trade regulation. Elite liberals usually represented commercial and professional interests and opposed Church privileges, favoring either a federal or otherwise less centralized government, and supported free trade.

In the first half of the twentieth century, some of the more successful of these elite parties grew into mass parties, somewhat in parallel to the rise of mass parties in Europe during the same period. The establishment of Latin American mass parties was fueled much more by clientelism and patronage than in Europe (although those mechanisms were certainly common in Europe as well), reflecting the higher levels of poverty and inequality. The left-right spectrum that defined much of European party life in that period was less clear in most parts of Latin America. Mass parties growing out of the earlier elite parties favored vague ideologies rooted in broad ideas such as national unity, populism, or tradition. Party development was deformed and often disrupted by the repeated, and in some cases sustained, periods of authoritarian rule that occurred in many countries (as also occurred in parts of Europe).[9]

Whereas the rise of mass parties in Europe was led by the emergence of socialist or social democratic parties, in Latin America the same pattern did not hold. Such an evolution was impeded in Latin America by weaker processes of industrialization (and hence a smaller, less dynamic working class) as well as the higher level of political repression in some societies. Some elite liberal parties did broaden into parties with wide membership but they maintained strong elite roots and vague programmatic priorities. In some countries elite liberal parties were crowded out by new mass-based parties, although these groups were different from the European workers' parties of the early twentieth century. They were what Torcuato di Tella has called "multiclass integrative parties" (such as the Institutional Revolutionary Party [PRI] in Mexico or the Colorado Party in Paraguay) or middle-class populist parties (such as the American Popular Revolutionary Alliance [APRA] in Peru or Democratic Action [AD] in Venezuela).[10] Some were undemocratic parties that sought to capture the entire political system and once in power resisted free and fair multiparty competition.

The two- or three-party systems that established themselves over time in these countries were deformed and disrupted but not decimated by the various bouts of authoritarianism that most of these countries suffered. Thus these countries entered the Third Wave of democracy in the 1980s with generally longer-established and more stable parties than countries in other regions joining the democratic trend. The "crisis of parties" that they are now experiencing is primarily about party decay—the decline of established parties.

A smaller but still significant number of Latin American countries including Bolivia, Brazil, Ecuador, El Salvador, Guatemala, Nicaragua, and Peru did not develop stable party systems in the twentieth century. Political parties were an active element of political life in these places but specific parties came and went from the political scene without putting down roots. No single factor explains why these countries failed to establish stable two- or three-party systems as some of their neighbors did. In some cases, such as Guatemala and Nicaragua, longer, harsher periods of authoritarian rule are one possible explanation. Contingent factors, such as the absence of political figures who happened to have the energy and vision needed to build lasting national parties, are also relevant. These parties entered the Third Wave with considerable experience with parties, yet without stable party systems. Their experience in the current "crisis of parties" is therefore not about the decay of well-entrenched two- or three-party systems but rather the consequences for democracy of persistently unstable, fragmented party systems.

Two exceptions in this regard are El Salvador and Nicaragua, which entered the recent period of democratization without established two- or three-party systems but have developed such systems since. In both cases, two-party systems emerged out of the resolution of civil wars, with the former warring sides transforming into political parties and continuing their competition peacefully through electoral politics. Mexico is also a somewhat exceptional case in the region in terms of its political party development. After nearly seventy years of a dominant party system with only limited party competition and constrained political party development, Mexican politics opened up in the 1990s. The two main alternative parties, the National Action Party (PAN) and the Democratic Revolutionary Party (PRD), took advantage of the new space to become real challengers. Although all three of Mexico's main parties today have serious defects, political party life is more vital than before.

Speaking very generally therefore, the current crisis of parties in Latin America comes in countries with long histories of political parties, some of which developed fairly stable party systems during the first half of the twentieth century and some which did not. The question naturally poses itself: Why are parties in Latin America—both where stable systems exist and where they do not—faring poorly in what is proving to be the most sustained and broad period of democracy in Latin American history?

One set of reasons arises from the wave of market-oriented economic reforms in the region that coincided with the return to democracy in the 1980s and 1990s. These reforms negatively affected parties in several ways.[11.] To start with, reforms have entailed shrinking the state through cuts in public service payrolls, reducing government spending, and privatizing state enterprises. This shrinkage has diminished the capacity of governing parties to engage in patronage (especially the provision of state jobs to party loyalists), which weakens a key method parties have used to bolster their organizational base. It has made it harder for governing parties to give the fat wage increases and industrial subsidies to favored constituencies useful for building party support. At the same time, in most Latin American countries market reforms have not produced very substantial economic growth, whether because the reforms were not fully or effectively implemented or because they were not the right remedies for the problems at hand. With poverty not diminishing in most countries, middle-class incomes slipping or stagnating, and inequality remaining high or even rising, many Latin Americans believe that their lives are not improving under democracy. They blame the main political parties for this fact, thus weakening the parties' position.

The embrace of market reforms has had another damaging effect on parties. At least until the last few years, the market reform approach was adopted, in practice if not always in principle, by almost all the main parties in the region. The effect for citizens was that no matter which parties or presidential candidates they elected, the same basic policies were pursued. The rise of democracy coincided with a decline of core socioeconomic policy choices, a fact that inevitably undercut citizen interest or belief in parties.[12]

Another reason parties have not been doing well has to do with the clash between the expectations that democratization unleashed among many Latin Americans for better treatment by the state and the continued weakness of most Latin American states. This is about more than just the disappointing performance of Latin American economies. For many Latin Americans, democratization brought with it the hope not just for a better material situation but for a life marked by greater dignity and justice. This hope was rooted in the idea that democratic governments would act on their behalf rather than to further the interests of a privileged elite, that old patterns of endemic state corruption and ineptitude would diminish. Yet for a whole set of reasons, basic state performance—in terms of the delivery of services and the reduction of corruption—has not markedly improved in many places. A core sense of injustice remains a cardinal feature of life for many people in the region. Again, as the governing entities in this period, parties have taken the blame for the continued weaknesses of Latin American states.

These are of course not the only reasons parties are struggling. As in European and North American societies, the ever more powerful influence of mass media and the rise of electronic communication technologies that foster heightened individualism hollow out the place of parties in the fabric of sociopolitical life. Also, as Christopher Sabatini has pointed out, established parties in some countries, such as Bolivia, Colombia, Peru, and Venezuela, have been weakened by decentralization policies that empower local political actors, and sometimes small local parties, eroding national parties from below.[13] Introducing direct elections for governors, for example, has empowered some local notables and weakened the hold of national parties. Thus Latin American parties are hit both by some of the region's broader problems—such as weak economic performance—as well as by some of its areas of progress—such as the spread of communication technologies and increased political decentralization.

Sub-Saharan Africa

Political parties are a fairly new institution in sub-Saharan Africa.[14] They emerged in most African countries only during the last phase of colonialization, around the 1950s. They first took form as independence movements that then evolved into ruling political parties when independence was gained. Many African countries experienced a brief phase of multipartyism and attendant growth of political parties in their initial postcolonial life. It came to a rapid end, however, as presidents all around the continent adapted the single-party model and forced opposition parties either to disband or merge with the ruling party.

Decades of severely circumscribed party development followed, opening up again only at the end of the 1980s and early 1990s when the postcolonial leaders began to give way and multipartyism enjoyed a new boom. Forty-one African countries held multiparty elections between 1989 and 2000. As Nicolas van de Walle notes, "Between the 1989 transition election in Namibia and the end of 2000, some 87 legislative elections involving at least two parties were convened in 42 of the region's 48 states ... [i]n addition over 65 presidential elections involved more than one candidate during this period."[15] The institutionalization of elections throughout most of the continent stimulated an enormous growth of political parties, with most countries seeing the establishment of dozens of parties. Hundreds of African political parties exist today, a sharp contrast to the situation of just twenty years ago.

Although multiparty elections have spread widely in Africa, often as a result of pressure from a donor community tired of what it perceives as dysfunctional patterns of authoritarian governance in Africa, democracy is struggling in most parts of the region. Entrenched leaders, often associated with dominant parties, use elections as a tool in many countries to legitimate their hold on power, rather than a means of deepening representational institutions or advancing democratic values. Civil conflict continues to rear its violent head in some places struggling to make pluralism work. A small number of countries, including Benin, Ghana, Mali, and South Africa, have made notable democratic progress. Yet even in successful cases such as these, democratic institutions and norms remain fragile and subject to constant challenges and limitations.

African political parties are part of this variegated, precarious political context. Some parties are instruments of semiauthoritarian power. Many others are insignificant institutions consisting of little more than a leader and a few followers. Even those that are both committed to democracy and have some real political weight have serious organizational weaknesses.[16] All around the continent, "parties are regularly perceived to be a weak link in the chain of elements that together make for a democratic state, or even to have helped undermine democracy through the irresponsible and self-interested actions of their leaders."[17]

African political parties generally exhibit the same types of organizational and operational weaknesses as parties in other parts of the developing and postcommunist worlds. They are mostly personalistic, centralized entities, usually with a weak presence outside the capital, a tendency to be active only around elections, no clear programmatic platform, and weak ties to civil society or the citizenry more generally. The main exceptions to this are some ruling parties, which although still often personalistic and centralized, have managed over time to build up substantial party organizations, including branches around the country.

Ideological incoherence is a feature of parties in most parts of the developing and postcommunist worlds but is especially visible in Africa. Few African parties have any recognizable ideological identity; the left-right spectrum is invisible or largely symbolic on most of the continent. Although often tied to ethnic constituencies, African parties rarely identify themselves explicitly as ethnic parties. They instead base their public appeals on vague, inoffensive concepts like national unity, national development, or democratic governance. In part this reflects the traditional pattern of African postcolonial politics in which efforts to appeal openly to any one subgroup of people in a country are viewed as divisive and not consistent with the spirit of a single national community. It also reflects the fact that an unusually high level of donor dependency of many African states gives the donor community considerable influence over their socioeconomic policies, draining most of the possible ideological life out of the party arena.

A characteristic feature of party life in Africa is the prevalence of dominant party systems. By far the most common party system in the region is one in which the ruling party has a long-term hold on the presidency and the national legislature while various opposition parties, possibly with some presence in the legislature, weakly attempt to challenge the ruling party. The ruling party allows elections to be held at regular intervals but uses state resources, its control of the state television and radio, and other means to ensure that its hold on power is not threatened.

Some of the dominant parties in power in Africa today are parties that ruled during the period of single-party politics and managed to make it through transitions to multipartyism without losing their grip, such as in Cameroon and Gabon. Others are parties that arose as challengers to discredited single parties in the late 1980s and early 1990s, such as the Movement for Multiparty Democracy in Zambia. Some dominant parties, such as the African National Congress (ANC) in South Africa and the Botswana Democratic Party, are politically benign or even somewhat democratic. They tolerate political opposition and independent civil society and generally respect political and civil rights. Others are ambivalent about democracy or actively subvert it, manipulating elections as needed to stay in power, and undercutting any political figures or forces that mount a strong challenge. Most of the dominant party systems that solidified or resolidified in the early 1990s have proven fairly stable, although alternation of power has occurred in a few places (at least within the overall circle of elite-led parties), notably in Kenya and Senegal.

The reemergence of multiparty systems in Southern Africa since the late 1980s has been associated with the coming to power of a certain kind of dominant party—a party based on the former national liberation movement, such as the ANC in South Africa, Frelimo (Mozambican Liberation Front) in Mozambique, and SWAPO (South-West African People's Organisation) in Namibia.[18] The top figures in these parties have a certain political mind-set that fuels the dominant party syndrome. They view themselves as the rightful inheritors of the state they fought to capture (boosting a tendency of the party to blur the line between state and party) and the rightful representatives of all the citizens of the country (weakening the rationale for the existence of other parties). As former military movements, these parties have strong hierarchical traditions. Their roots in struggle often make their leaders deeply suspicious of opposition and prone to confusing political opposition with disloyalty to the nation.

Another characteristic feature of political parties in Africa is the ethnic basis of many parties. As van de Walle notes, "In most countries, the single most important factor explaining party loyalty is ethnicity or region, and ethnic identity provides a remarkably precise prediction of voting behavior."[19] The ethnic basis of parties is the result of the lack of other pronounced cleavages. Most African societies have flat class structures, that is to say, very large numbers of rural and urban poor, tiny middle classes, and small circles of wealthy elites. The lack of broad well-developed social organizations that are willing or useful partners for parties is another factor. One consequence of the ethnic basis of many African parties is a greater concern in Africa than in many other places about whether multipartyism is a formula for civil conflict.

African political party development has been strongly shaped by the pervasive neopatrimonialism in Africa.[20] Although political systems in many parts of the world evidence some features of neopatrimonialism, Africa's endemic poverty and very weak postcolonial states have contributed to especially high levels of it. In neopatrimonial political systems, power holders treat the state as their own instrument of patronage, using state resources to buy support or merely to enrich themselves. Internal channels of political loyalty and influence outweigh the formal political institutions. Political relationships based on kin, clan, or tribe outweigh any formal concept of citizenship.

The conventional logic of party development does not hold when politicians are patrons and citizens are clients. Money flows down from the state through the ruling party to citizens rather than up from the citizens' parties and to the government. Parties secure votes not by programmatic appeals and persuasive campaigning but through the distribution of state resources to favored groups. The central goal of political competition becomes not simply to gain a place in or gain control of the government, but to capture the state. Those political forces that succeed in capturing the state are then able to wield its resources to solidify their client base and fend off challengers. Those parties or candidates that fall short of the prize are banished to a bleak, resource-deprived political wilderness. Neopatrimonialism thus contributes to dominant party politics and the centralization of party structures, as well as to the weak programmatic basis of party competition, the prevalence of corruption, and the low citizen regard for parties.

The institutional design of African systems—strong presidential systems with weak legislative branches—also contributes to the prevalence of dominant party politics and to weak party development overall. In such systems, parties concentrate the great bulk of their energy and resources on the presidential contests, which contributes to the centralization and personalization of party structures. The inconsequential role of most legislatures undercuts any efforts by opposition parties to build themselves up during their time out of power.

Finally, it must be noted that the inescapable reality of Africa's terrible poverty is a powerful factor shaping Africa's political party development in manifold ways. In small, weak economies, few sources of money exist outside the state and the narrow privileged circles close to the state for opposition forces, reinforcing the tendency toward dominant party systems. Widespread poverty results in a low level of class differentiation, which contributes to the prominence of ethnic divides as the sharpest cleavage around which parties can organize. Poverty fosters the donor dependence that undercuts domestic ideological debates and alternatives, robbing party life of vitality. As noted previously, poverty puts most citizens in a state of high socioeconomic vulnerability, thereby paving the way for the neopatrimonialist patterns that have such debilitating consequences for party development.

The Middle East

Political parties are very weak in the Middle East, reflecting the broader weakness of democracy in that region.[21] More than half of the countries of the region either have no parties at all or are de facto one-party states. Parties are banned in Saudi Arabia and the smaller Gulf monarchies. Some of these countries, including Bahrain and Kuwait, have competitive legislative elections, but candidates either compete as independents or are put up by nonparty associations. Some of the region's republics either ban political parties (Libya) or allow opposition parties but so severely circumscribe their activities that they are effectively one-party states, such as Syria and Tunisia.

Only eight Middle Eastern states, plus Palestine, have what can be considered significant multipartyism. Unlike in other regions, the emergence of parties in these states was chronologically quite heterogeneous. In Egypt, for example, parties emerged in the early twentieth century, around the time of Egypt gaining independence. Between independence and the Free Officers' coup of 1952, Egypt held ten multiparty parliamentary elections. In the countries that gained independence later, such as Jordan and Morocco, parties first formed in the 1940s as part of the broader regional process of decolonization. Others, such as Algeria and Yemen, have seen the development of parties (beyond a dominant ruling party) only in the past twenty years.

Even in the small set of Middle Eastern countries that have multiparty political life, the boundaries of political competition are fairly constrained (except Israel, with its open party life). Those countries that are republics, such as Egypt, Iran, and Yemen, are authoritarian or semiauthoritarian states with dominant parties or groups holding most of the levers of political power and only very weak opposition parties operating in a limited political space. In those countries with multiparty systems that are monarchies, namely Jordan and Morocco, party competition is not dominated by any one party, but the parties compete only for a very limited institutional share of power—that is, for representation in parliaments that are largely subservient to the ruling monarchs. Iraq and Lebanon are exceptions to these two main patterns. Iraq after Saddam Hussein is struggling to establish a multiparty system in the face of a persistent insurgency and a violence-ridden process of state reconstruction. Lebanon has had active multiparty politics for decades but they were long constrained by Syrian political domination. Following Syria's withdrawal from the country in 2005 after the Lebanese Cedar Revolution, political life became more open but the parties are still locked into a confessional system with some significant undemocratic features.

Where it exists in the Middle East, multipartyism takes a different institutional form in the republics compared with the monarchies.[22] The presidential regimes protect the place of whatever party or parties are close to the president and therefore have a series of features designed to frustrate opposition parties: large voting districts, high thresholds for parliamentary representation, closed party lists, and multimember districts (to block vote-swapping schemes by opposition parties). In contrast, the monarchies do not associate closely with any one party and instead disperse power among competing parties or other political groups to make sure no one gains too much power. They do this through electoral laws that create small districts and allow victory by plurality within the districts. As a result, in monarchies opposition parties are better represented in parliaments and there is more alternation of power within the parliaments.

Although there is considerable desire on the part of many citizens of the Middle Eastern states for political reform and liberalization, few see parties as positive partners in this cause. Parties are highly unpopular almost everywhere when they exist in the region. A recent survey in Morocco, for example, the Arab country with perhaps the best developed set of political parties, found that only 8.7 percent of voters had sympathy for any party at all.[23] The specific features of parties that citizens lament are largely the same as those that cause people in Latin America, the postcommunist countries, Africa, and elsewhere to distrust and dislike their parties. Corruption and co-option come in for particular attention, due to the fact that as in Africa, neopatrimonialism and clientelism are endemic in the politics of most Middle Eastern states. One should note, however, that the patronage politics are often based on relative financial plenty rather than penury. Many of the regimes in the region wield far more resources than their African counterparts, whether due to their oil revenues or, in the case of Egypt and Jordan, unusually large inflows of U.S. aid.

Looking past the familiar nature of citizens' main complaints about parties in the Middle East, one can see these parties often suffer from a kind of chronic weakness that is somewhat particular to the region. Where parties have emerged and multiplied in the Middle East they have not done so as part of democratic transitions, as in other regions. Instead, multipartyism is an element of processes of controlled liberalization, or defensive liberalization, that Arab governments have carried out during the past twenty years. They have used such processes to relieve some of the accumulated domestic pressure for political participation, to share the burden of (and blame for) the often daunting socioeconomic challenges at hand, and to win some credibility domestically and internationally as reformers. As Daniel Brumberg has argued, political liberalization in the Middle East since the mid-1980s is best understood not as the early phase of democratization, but rather as a defensive strategy aimed precisely at avoiding real democratic change.[24]

Opposition parties in the region therefore must struggle not only against specific measures of repression, harassment, and co-option, but also more broadly against political frameworks in which they are allowed to exist but have no real possibility of competing for access to the main levers of power. In those monarchies where political parties or nonparty associations are allowed to compete in legislative elections, parties face the stubborn fact that the core political power in the country is held in a reserved, protected space, out of reach of the parties. In the multiparty republics, the core political power is not formally outside the arena of multiparty competition but de facto it is, with strongman presidents, backed by military and internal security forces, maintaining a stranglehold on power.

These structural realities concerning the place of parties also contribute to weakness not just of opposition parties but also of parties close to the centers of power. Such parties are generally not that strong because the regimes do not use parties as the organizational basis of their power. In the monarchies, the power and legitimacy of the royalty is purposely kept at least somewhat separate from the whole partisan fray, including from those parties traditionally close to the crown. In the republics, power resides not so much in the presidential parties but in the presidents themselves and the security forces behind them. Even when there is a long-standing party of power, such as the National Democratic Party in Egypt, the party itself is surprisingly weak as an organization.

Political party development in the Middle East is also complicated by the fact that the most significant political opposition to many Arab regimes comes from Islamist movements. These movements are formed around and operate through socioreligious institutions, including mosques, religious schools, and Islamic charities, although they extend their reach into many nonreligious institutions as well, such as professional associations. They are usually deeply distrusted by the ruling elites and they coexist uneasily with them in relationships marked both by selective repression and informal line-drawing concerning permissible areas and modes of action.[25] Despite the obstacles placed in their path, through persistent social activism and local-level service delivery, Islamist movements have established strong grassroots networks.[26] Some countries, including Algeria, Jordan, Kuwait, Morocco, Palestine, and Yemen, permit Islamist parties or associations to form and compete in elections. In most of these cases, however, the institutions for which they are allowed to compete for representation only have limited political power and thus the inclusion is very partial. In other countries, notably Egypt, Islamist parties are banned altogether, with the result that a very significant part of the society is openly unrepresented by the political parties that are allowed to exist.

South Asia

South Asia is an unusually heterogeneous region politically, with vividly divergent political conditions in a small number of countries—spanning well-established democracy, military dictatorship, and open civil war. In such varied political contexts, the political parties and party systems also naturally vary greatly and it is difficult to identify regional trends or patterns.[27] Nevertheless there have been some common elements in the evolution of the parties in different countries and it is possible to talk about a characteristic South Asian type of political party, at least in the formative years of party development.

Parties emerged in South Asia as part of decolonization, starting with the establishment of the Indian National Congress in 1885 (if one takes the long view of the decolonization of India), then more widely around the region in the 1940s and 1950s.[28] In Nepal, the noncolonized exception, parties got a start in the 1950s, during the initial, largely blocked attempt to move away from monarchial rule. In Bangladesh, parties did not become active until the 1980s, due to the country's later independence and initial postindependence period of military rule.

The initial decades of party development in most South Asian countries followed a dualist pattern. On the one hand, broad, umbrella-type parties formed from the independence movements and stood as the architects of national emergence. The archetype of such parties was of course the Indian National Congress. These parties became dynastic organizations over time, family affairs, with power held in tightly knit familial structures, and leadership of the party passing within the same family across generations. They have been marked by grand personalities, family intrigues, and heavy doses of politico-cultural symbolism in which the fates of ruling families become symbols for the destinies of their countries. These parties have also been highly elitist organizations, rooted in narrow circles of social elites arrayed around a dynastic core. Political parties in many societies around the world are elite-based organizations, but in South Asia the elitist character of party organizations has been especially marked, reflecting the unusually high degree of social (and in some cases ethnic) stratification of these societies. The negative consequences for the representational function of these parties have been serious. These parties are also deeply enmeshed in patronage and clientelism. With their widespread poverty and neofeudal socioeconomic structures in many rural areas,

South Asian societies are prone to the high degrees of neopatrimonialism that are found in Africa and some other parts of the developing world.

On the other hand, some opposition to these broad national independence parties also emerged, usually concentrated in leftist parties, communist or socialist depending on the context. These parties struggled for traction, gaining power in some local areas but usually not at the national level. This initial two-part configuration of the political party landscape, which lasted from the 1940s into the 1970s, reflected the two main ideological currents— nationalism and socialism—that dominated postcolonial states throughout the developing world.

In recent decades, South Asian parties and party systems have evolved along quite varied paths as part of the significant political changes and upheavals around the region. The dynastic parties have aged and faded somewhat. In India, for example, the Indian National Congress has followed a somewhat conventional pattern of evolution, from an elite-oriented party to a mass party to a catchall, electorally focused organization, while losing its dominant position on the national stage.[29] The Bharatiya Janata Party (BJP, Indian People's Party), an ethnonationalist Hindu party, has emerged as a major challenger at the national level. Many smaller parties have become active at the state level, with some of the most successful among them being parties that represent the traditionally excluded castes. Party politics in India, although still operating within a democratic framework, has become a hard-nosed business crowded with opportunistic, largely unprincipled parties enmeshed in corruption and unbridled electoralism. Secularism, the rule of law, and broader values like national unity and political ethics have all declined in political party life.

In Pakistan, in contrast to India, the period of party formation around independence did not gel into well-established national parties. What national parties have existed have been buffeted by the chaotic course of postcolonial political life: five constitutions, two periods of nonconstitutional rule, repeated military interference in political life, and relentless, often violent political conflict between the contending elite groups. The main parties have never put down deep roots in the society and have largely been personalistic vehicles focused on electoral mobilization, and when they have succeeded in gaining power, on patronage and self-enrichment.

Sri Lanka and Bangladesh have established somewhat stable two-party systems, although each has glaring shortcomings. In Sri Lanka the two main parties are coherent (albeit deeply enmeshed in patronage) but do not penetrate the Tamil areas of the country (Tamil parties compete in government-held

Tamil territories but participation is low due to insecurity and low support for the parties).

Bangladesh party life is viciously polarized, afflicted by a poisonous zero-sum mentality, and beset with rising political violence.[30] Moreover, although the main parties are solidly entrenched, they are weak in terms of governmental capacity and overshadowed in important ways both by a dense set of international donor organizations that provide more than half of the country's budget and by a thicket of local service delivery NGOs through which much of the aid is channeled.

Nepal emerged from monarchial rule in the early 1990s with what looked like the start of a stable three-party system, even though all these main parties were widely criticized in the country as extremely elitist entities concerned only with the interests of the highest castes, as well as caught up in endless partisan squabbling and incapable of taking on the country's profound developmental challenges. Starting in the late 1990s, however, the parties were battered and repeatedly marginalized by a royal family determined to keep dominating politics and a brutal Maoist insurgency that has gained control of significant amounts of the national territory. Only in 2006 after years of conflict was a settlement reached that appeared to give the parties a second chance to preside over a pluralistic, peaceful country.

Although there is no consistent pattern in the evolution of South Asian parties and party systems since their emergence in the decolonization period, several crosscutting trends are identifiable. Parties throughout the region have largely left behind their founding ideas and ideals and transformed into electoral vehicles steeped in corruption and self-interest. Patronage politics is the norm throughout the region, both at the national and local levels. Some of the traditional dynastic parties have lost their positions of preeminence but the dynastic tendencies of personalism, family control, and family drama still color party politics. Religion and ethnicity have become much more present in party life. Hindu nationalism in India and Islamism in Pakistan are now central elements of political life in those countries and politics all around the region are immersed in issues of ethnic and kinship-based cleavages and loyalties. Antidemocratic forces and civil conflict have overwhelmed or crippled party life in several countries.

East and Southeast Asia

East and Southeast Asia present a sharply divided political party landscape.[31] One major set of countries in these regions, including Burma, China, Laos,

North Korea, and Vietnam are dictatorial states controlled either by an authoritarian single party, or, in the case of Burma, a military junta. Another set are multiparty systems, divided between dominant party systems such as Cambodia, Malaysia, and Singapore, and others that are more pluralistic, such as Indonesia, Mongolia, the Philippines, South Korea, Taiwan, and Thailand. Whereas party development is fundamentally blocked in the authoritarian countries, it has experienced a surge during the past twenty years in the multiparty systems.

Most of the current multiparty systems in East and Southeast Asia got their start in the 1940s and 1950s as part of decolonization or, in the case of countries that were never colonized, as part of transitions away from traditional autocracies. Multipartyism was shaky for decades. Parties were often overshadowed and manipulated by powerful rulers or ruling cliques who viewed parties as insignificant instruments to be used or discarded as needed. Some of these countries experienced periods of authoritarian rule that abrogated or severely circumscribed fledging multiparty systems, such as the decades of dictatorship in the Philippines under President Ferdinand Marcos or in Indonesia under President Suharto. It was only in the 1980s and 1990s, when some of the authoritarian regimes fell or stepped aside, that multipartyism began to get on more solid footing.[32] Thus many parties in East and Southeast Asia are less than twenty years old. There is a strong sense in the region that multipartyism is an ongoing experiment whose value, at least in some places, is still subject to debate. The most notable exception of course is Japan, the longest-settled democracy in the area, although even there, political party life has primarily been a narrow story of dominant party politics.

With the spread of multipartyism in East and Southeast Asia has come a predictable explosion in the number of parties. Also with that has come the equally familiar wave of public dissatisfaction with and even disdain for parties. All the same complaints about parties are heard as in other new or struggling democracies. The parties appear, often quite manifestly, to suffer the same sorts of organizational and behavioral shortcomings as their counterparts in other parts of the developing and postcommunist worlds. Unlike with South Asia, it is not possible in such a politically heterogeneous region to identify a characteristic regional type of party. Nevertheless, two attributes of parties in the multiparty systems of East and Southeast Asia stand out.

The first is personalism. Parties in many new or struggling democracies are personalistic entities in which party organizations and ideologies are completely subordinated to the interests and direction of party leaders. In East and Southeast Asia this is especially so. Party politics is synonymous with the power battles of titanic, domineering political figures. "Big man politics" is the order of the day, in Cambodia, the Philippines, Singapore, South Korea, Thailand, and elsewhere. Many parties are clearly little more than fiefdoms of the party leaders and their close associates. Party switching is a further symptom of the pervasive personalism. Because party leaders are mostly using parties as electoral vehicles, they have little inhibition against dropping their party if it does not do what they want. To take just one example, a recent study of Thai elections found that 45 percent of legislators elected were defectors from other parties.

Second, the party systems are soaked in money and corruption. Like personalism, problems relating to money in politics are common all around the world. In East and Southeast Asia, the term "money politics" is ever-present, with constant charges of vote buying, influence peddling, illicit corporate-party ties, and other such practices. In its recent study of Asian political parties, for example, the National Democratic Institute highlights the centrality of the money politics problem:

> [Asian] parties are also threatened by the influence of money, which can affect key aspects of the parties' operations, such as selecting leaders and candidates and establishing legislative priorities. The corrupting influence of money is particularly evident in the electoral process where vote buying and patronage are key aspects of the political system.[33]

The depth and extent of money politics is partly due to the fairly abrupt transitions in some countries from semifeudalistic political structures to multiparty politics. The continuing culture of reciprocal favors and instrumental gift-giving in many Asian societies is also likely a factor, especially in relation to vote buying, which is more an issue (at least more often thrown around as an accusation) in Asia than any other region. There is the fact that in some of these countries, such as South Korea and Taiwan, there is a lot of money to be thrown around in political life. The rapid economic growth in many parts of East and Southeast Asia has produced many wealthy new businesses, or enriched older ones. These businesses have spent heavily on politics to ensure the influence or protection they believe they need.

The Philippines is an example of a country where the tendencies toward personalism and political corruption have severely marked party politics.[34] Party competition is vigorous but perceived by many citizens as a sordid game of ambition, money, and greed played by members of a socioeconomic elite that cares little for ordinary people and uses parties simply as instruments of their own needs and interests. The unstable and theatrical patterns of presidential politics in recent years in the Philippines highlights the shallowness and intensive personalism of the country's party politics. Much the same could be said about party life in Thailand.[35]

Although party politics all around the region evidence these problems of intense personalism and money politics, some of the party systems function fairly well at least in the sense that they offer citizens a real range of choices and the major parties have some genuine roots in the society. Taiwan, for example, has a fairly stable, coherent party system in which the two main parties have each over decades built up a grassroots base and stand for distinct policy choices. Both parties have shown a long-term positive evolution as democratic political actors. The Kuomintang (KMT), which dominated Taiwanese politics for almost half a century after the mainlanders arrived in Taiwan in flight from the Chinese Communist revolution, has painfully but genuinely learned to accept democratic rules of the game. The main opposition to the KMT, the Democratic Progressive Party, went from being a weak political force to a governing party over the course of several decades through a process of serious, diligent party building.

Similarly, in post-Suharto Indonesia, parties are much criticized by ordinary citizens and expert observers for being elitist, opportunistic, and corrupt. Yet some of the larger parties have identifiable constituencies as well as close ties to broad-based social organizations, such as the two main Muslim organizations in the country. Given the short amount of time that has passed since the old authoritarian order passed away, multiparty politics are actually doing relatively well in Indonesia.

In sum, party development in East and Southeast Asia resists easy characterization. It is more heterogeneous than in any other region. On the one hand, East and Southeast Asia have a higher proportion of one-party states than any other part of the world. Yet they also have a number of assertively pluralistic systems in which multiple parties, most of them relatively new, compete furiously. Only in a small number of this latter set of countries have parties evolved beyond personalistic vehicles to become representative organizations with stable ties to broad-based constituencies. The remarkable economic dynamism of the region continues apace and Asian political systems are struggling to keep up. Political actors are being asked by increasingly wealthy, educated citizens to provide some reasonable levels of accountability, fairness, and good governance in place of the common patterns of crony (albeit high-growth) capitalism. Political parties are still seen more as part of the problem than the solution in this vein and a critical question for these countries is whether parties can respond more effectively to this rising demand.

CHAPTER THREE

Diagnosing the Condition

The global tour of parties in the developing and postcommunist worlds highlights some important differences among parties in those regions. One of these differences is age. Parties in the developing and postcommunist worlds fall roughly into three generations. The most recent generation are parties created since the late 1980s, as part of the latest wave of political openings or democratization. Most parties in new or struggling democracies, at least in sheer numbers although often not necessarily in significance, fall into this generation. In fact, in some countries that are experiencing multiparty politics in a sustained way for the first time during these past few decades, such as the former Soviet republics and many African countries, all or almost all of their parties are of this recent generation.

The previous generation are parties formed in or around processes of decolonization, mostly from the 1940s through the early 1960s. Parties of this generation are especially common in South Asia and Southeast Asia, and some parts of the Middle East. They are also found in those African countries where the country's original postcolonial ruling party still survives.

A third, older generation of parties also exists—parties that emerged in the second half of the nineteenth century or the first few decades of the twentieth century as part of the spread in some parts of the world in those years of constitutional liberalism and parliamentarianism. Some parties of this early generation are found in Latin America, primarily in South America. Other parties of this early generation were established in Central and Eastern Europe but they were decimated by the arrival of Communist regimes there in the 1940s. Some of the parties in Central and Eastern Europe today are re-creations of parties of that earlier generation.

Another difference, one closely related to age, is in the size of parties. As noted in chapter 1, most parties in new or struggling democracies are weak, thinly institutionalized organizations with a limited number of full-time cadres in the central headquarters and a weak presence around the country. A small but important set of parties in these countries, however, have exten-sive organizations, at least in size (although their size is rarely matched by their organizational efficiency and capacity). Some of these are older parties, such as some of the main South American parties, that have managed to build up sizeable organizations. Others are parties that were built on or evolved from mass-based movements (such as African liberation movements) or powerful former ruling parties in one-party systems (such as Communist parties in Central and Eastern Europe).

The global tour also makes clear, however, that underneath these and other differences, a distinct sense of sameness pervades the world of political par-ties in new or struggling democracies. The core set of commonly lamented organizational characteristics of parties turns up all over in the developing and postcommunist worlds: their leader-centric, top-down nature; their self-interestedness and corruption; their weak capacity for organizational devel-opment; their lack of strong ties to a defined constituency; and their lack of well-defined ideologies, clear party programs, and ability to formulate and implement policy. These characteristics vary in intensity. They are generally less severe, for example, in parties of Central Europe compared to the parties of the former Soviet Union, and less marked in some South American coun-tries, such as Chile and Uruguay, than in others, such as Brazil and Peru. Their general ubiquity, however, is striking. If one set about to assess the political parties of a country that is part of the Third Wave of democracy, one could safely assume that the main parties have this set of organizational character-istics and from there assess the severity of these attributes and identify other distinctive characteristics and features.

The fact of this common set of characteristics gives rise to a crucial ques-tion. Given the very wide range of sociopolitical traditions, structures, and val-ues throughout the new or struggling democracies, why do their political parties generally share a core set of organizational and operational character-istics? Or to put it in the terms that democracy promoters use, why are the essential problems of political parties so similar across such widely varying places?

The easy answer to this question, and the answer that many who work in party aid organizations instinctively gravitate toward, is age. In this view, parties in new or struggling democracies have the problematic characteristics that they do because they are new. They have either just formed in the past ten or twenty years, or, if they are of the earlier two generations of parties, have only started operating in a democratic environment in the past ten or twenty years and are thus effectively new. Being new at democratic life, the argument goes, these parties lack knowledge and experience in the basics. They are still learning the roles of parties in a democracy—how to campaign effectively, how to build up their organizations, and how to govern. There is no guarantee parties will move along the developmental continuum, that is, replacing these characteristics with the attributes of well-functioning parties, such as internal democracy, lawfulness, strong ties to well-defined constituencies, and clear ideologies. But injections of knowledge and experience from the outside should at least help move them along this path.

Certainly many parties in new or struggling democracies lack knowledge and experience about democratic practices. There is little indication, however, that their youth and inexperience are the main causes of their troubled organizational and operational characteristics. Many of the older parties in these countries that have had considerable experience with competitive pluralistic politics, such as the Peronist Party in Argentina or the Indian National Congress, exhibit the same tendencies toward leader-centrism, ideological incoherence, corruption, and so forth as do parties in their first or second electoral cycle. As the political trajectory of the past twenty years in most new or struggling democracies makes clear, political parties seem only to become more marked by such tendencies as they age. The accumulation of experience is not producing any noticeable ameliorative effect. It is necessary, therefore, to look elsewhere for answers to explain why parties in these countries so consistently show the common organizational and operational features that they do.

Compression

The Long Path to Electoralism

One key explanatory factor is the political context of the emergence of parties in new or struggling democracies—or reemergence in the case of parties that survived through earlier periods of authoritarian rule. Many of these parties have come to life in a context of immediate, intense electoral competition, with significant consequences for their organizational development. To elaborate this factor fully it is useful to review briefly some basic elements of the evolution and types of parties in established democracies. The aim is not to hold up parties or party development in those countries as an automatic ideal against which parties in new or struggling democracies must be measured (something that Western party aid organizations do, as discussed later in this book). Rather it is simply to use this experience to gain some comparative insight on patterns of party formation and evolution.

The scholarly literature on party development in the established democracies is a thicket of contending typologies and evolutionary schemas. In delving into this literature it is hard not to think that parties are so tremendously varied that efforts to sort them into clear categories is futile. Nevertheless a broadly agreed-upon framework of party evolution prevails and provides a useful analytic base.[1] It holds that parties in these countries (at least Western Europe; the applicability of the framework to Australia, Japan, New Zealand, and North America is debated) have followed a four-stage evolutionary path.

In the first stage, which unfolded during the spread of parliamentary government in the nineteenth century, cadre parties (or, as they are sometimes labeled, elite-based parties) emerged. These were small parties representing the interests of narrow circles of socioeconomic elites. They had limited numbers of members and minimal organizational structures. They often derived from contending parliamentary groups (such as landholders versus urban merchants) and they were very much a product of the limited suffrage (restricted in many countries to male property owners) and the shallow political participation of that era.

As industrialization spread in Europe in the nineteenth and early twentieth centuries, the urban working class grew, suffrage expanded, social organizations (notably unions) multiplied, and a new kind of party emerged—the mass-based party. These parties had large numbers of members, usually dues-paying members, who were brought into the party through grassroots party work and were served by the party through extensive party organizational networks and structures. These new parties developed close associations with various types of social organizations, including unions and religious organizations. They were often ideologically or programmatically oriented. The archetypal mass-based party was a socialist party representing a newly expanding industrial working class. In the early decades of the twentieth century other types of mass-based parties emerged, such as nationalist, fascist, and religious parties. Although mass-based parties competed in and strove to win elections, they were not narrowly focused on short-term electoral goals.

They had long-term, movement-building goals. Thus they sought to develop stronger, deeper ties to their adherents than merely getting their vote. These parties became social networks, creating social institutions, relationships, and protection for their members.

The next stage of party development occurred after World War II. The rise of mass consumer culture and the broader evolution of working classes into middle classes, combined with the emergence and spread of television, produced significant changes in political parties. Mass-based parties evolved into or in some cases gave way to electoralist parties. Electoralist parties focus primarily on winning elections. They are organizationally somewhat thinner than mass-based parties and use electoral professionals to plan and run campaigns. They place greater emphasis on television and other forms of mass voter outreach than on long-term membership development. They are more candidate-centered and personality-oriented. The archetypical electoralist party is the "catch-all" party, meaning that these parties downplay any strong ideology or cause in the interest of gaining as many votes as possible. Most of the major European parties evolved in the postwar years from mass-based to catch-all parties, moving somewhat toward the center and seeking to go beyond their core constituencies to attract a wider voter base.

The other main variant of electoralist party besides the catch-all party in the established democracies are programmatic parties. Like catch-all parties these are also organizationally thin and electorally focused but they adhere to a distinctive ideology or political program. In proportional representation systems, such parties are usually more willing then catch-all parties to accept a defined, circumscribed voter base. The contemporary British Conservative Party, at least in its Margaret Thatcher phase, is an example of a programmatic party. Some observers consider the U.S. Republican Party, from the Reagan years on, such a party. Smaller programmatic parties would include the main conservative parties in Sweden or some of the main Dutch parties.

Some political party experts believe that beginning in the 1970s another stage of party development started to occur.[2] After a brief golden age in the 1950s and 1960s, catch-all parties came under increased stress and criticism due to a variety of factors. These included economic challenges (such as stagflation in the 1970s and diminishing big government policies in the 1980s) and sociological ones (like the continued increase of individualism and the tendency of citizens in postindustrial societies to reduce their attachments to traditional social organizations, including parties). Some parties have responded by searching for ways to develop renewed links with voters using new information technologies or other methods. Scholars have offered a host of contending concepts to characterize what they believe to be new types of post–catch-all parties including cartel parties, new politics parties, and network parties.[3]

Catch-all, programmatic, and post–catch-all parties have been the dominant types of parties in established democracies for the last fifty years but not the only types. They share the political space in some countries with movement parties—small parties that espouse a clear cause, usually in sharp opposition to the existing set of parties, and appeal to a well-defined, though limited constituency. Although they are active electoral competitors, some of them focus more than many large electoralist parties do on developing an active, relational concept of party membership. Movement parties exist on the right, such as Jean-Marie Le Pen's National Front in France or Jörg Haider's Freedom Party in Austria, and on the left, such as Green parties or some leftist liberation parties.

In short, the evolution of parties in established democracies has been a long trajectory toward electoralism. Electoralism became the dominant mode after World War II and since then has only intensified. The trajectory toward electoralism was long and slow, reflecting the gradual development of liberal democracy that characterized European political life from the late eighteenth century to the mid-twentieth century. By the time parties in what are now the established Western democracies became primarily electoralist organizations, many had built up considerable organizational capital from their time as mass-based parties. Parties had gained a solid place in their societies, having become embedded in the existing socioeconomic cleavages. Thus although fifty years of electoralism has produced an organizational attenuation of these parties (the thinning out associated with the transition from mass-based parties to catch-all parties), Western parties are still living off the traditions and forms of party organization built up over a much longer earlier period. Similarly, although the economic and sociocultural modernization that has occurred in these years has reduced the place of parties in citizens' lives, these parties are still living off the inheritance of their earlier period of greater centrality in sociopolitical life.

The Short Path to Electoralism

The evolution of parties in new or struggling democracies has been very different. Most parties in these countries have not evolved slowly from cadre parties to mass-based parties to electoralist parties. Instead they emerged as electoralist entities from the start, during the recent spate of political openings and democratic transitions that have made up the Third Wave of democracy.[4] The fact that they are electoralist parties, like most parties in established democracies, does not mean that they resemble those parties in terms of their place in society, their rootedness, organizational capability, policy capacity, or in many other ways. The category of electoralist party (according to Diamond and Gunther's highly useful party typology) includes several very different types, including catch-all parties, programmatic parties, and personalist parties.[5] The common element of the different subtypes is that all are primarily focused on electoral campaigns. Most electoralist parties in established democracies are catch-all parties that evolved from mass-based parties. Some parties in new or struggling democracies, especially the older ones, are catch-all parties or at least weak forms of catch-all parties, but most are electoralist parties of a personalist nature.

This "electoralist-from-the-start" character has had major consequences for shaping parties in new or struggling democracies. It can be understood as one element of a broader political phenomenon—the compression of attempted democratic change in Third Wave countries. In these countries, once the old authoritarian regime falls, every possible element of democratization—elections, civil society development, rule-of-law development, parliamentary strengthening, decentralization, and many more—is suddenly on the table at once. The slow, evolutionary patterns of political development that characterized democratization in much of Western Europe and North America—such as the gradual consolidation of the rule of law in parallel with establishment of universal suffrage—have no place in the contemporary context. The international community now arrives in countries immediately after authoritarian regimes fall bearing a wide-ranging agenda of expectations, policy support measures, and aid programs aimed at stimulating progress on as many dimensions of political reform as possible. Newly democratizing countries are immediately subjected to indexes and other rating schemes to monitor their performance on a host of governance, rights, and other politically related dimensions.

Moving quickly forward on elections is one of the core features of this democratic compression. Almost all countries that manage to shed an authoritarian regime now hold national elections as soon as possible, almost always within two or three years. The international community does often encourage and usually facilitate new democracies' first elections, frequently with substantial amounts of assistance for the administration of the elections. Yet the almost reflexive tendency of postauthoritarian countries to proceed rapidly to elections is in most cases not primarily a result of international encouragement or presence. Rather it is driven by a basic normative change that has occurred in the world in the past thirty years: more and more people in the developing and postcommunist worlds view elections as the sole path for establishing the legitimacy of a government. Therefore when a dictator dies in his sleep (as in Nigeria in 1998) or is driven out of power (as in Indonesia in 1998) citizens push for immediate elections no matter how unprepared for elections the society may be in traditional political development terms. Even when international actors step out of a proelectoral role and try to slow the rush to elections, the domestic pressure in favor of elections is usually too strong to resist, as the U.S. government discovered in Iraq after it ousted Saddam Hussein.

Political party development is one item on this compressed, all-at-once democratization agenda. With many new or struggling democracies moving abruptly from no multiparty elections (at least no genuine elections) to successive national and local elections with universal suffrage and a fairly open field for political competition, the door to party formation is suddenly thrown open. Election schedules often have been established and administrative preparations for elections commenced while political parties (other than the outgoing ruling party) are still scrambling to get established. Parties have to get going very quickly and plunge right into electoral competition, often before they have anything more than a handful of candidates, a skeletal organization, and some initial financial backing.

Moreover, parties have had to develop quickly in contexts where civil society development is also in high gear. In many established democracies not only did parties have a long developmental path before they faced strong electoral pressures, but civil society was also developing quite slowly alongside them, allowing a gradual interaction and building up of mutually beneficial ties over time. In contrast, a signal characteristic of Third Wave transitions is the mushrooming of (usually donor-funded) civil society organizations immediately after the fall of the authoritarian regime. As discussed in chapter 5, many of these new civil society organizations are advocacy NGOs that are wary of parties and uninterested in being closely associated with them. These organizations compete with parties, often aggressively and effectively, for citizens' attention and support, for talent, and for policy influence. Stiff competition right from the start for creating ties to citizens further encourages parties in these contexts to focus almost exclusively on their electoral role because it is the one role not open to civil society groups.

Parties are affected not just by this democratic compression but also by what might be called a certain type of socioeconomic compression as well. In established democracies, parties got under way and were institutionalized well before mass electronic communication was developed. They adapted to the rise of such communication methods, but were not originally built around them. In contrast, most parties in new or struggling democracies have been born right in the middle of ever-expanding forms of such communication. Thus from the start their very organizations and methods are built around the imperatives of mass-based electronic campaigning, with its emphasis on personalities, images, repetitive and superficial messages, and the consequent de-emphasis on personal relationships, grassroots contacts, and sustained communication.

These two types of compression combine to have decisive effects on patterns of party development. With political space suddenly opened up, elections coming in a hurry, and a paucity of established parties, new political parties naturally mushroom. Slow processes of party formation—such as small, horizontally structured groups of people united around a political ideal who form a party and gradually build its presence in the society through long-term, person-to-person grassroots work—do not fit with the imperative of sudden, full electoral competition. Instead, rapid processes of party formation dominate. These are processes in which strong-minded, ambitious people who want to gain an important place in the new order start parties with little organizational basis other than a small circle of loyal friends and little underlying political vision other than self-advancement. Because they are thrown immediately into the electoral fray, these new parties are under intense pressure to get immediately to work attracting votes. A failure to make a good showing in the first election or two is devastating—it almost guarantees that money, talent, and attention will quickly abandon the fledging party in search of more promising ones. Developing campaign messages, slogans, and symbols, raising money, and getting the message out become top priorities. There is no time to build a voter base slowly from the ground up. To the extent they have access to them and can afford them, parties will focus on mass media outreach and other rapid, large-scale methods of communication. Developing a stable, long-term constituency, a well-developed party platform, and a well-grounded organizational structure with real roots all over the country are secondary priorities at best.

Those parties that do well in the first or second elections may have some room to adopt a longer-term horizon of party building. By then, however, the forms of their organizations—especially the top-down, leader-centric, "large head, small body" shape is set. Moreover, in an environment of regular, often frequent elections, the long-term incentives for engaging in gradualistic, decentralized membership development and local party capacity-building remain low relative to the pressure for near-term vote-getting. The pattern of electoralist politics—with its emphasis on raising money, selling candidates, and pushing images—has taken hold. Parties have little choice other than to swim in these new political waters around them.

The syndrome of "electoralist-from-the-start" affects not just parties recently established in the early years of Third Wave democratic transitions but also many older parties too. Parties that predated recent democratic openings (having been born in an earlier pluralistic era and having survived an intervening period of authoritarianism), such as the older South American parties, were effectively relaunched once democracy returned to their countries. Their relaunch, which often entailed a significant remaking of party apparatuses that had been greatly reduced under authoritarian rule, took place in this new context of intense, rapidly unfolding electoralism. They, too, faced similar pressure to run electorally before they could hardly walk organizationally.

The powerful shaping effects of early, intensive electoralism on the organizational structures and operating methods of politics in new or struggling democracies is underlined by some contrasting cases. In a few countries in the developing world, certain strong parties (from the point of view of organizational development) have evolved. Tellingly, they have grown up in situations of electoral blockage, that is to say where they are allowed to exist but their electoral prospects are constrained by a nondemocratic ruling party. In Taiwan for example the Democratic Progressive Party and the precursor opposition groups that formed the basis of the party when it was formally established in the mid-1980s, were forced to operate politically for many years in a situation of only partial electoral freedom. Knowing that an electoral victory would not be allowed any time soon, the party took a long-term, serious approach to building a political base and ties to supporters, rather than concentrating all its efforts on maximizing votes in any one election.[6] The party developed over time into a well-grounded party with a greater rootedness (although not necessarily a coherent organizational structure) than the typical party in new or struggling democracies.

The National Action Party (PAN) in Mexico, founded in 1939, was forced to live through many decades in which it was allowed to operate and compete electorally at the local level but had no possibility of victory on the national level. This period of electoral blockage impelled the party to concentrate on building a strong grassroots network and finding ways to connect with citizens other than through national campaigning. It encouraged a strong form of party organization that served the party well once the electoral space opened up in Mexico in the 1990s.[7]

Interestingly, a similar pattern is being produced today with Islamist movements and parties in the Arab world. Some Arab governments allow moderate Islamist movements and sometimes parties to exist, but try to keep closed the possibility of their actually gaining power. They do this by not allowing them to compete as a party (as in Egypt), maintaining behind-the-scenes military control over the political party sector (as in Algeria), or only allowing parties a very limited place overall in the political system (as in Morocco). Faced with no likely prospect of being allowed to take full power in the near term, most Islamist movements and parties in the Arab world have concentrated—often with impressive success—on developing strong grassroots organizations and a broad base in their respective societies. Ironically, although they have been intent on limiting Islamist movements and parties, many Arab states have created the very conditions that may lead them ultimately to become strong, well-rooted parties: high incentives for grassroots organization building and low incentives for an electoral focus.

Structural Factors

The compressed nature of political transitions and the instant electoralism that it forces upon many parties in new or struggling democracies is a major factor contributing to their characteristic forms and methods. It is not the only one. Obviously, just as factors such as industrialization, the rise of mass consumer culture, and mass communication technologies have shaped party development in the established democracies, a plethora of socioeconomic and sociopolitical trends and conditions have shaped and continue to shape parties in new or struggling democracies. The previous chapter highlighted some of these elements in particular regions. Their diversity across the many different regions in the developing and postcommunist worlds may at first glance seem too great to offer any explanations of the commonality of the characteristics of parties in these places. A careful look, however, reveals some crucial common factors.[8]

Weak Rule of Law

In many established democracies, substantial progress in the development of the rule of law occurred simultaneously with the slow, early phase of political party development. As universal suffrage was being achieved and modern electoral systems put in place, the rule of law was being substantially strengthened. This does not mean that judicial systems functioned perfectly, core legal norms were always agreed on and respected, state officials never put themselves above the law, or larger breakdowns in the rule of law did not sometimes occur (as in Germany and other parts of Europe in the 1930s). On the whole, however, parties in what are now the established democracies have had to learn to live within law-bound environments.

In contrast, party development in new or struggling democracies is taking place, and where parties are older, has long taken place, in societies where the rule of law is very weak. The degree of weakness varies considerably but in many places a basic picture is familiar. The institutions responsible for drafting and enacting laws function poorly. The institutions for implementing and enforcing laws are weak and politicized. Political and economic elites ignore or manipulate laws to protect their own interests and law acts only as a feeble check on the exercise of political power. Rules about financial transparency, both in the political and business sectors, are often especially poorly developed or enforced.

When electoral competition is thrown open in such contexts and highly ambitious, power-seeking actors—political parties—enter the fray, a predictable pattern occurs. As such organizations gear up campaigns and assert themselves in political life, they push at whatever legal boundaries they confront. They try to circumvent restrictions on their activities, ignore rules that constrain them, or intentionally violate norms they view as unfair or simply inconvenient. Their relentless interest in power ends up outweighing the low incentives for obeying the law that exist in weak rule-of-law systems. Although the people who found and lead political parties may not start off as being especially unethical or prone to violating the law, many or perhaps even most of them end up engaging in legally questionable electoral behavior, either in the electoral scramble for power or in official positions if they make it into government. This fact usually becomes well-known among the citizens of the country and contributes significantly to the low regard in which parties are held, and often to a broader disillusionment with democracy.

The weakness of the rule of law in most new or struggling democracies has become a major item on the international community's agenda and donor efforts to help these countries strengthen the rule of law are now common. Such efforts sometimes produce progress on specific challenges, such as improving the management of the courts, or introducing more modern administrative procedure.[9] They are almost always too small and piecemeal, however, to make a significant dent in the overall situation of the rule of law of the country in question. In other words, most new or struggling democracies are living with serious deficiencies in the rule of law that will not be solved anytime soon. The juxtaposition of multiparty competitive politics with the weak rule of law is another part of the challenge of democratic compression, one that cannot be avoided by waiting for rule-of-law development to occur first, given that autocracies in many cases have been responsible for the debilitated legal and judicial systems.

Poverty

Poverty also contributes to the characteristic pattern of party development in new or struggling democracies. A sizeable proportion of such countries, especially in the Caucasus, Central America, South Asia, and sub-Saharan Africa, are poor, with per capita incomes less than $2,000. Others are middle income countries, but many of them, especially in South America, still have large numbers of poor citizens due to high levels of inequality. Building and maintaining parties in poor societies, or societies where large numbers of citizens are poor, is much harder than in wealthy societies and produces or reinforces certain types of party development.

To start with, most parties in poor societies have great difficulty raising funds. Most citizens have little money to spare, the business community is small and usually under stress, and the government is also short of funds, meaning that public financing for parties is likely to be minimal. The low availability of funds for most parties contributes to the weak party organizations that are so common in these countries. Parties are unable to hire many staff or set up training programs, to buy transportation and communication equipment, to finance branch offices, and so forth. Although the societies are poor, campaigns are still expensive, with parties under pressure to hire staff; buy television, radio, or newspaper ads; print posters and brochures; pay for rallies and other events; and much more. Given the overriding importance of electoral performance, parties put most of what money they have into campaigns, starving the side of long-term organizational development.

The money available for parties (beyond public funding, which even when available is usually very limited) comes primarily from a small number of wealthy businesspeople who invest in politics to advance or protect their own interests. The dependence of parties on these secretive and often shady financial backers has serious negative consequences for party development. It magnifies party corruption because parties are often put in situations where they choose between doing illicit favors for their backers or losing the only significant source of funds that they have. It also reinforces the top-down structure of parties because party leaders have inordinate amounts of power and influence within parties due to the fact that they maintain personal relationships with the funders. The pattern of funding reduces the range of likely political alternatives. In poor societies, or middle income countries where most wealth resides in a narrow elite sector, almost anyone who has a lot of money is tied, formally or informally, to the ruling elite. As a result they are little inclined to support opposition parties or any parties that would try to shake up the status quo, greatly reducing the chances of such parties gaining strength. Thus political alternatives are weak and a tendency toward dominant party systems is strengthened, as evidenced in the former Soviet Union and sub-Saharan Africa.

More generally, widespread poverty contributes significantly to the rise and endurance of the neopatrimonial politics that are so common in many parts of the developing world, with significant consequences for party development. Poverty renders citizens socioeconomically vulnerable and poorly equipped to assert their own interests. They look to parties as sources of largesse and protection rather than as representational vehicles. Parties look at citizens as passive blocs of potential voters to be bought or co-opted rather than as a potential base of members to recruit and constituents to represent. When parties achieve power they use it to deliver patronage to their supporters. Corruption and organizational centralization are thus woven into the fabric of party development.

Constraints on Policy Choices

As mentioned previously, a lack of ideological definition and differentiation characterizes most parties in the developing and postcommunist worlds. As voters in those countries habitually complain, parties do not seem to stand for anything, or else they all stand for the same bland, overarching goals such as democracy, national unity, and development. The youth and institutional underdevelopment of these parties may at first glance appear to account for this shortcoming. In fact, however, deeper causes are at work, relating both to the broader international context in which the parties operate and some structural features of the societies of which they are a part.

Many parties in new or struggling democracies were born in the "end of ideology" context of the 1980s and 1990s. Of course parties in established democracies have been affected by the softening of the left-right framework as well, with many gravitating toward the center as a result. These parties, however, have been able to continue to live off the legacy of ideological identities formed at an earlier time, when the left-right framework was stronger, a tactic not available to many newer parties in new or struggling democracies.

The softening of the ideological ground for parties is compounded by the international economic context in which developing and postcommunist countries exist. New or struggling democracies are fighting for a place in a globalized, intensely competitive international economic system. Many are dependent on aid or other capital flows from abroad. All countries today face reduced economic policy sovereignty due to globalization. The weak economies of most new and struggling democracies are especially constrained. Basically they are obliged to try to follow what has become a largely uniform set of market-oriented economic policies. As a result, one of the core bases for ideological differentiation among competing political groups that has underlined party development in established democracies—basic economic policy choices—is largely unavailable in these countries.

Of course some parties advocate an alternative to the dominant economic policy framework—usually a softer line toward marketization, with a social democratic coloring. As the case of Brazilian President Luis Ignacio (Lula) da Silva and his Workers' Party demonstrates, however, if such parties manage to gain power they face sharp constraints on their actual policy choices due to the realities of international capital flows and other elements of the international economic context. With occasional exceptions, such as Venezuelan President Hugo Chávez's oil-fueled populist redistributive policies, they rarely end up moving more than a few degrees away from the standard market-oriented policy script. Voters learn that although they can vote for promises of different economic policies, in most cases no matter which party or parties they elect, they will end up with approximately the same economic policy. The most meaningful dimension for differentiating parties on core socioeconomic issues thus becomes the "how" rather than the "what"—how competently and honestly they will govern. Therefore issues of corruption and competence rather than ideology dominate the electoral campaigns of many new or struggling democracies.

The constrained international economic policy environment is not the only factor weakening the ideological identity of parties in these countries. Many of these societies do not have the sort of socioeconomic cleavages that historically gave rise to the left-right divide in established democracies. That is to say, they are not differentiated, industrialized economies in which a large and rising working class is pitted against an owner class made up both of urban commercial entrepreneurs and rural property owners. Instead quite a few of the Third Wave countries, especially in Central America, South Asia, and sub-Saharan Africa, have very large sectors of urban and rural poor, with a very small, often precarious middle class, and even smaller circles of the very rich. They do not therefore have the socioeconomic basis for a "normal" ideological differentiation of the party spectrum into a roughly balanced division between the center-left and the center-right. The much flatter (in the sense of large numbers of poor people and very small numbers of rich people) socioeconomic structures in many of the poorer Third Wave countries mean that other cleavages, such as ethnicity, religion, and regional identity, are more prominent as potential determinants of party differentiation.

Antipolitical Legacies

Many of the attempted democratic transitions of the past several decades have come after long, harsh periods of dictatorial rule. The experience of such rule inevitably leaves behind serious damage to a society's sociopolitical fabric, damage that complicates the process of party development when it does get under way again in a new period of openness. Although these wounds naturally vary from place to place depending on the particularities of the political experiences, a general syndrome is identifiable.

In many of the new or struggling democracies, citizens come to the whole issue of democratization with a deeply antipolitical outlook. They are cynical about the very idea of politics. They see political life of any type as an irretrievably dirty domain dominated by greed, hypocrisy, and unfairness; the hopeful idea that multiparty competition will be a method for balancing and resolving diverse societal interests in a roughly fair way appears a chimera. In fact, the very idea of partisan differences and all the partisan squabbling and debates that come with more open political systems seem at best necessary evils and often a depressing waste of time and energy.

Such attitudes pose formidable challenges for political parties seeking to gain a footing or strengthen an already established position. Citizens of countries coming out of authoritarian or totalitarian rule are typically happy to be given the chance to vote, and they turn out in large numbers, at least for the first few rounds of elections. Their voting, however, is often an expression of their own sense of personal empowerment and independence, not their loyalty or attachment to any one political grouping. They are often reflexively suspicious of political parties, seeing them only as intrinsically self-interested actors in the tainted domain of politics. This is especially true in the former communist countries where the previous regime ruled through a party, thereby poisoning the whole idea of political parties for many people.

Thus as parties in new or struggling democracies seek to develop a base they not only face the many logistical hurdles intrinsic to such an endeavor, from raising money to creating organizational capacity, they also have to make inroads against strongly negative public attitudes about the very concepts of politics, politicians, and political parties. Representatives of a party engaged in outreach are not simply competing to persuade citizens to support them rather than another party. They are struggling to convince citizens to get interested in supporting any party at all. Adding still further to these challenges is the social atomization that dictatorships leave behind. Repressive systems teach people to distrust each other concerning anything to do with politics, at least outside of very limited circles of secure personal loyalty. Such engrained distrust, and the related habits of political caution and inhibition, frustrate the efforts of parties to build wide networks of support once the political environment opens up.

In short, parties are starting in a hole in postauthoritarian societies. Although the citizens may be thrilled to have gotten rid of the old regime, pervasive skepticism about politics represents an uphill terrain for party development. In simple terms, a politically cynical public encourages cynical parties and politicians, who in turn only confirm the public's worst suspicions. These attitudes and patterns are not unchangeable but they make the challenge of party building in new or struggling democracies that much more difficult.

Presidential Systems

Western political scientists have devoted large amounts of attention over the years to analyzing the effects of different kinds of electoral systems on party development in established democracies.[10] The contrasting effects of proportional representation systems versus majoritarian systems has, for example, been a topic of extensive attention. These same issues are also at work of course in new or struggling democracies but have been researched in less depth. It is very likely that the type of electoral system has similarly important consequences in new or struggling democracies for the numerical shape of the party systems in these countries (whether they have two- or three-party systems, which tend to arise under majoritarian electoral systems, or more multiple party systems). However, with respect to the core set of organizational characteristics of parties in many new or struggling democracies, a different issue concerning political structures is of greater relevance: the prevalence in these countries of presidential systems.

Unlike in established democracies, where parliamentary systems are by far more common, presidential systems are dominant in new or struggling democracies. They are almost the rule in Latin America and the Middle East (outside the monarchies), the former Soviet Union, and sub-Saharan Africa, and common in East and Southeast Asia. The only regions of the developing and postcommunist worlds where they are not dominant are Central and Eastern Europe and South Asia.

Presidential systems are hard on parties.[11] This is true in established democracies but even more so in new or struggling democracies where other institutional sources of power, such as legislatures and judiciaries, are usually extremely weak. Competing in political systems in which capturing the presidency is the central, even overriding goal, reinforces the already marked tendency of parties in new or struggling democracies to be top-down, leader-centric organizations. Most of the attention within the parties becomes focused on who will be the presidential candidate. Most of the resources are directed to the presidential campaign. Parties often end up as vehicles for presidential campaigns with other functions and roles given short shrift.

The very weak parliaments that are an endemic feature of presidential systems in developing and postcommunist countries also hamper party development. When parliaments have little power, parliamentary elections become sideshows and parties have trouble attracting good candidates or generating much organizational involvement in the process. Feckless, unimportant parliaments undermine parties in the public's eye. Citizens become dismissive of parliamentarians and the parties they represent when they see parliament accomplishing little.

Rocky Soil

To summarize, it is natural but substantially mistaken to assume that the characteristic organizational and operational features causing the standard lament about political parties in new or struggling democracies are the result of the relative youth of most of these parties. The fact that the older parties in these regions, such as many of the parties in South America and South Asia, largely share many of the same problematic features, casts doubt on the value of party age as a central explanatory factor. Parties in many countries seem to be becoming more rather than less problematic as the attempted democratic transitions unfold. Instead, the structural and contextual conditions in which party development occurs in these countries appear to be responsible. Although there are obviously tremendous variations in the underlying settings in which parties attempt to operate in the developing and postcommunist worlds, a certain number of conditions found in many of these countries contribute to the characteristic patterns of party development that cut across the many regions and countries in question.

In other words, parties emerging where broad-based electoral competition is an immediate, overriding priority, the rule of law is weak, widespread poverty or economic inequality is present, the choice of basic economic policies is strongly constrained, deep-seated antipolitical attitudes created by the experience of dictatorship persist, and strong presidents overshadow weak legislatures and judiciaries have certain characteristics. That is to say they are usually top-down, leader-centric, organizationally thin, corrupt, patrimonial, and ideologically vague. Not all Third Wave countries have all of these underlying conditions of course, but they are widely present. These conditions do not create uniform parties. Parties vary widely in many new or struggling democracies along certain dimensions—such as size, degrees of religious or ethnic orientation, and electoral capability—but they do produce common patterns of organization and operation.

It is noteworthy in this regard that in the one part of the developing and postcommunist worlds where some parties are doing fairly well (in the sense of becoming somewhat like Western European parties)—that is, Central and Eastern Europe—these various structural and conjunctural conditions cited above are generally less present. Although the rule of law is highly imperfect, legal institutions and norms in Central and Eastern Europe are more solidly entrenched than in many other parts of the developing and postcommunist world. Poverty is less present and economic inequality is not high. Economies are much less dependent on external aid than in many other places and open to at least some economic policy choices. Parliamentary or mixed presidential-parliamentary systems are more common than presidential systems.

A Common Crisis?

At the same time that many people in new or struggling democracies talk about their political parties as being in a state of crisis, talk of party crisis, or at least party decline, is also fairly common in many established democracies. Many writings in the Western political science literature identify and analyze this phenomenon.[12] The most-cited symptoms of party decline include a reduction in the overall vote for the traditional parties in a country and a rise in the vote for protest figures or protest parties; the increasing "dealignment" of voters from parties, that is to say, a weakening of voter loyalties toward parties and the replacement of deeper ties between parties and voters with more superficial relations based on short-term electioneering; declining voter turnout; declining party membership; and diminished public regard for parties. Many of these symptoms sound similar to the characteristics of parties in new or struggling democracies that give rise to the standard lament about parties in these countries. This partial parallelism raises the question of whether the problems with parties in new or struggling democracies are really just part of a larger trend of problems with parties everywhere. From that follows the question of whether the travails of parties in new or struggling democracies should be viewed as an inevitable condition of contemporary politics rather than a shortcoming of attempted transitions.

No simple answer to this question of parallelism is possible. There certainly exists some similarity in the symptoms of party decline in established democracies and the weaknesses of party development in many new or struggling democracies. The common link is that of electoralism. The pervasive, relentless electoralism common in established and new or struggling democracies alike creates similar patterns of political opportunism, professionalized electioneering, narrowed party-voter ties, personalism over ideological substance, and other problematic elements of contemporary political party life.

Despite this common link, however, there are significant differences. To start with, as noted earlier in this chapter, the effect of electoralism on parties in established democracies is a gradual hollowing out of organizational resources and of a place in society that parties had already accumulated over a long period. In contrast, with most parties in new or struggling democracies, electoralism is a starting condition. These parties are not hollowing out slowly over time; they are formed (or relaunched after living under authoritarianism) around the electoral imperative and struggle to achieve any hold at all on citizens. Thus one can speculate that parties in new or struggling democracies represent in a sense the future (albeit a troubled one) of parties generally—they are pure entities of electoralism, something that parties in established democracies are slowly moving toward but are still somewhat distant from due to their inherited political capital from earlier periods. In this view, trying to help parties in new or struggling democracies take on the organizational forms and methods of parties in established democracies may be a futile endeavor—it is effectively asking them not to develop "forward" but actually to evolve "backward" against the main currents of political development in the world.

Second, it is true that there is some similarity in the types of conditions that electoralism produces in new or struggling democracies on the one hand and established democracies on the other. The severity of the problems of parties in the former set of countries is much greater due to the various structures and conditions outlined in the previous section. For example, although irregularities in party finance have been an issue in France, Germany, Italy, Spain, the United States, and other established democracies, they are generally less serious than the sort of deep party corruption that has plagued many new or struggling democracies, such as for example, Argentina, Mexico, Nigeria, South Korea, and Ukraine. Similarly, although the dealignment of voters from parties is a measurable phenomenon in many established democracies, in most cases (Italy is one notable exception) it is mild compared to the sort of instability that afflicts party systems in some parts of the developing and post-communist worlds, such as in Brazil, Guatemala, Peru, and Poland. Although parties are less important to citizens and have less of a place in their life today than they used to in most established democracies, they still have an important place compared with the precarious or sometimes marginal place parties have in some new or struggling democracies, such as Morocco, Pakistan, Russia, and Uganda.

Third, electoralism is a common causal link between the situation of parties in new or struggling democracies and in established democracies. Beyond that one link, the causes of the crisis of parties in many of the former set of countries are quite different in nature from those in the latter. Very generally speaking, the characteristic features of parties that underlie the standard lament in new or struggling democracies are the result of societal shortcomings or failures, from the parlous state of the rule of law to persistent poverty and a broad sense among citizens of poor performance of the political system. In contrast, the crisis of parties in the established democracies is substantially related to what can be considered societal successes. Rising affluence, higher levels of education, a lack of serious threats to most citizens' well-being, the wide, rapid adoption of new communication technologies, and other areas of sociopolitical progress contribute to the heightened individualism and boredom with partisan politics that are taking a toll on parties in these countries.

Thinking about Party Systems

As we will see in the next several chapters, when outside actors decide to try to bolster parties in new or struggling democracies they focus on the problematic organizational characteristics underlying the standard lament. In other words, they craft programs aimed at decentralizing power within parties, fostering financial transparency, developing coherent party platforms, increasing contacts with ordinary citizens, and other such objectives. The similarity of the key organizational characteristics of parties in these countries leads to a great deal of sameness in party programs across widely different countries. Yet although parties in many places embody similar organizational and operational features, the party systems that they make up often vary quite significantly. The variations in these systems have implications for how parties are or are not contributing to democratization and thus for the question of how external democracy promoters might address the issue of party development. Stated differently, an alternative way to view (and try to assist) party development is by focusing not on the general organizational characteristics of parties but on the shape and functioning of the party system as a whole. This section outlines one way to think about the differences in party systems in this vein, a way that may be helpful in exploring such an alternative approach to party aid, a subject I take up in chapter 9.

Much of the political science literature on party system types is based on established democracies. It usually focuses on variables such as the number of parties, the degree of ideological variability, and the amount of volatility in voter support for parties. Although revealing in various ways, these variables do not necessarily get at the crucial differences among party systems in countries outside the European and North American democracies. Differentiating among party systems in other countries where democracy is less secure requires attention to other dimensions, in particular two: First, what is the relationship of parties as a whole to the exercise of political power in the country? Second, how is power distributed among the parties (or conversely, is power highly concentrated in one party)? By concentrating on these two dimensions, what might be called a power-oriented taxonomy of party systems in countries other than the established democracies can be constructed. This taxonomy has two halves, party systems in nondemocratic countries (authoritarian or semiauthoritarian countries) and party systems in countries that have achieved at least a fragile state of democracy.

In authoritarian or semiauthoritarian countries that have political parties (leaving aside those countries where parties are banned, such as the Gulf monarchies) three types of party systems can be identified:

1. *Single-party systems.* Some authoritarian governments are single-party states—only one party, the ruling party, is allowed to operate and political opposition is harshly repressed.

2. *Emasculated party systems.* In some semiauthoritarian contexts, multiple political parties are allowed to organize and operate and to compete in at least some elections but the main political power in the country resides outside any political party, for example in a monarchy (as in Jordan or Morocco, or until recently in Nepal) or in a power apparatus that is not primarily rooted in a party (as in Algeria or Russia). The party system therefore exists as a political sideshow, which may absorb the energy and attention of many political actors but is of only limited consequence in the country's political life.

3. *Malign dominant party systems.* In some nondemocratic contexts, both authoritarian and semiauthoritarian, the main powerholders operate

through a party and other parties are allowed to exist. The ruling party maintains a high enough level of control over the system and has a great enough willingness to abridge rights, manipulate elections, harass and persecute the opposition, and commit other antidemocratic acts to ensure that its hold on power is not seriously threatened by the other parties. Such systems are common in Africa, the Middle East, and the former Soviet Union.

In Third Wave countries that have achieved a basic level of democracy, three different types of political party systems (viewed through the lens of power relationships) can be identified:

4. *Benign dominant party systems.* In some countries one party maintains a long-standing lock on the principal levers of political power but it does so primarily by virtue of genuine political support from a majority of the citizenry rather than through political intimidation and manipulation. Regular elections are held and the elections are free and fair. Several southern African countries, such as Botswana, Mozambique, Namibia, and South Africa, are examples of such a system.

5. *Unstable distributed party systems.* These are multiparty systems in which parties are central to the exercise of power, reasonably free and fair elections are regularly held, and no one party has a lock on power. Yet many or even most of the parties are chronically unstable, coming and going continuously on the party scene, and failing to develop stable constituencies and lasting identities. Such systems are most common in Latin America, such as in Brazil, Guatemala, and Peru, although significant party instability is also found in other parts of the world, such as in the Philippines, Poland, and Thailand.

6. *Stable distributed party systems.* These are multiparty systems in which parties are central to the exercise of power, reasonably free and fair elections are regularly held, alternation of power is common, and at least the core set of main parties is relatively stable. Although such systems have various solid prodemocratic characteristics the parties are often the source of significant public dissatisfaction and perceived to be in a state of decline. Some of them face serious particular problems, such as a high level of conflict between the main parties (as in Bangladesh), a degradation of the opposition and troubling antidemocratic signals from the ruling party and therefore a danger of a slide toward a dominant party system (such as in Argentina), or the challenge of incorporating surging new political actors that fit uneasily within the existing

system (such as in Bolivia). Stable distributed party systems are the most common (outside Western Europe and North America) in Latin America and Central and Eastern Europe, although they are also found in different parts of Asia as well.

The lines between these different party systems are not always sharp and movement among categories certainly occurs. In some malign dominant party systems, the ruler or ruling party allows opposition parties to operate but persecutes them so relentlessly that the country is close to a de facto single-party state. Belarus is an example of such a system. Similarly the line between malign and benign dominant party systems is sometimes fuzzy. A dominant party may start off with genuine majority support and a willingness to respect democratic rules of the game but then lapse into antidemocratic behavior over time. President Hugo Chavez's rule in Venezuela is an example of a regime that is probably in the process of such degeneration. The line between dominant (both malign and benign) party systems and distributed party systems (unstable and stable) is fairly sharp—alternation of power is key. Countries do move across it, such as when Kenyan President Daniel Arap Moi stepped down from power and his party lost the 2002 elections, ending a long, dominant party period.

Parties in all these different types of systems exhibit similar sorts of organizational shortcomings and syndromes. The standard lament cuts across the whole spectrum of party systems in these countries. Yet the challenge of party development has a distinctive cast in each of these systems, one that must be taken into account in any effort to assess how to assist parties in a particular national context. Figure 3.1 contains a list of these different types of party systems and the central challenge for prodemocratic party development in each one.

Single-party systems face a stark challenge regarding possible party development—the need for the creation of political space, including the legalization and tolerance of political opposition, and the institutionalization of multiparty competition. In emasculated party systems, parties face a fundamental problem of relevance, due to their powerlessness. No matter how much they work at developing their organizational structures, platforms, media skills, and so forth, the fact that they are kept at a distance from the main institutions of power badly undercuts them. Thus party building in such a context is much more than organizational development; it is about challenging the existing power structure and attempting to wrest from it more power for parties as a whole. Such challenges are about amassing and assert-

Figure 3.1. The Central Power-Related Challenges of Party Development outside the Established Democracies

Type of Party System	Central Challenge
Authoritarian or semiauthoritarian countries	
Single-party system	Creating political space, legalizing opposition parties
Emasculated party system	Empowering parties overall
Malign dominant party system	Reversing state-party fusion and checking the power of the ruling party
New democracies	
Benign dominant party system	Preventing state-party fusion
Unstable distributed party system	Facilitating party rootedness
Stable distributed party system	Stimulating party renewal

ing raw political force, although they may end up taking eventual form in orderly processes of constitutional reform or other legal changes.

In malign dominant party systems, the ruling party usually has taken over the state in some substantial ways or is in the process of doing so. The effacement of the state-party line has fateful consequences for the development of parties. From a democracy-building point of view, the ruling party is usually too strong in many ways and thus is not in need of basic organizational assistance. The opposition parties are faced with overwhelming competition from a party that has control over the state media, and often over the judiciary, civil service, and other state bodies, the ability to use state financial and organizational resources on its own behalf, and other fundamental advantages. Thus party development in such systems mixes the conventional challenges of organizational development with the broader task of taking on the state-party nexus and finding ways to limit the formal and substantive scope of the ruling party's power.

Benign dominant party systems present their own special challenges for party development. The central power-related challenge in such contexts is preventing the effacement of the line between the ruling party and the state. The ruling party usually has some real organizational strengths due to its sustained time in power and its ability to use patronage and other advantages to bolster the party. The challenge for party development (from the democratization point of view) is to block the natural tendency of the ruling party to start blurring the line between party and state—to not divert state resources to the party, to not politicize key functions like election administration and electronic media, and to not undermine the independence of the judiciary.

In distributed party systems where the parties are unstable, the overriding challenge of party development is that of establishing party roots. Parties are failing to develop sustained attachments either to key sociopolitical sectors or broader mass constituencies, with the result that they have no real staying power. Helping facilitate a situation in which parties will connect more deeply to the society generally is quite different from and probably much harder than the already daunting challenges of helping parties carry out the usual range of organizational and operational reforms.

In stable distributed party systems, a central challenge of party development is usually party renovation. In most such countries, as in parts of Latin America (for example, Chile, Colombia, and Honduras), overall party stability has meant gradual internal party decay. The overriding issue is how to achieve a renewal of entrenched, patronage-based party machines with calcified leadership structures and deeply stale political philosophies. As mentioned previously, some stable distributed systems face particular problems, such as conflict between the main parties or incorporating new political actors who wish to fundamentally change the system. In such cases, party development may hinge significantly on the ability to deal with those special issues.

PART THREE

The Assistance Response

CHAPTER FOUR

The World of Party Aid

political parties are seriously troubled throughout the developing and postcommunist worlds. There is, however, an international response: dozens of organizations, primarily Western foundations or institutes affiliated with Western political parties, and also a growing number of multilateral organizations, are attempting to help strengthen or reform parties in new or struggling democracies all around the globe. Although most persons in Europe and the United States involved in diplomacy, development, human rights, or international politics generally are somewhat aware of the world of international political party aid, many have only a hazy understanding of its core features. Within countries on the receiving end of party assistance, understanding about such activities is often even weaker. Many people in such countries mistakenly assume that party aid primarily consists of money from Western groups going directly to parties in other countries and that such money usually aims to help favorites and therefore influence the outcome of elections. Confusion reigns about the range and nature of the organizations involved, where they concentrate their efforts, how they decide where to work, what they do, and the scale of their work. Very few people have any idea what sort of effects or significance party aid has and what is reasonable to expect from it.

It is not surprising that knowledge about party aid is so sketchy. The organizations that carry it out are focused on their work on the ground. They have little incentive to publicly discuss and analyze what they do beyond providing the obligatory activity reports to their funders, maintaining moderately informative websites, and publishing glossy newsletters chronicling their accomplishments. It is a decentralized domain with numerous actors working all around the world. As is the case with most parts of the burgeoning (and also generally not well understood) world of democracy aid, it is no one organization's job to gather and disseminate information about who is doing what where, or to analyze and assess it.

This chapter sets out an overview of international party aid. After describing the main actors involved, their sources of funding, and the evolution of their geographic reach, it analyzes the principal types and goals of party aid. The final section of the chapter presents synopses of party aid in the six case study countries that underlie this book.

Party Aid Providers[1]

Party-Related Actors

Most international party aid is carried out by European and American foundations or institutes affiliated with major Western political parties. By far the largest of these organizations are the German *Stiftungen* (party foundations), the U.S. party institutes, and the Swedish party foundation affiliated with the Swedish Social Democratic Party, the Olof Palme International Center. The *Stiftungen* today number six: the Konrad Adenauer Stiftung (affiliated with the Christian Democratic Party), the Heinrich Böll Stiftung (Green Party), the Friedrich Ebert Stiftung (Social Democratic Party), the Rosa Luxemburg Stiftung (Party of Democratic Socialism), the Friedrich Naumann Stiftung (Free Democratic Party), and the Hanns Seidel Stiftung (Christian Social Union). The three largest, Adenauer, Ebert, and Naumann, all began doing international work in the late 1950s (the Ebert Stiftung was originally founded in 1925 but was closed from 1933 to 1947 and only entered the international domain actively in the 1950s), although this work was generally development-oriented and did not start including a focus on political parties until the 1970s. They were joined by the Hanns Seidel Stiftung in the late 1980s and the Böll and Luxemburg Stiftungs in the 1990s. The larger *Stiftungen* are generously funded organizations with staffs numbering in the hundreds and field offices all over the world. The Ebert Stiftung, for example, had a budget in 2004 of $148 million and more than seventy field offices worldwide, each staffed with an expatriate director and some local personnel.[2] Their international mandate (they are also active in civil and political education within Germany) covers work in both Organization for Economic Cooperation and Development (OECD) and non-OECD countries. In non-OECD countries they seek to provide support to partner organizations that contribute to "the realization of social justice, the promotion of broad political participation and to the strengthening of national political independence in accordance with the aims laid down in the Universal Declaration of Human Rights."[3] In practice this translates to a broad developmental approach in which democracy-oriented work is only one element, albeit an important one. Their work with political parties is in turn only one part of their democracy-related work, the principal component of which is civil society development. Thus although the German *Stiftungen* are among the largest party aid providers, they do not view themselves as party aid organizations per se but rather general international development organizations that include party work as one of many things that they do.

The U.S. party institutes, the International Republican Institute (IRI) and the National Democratic Institute for International Affairs (NDI), were established in 1983 as part of the creation of the National Endowment for Democracy (NED). They are two of the four core grantees of the NED, along with institutes affiliated with U.S. labor and business. Unlike the German party foundations, their mandate is exclusively international, and they only work in non-OECD countries. They focus only on democracy building, not more general socioeconomic development. They have grown significantly in the past ten years, to rival the larger *Stiftungen* in the size and scope of their international work. In 2005, for example, IRI and NDI had budgets of $75.5 million and $101.7 million respectively. Party aid is one of their core activities but still only one element of a wide portfolio of democracy aid that also includes election monitoring, legislative strengthening, governance reform, and civic education. Although they are the next largest party aid organizations, they too, like the *Stiftungen*, do not regard themselves as party aid groups per se but rather as democracy-building organizations that give some emphasis to party development.

In addition to the German *Stiftungen*, another approximately twenty-five European party foundations engage in international party work, from Austria, France, Greece, the Netherlands, Portugal, Spain, and Sweden.[4] By far the largest of these is the Olof Palme International Center. The Palme Center, both directly itself and through more than two dozen Swedish member organizations, works on many socioeconomic and political development issues internationally, of which political party development is one. All of the other European party foundations are small organizations. Five have annual budgets in the range of $1 million to $4 million (Fundación Pablo Iglesias [Spain], Fondation Jean-Jaurès [France], Constantine Karamanlis Institute for Democracy [Greece], Renner Institute [Austria], and Fondation Robert Schuman [France]), with the rest under $1 million. Almost all of these foundations were established in the 1990s. Like the *Stiftungen*, most of these foundations do a mix of different kinds of political and socioeconomic work. For most of them, however, party programs are the largest element of their portfolio. Some European parties engage in international party assistance not via separate foundations but through an international outreach office within their central party organization. The three main British political parties are examples of this approach.

These many party foundations or institutes are affiliated with or linked to political parties in their country, but the exact relationship varies considerably and is often hard to delineate precisely. The German *Stiftungen*, for example, insist that they are not party foundations in a strict legal sense but rather foundations that are close to political parties. In any event, each *Stiftung* represents the ideology and interests of its mother party abroad, both in symbolic ways (such as conferences to disseminate relevant ideological themes) and very practical ones (such as handling the arrangements for a visit to another country of a German minister who is from the relevant mother party). The chairpersons of the *Stiftungen* are usually former high-level politicians of the party and *Stiftungen* staff, many of whom have worked within the party, and regularly consult with the party.[5] Many of the other European party foundations or institutes have copied the German model and have a similarly close but still somewhat autonomous relationship to their parties.

The U.S. party institutes are less directly connected to their mother parties. They place much less emphasis on the role of representing their parties abroad and are less tied to the parties in terms of staff having worked for or within the party (a fact that partly reflects the much less coherent and robust central organizations of U.S. parties compared with European parties). Some staff members of the International Republican Institute for example are Democrats, and vice versa for NDI, a party crossover that almost never occurs on the staffs of European party foundations. Nevertheless the U.S. institutes are certainly linked to their respective parties. Their boards of directors are all senior persons closely identified with the party and the institutes do some activities (such as bringing international visitors to their party's presidential conventions) that are explicitly party related.

Four countries, Great Britain, Finland, the Netherlands, and Norway, have established specialized supraparty organizations to play a role in international party aid: the Westminster Foundation for Democracy (WFD) created by the British Parliament in 1992 as an independent institution sponsored by the

Foreign and Commonwealth Office; the Netherlands Institute for Multiparty Democracy (NIMD) set up by the Dutch government in 2000; the Norwegian Centre for Democracy Support, established by the Norwegian government in 2002, and Demos, established by the Finnish government in 2006. The WFD oversees the international party-strengthening work of the British political parties, playing a role in helping set strategic priorities for such work and monitoring its implementation. NIMD carries out multiparty programs primarily in Africa and Latin America, working in coordination with the seven Dutch party foundations (each of the seven parties has a representative on the NIMD board of directors and staff from the party foundations work directly on some NIMD programs), but with its own staff and projects. The Norwegian Centre for Democracy Support channels and oversees funds to the Norwegian political parties for international assistance work. The new Finnish organization does the same with Finnish political parties.

International Organizations Join the Scene

A central, although usually implicit, tenet of much Western party aid is that only political parties or institutions closely tied to them are qualified to do such work. Only they, the thinking goes, have the real knowledge and understanding of what parties do, how they operate, and how they can reform. This is by no means a unique outlook in the democracy aid world. Journalists are usually called upon to do media work, lawyers to craft rule-of-law programs, union representatives to help strengthen unions, and so forth. In this decade, however, a different, nonparty type of organization has entered the party aid scene—international organizations. The United Nations Development Programme (UNDP), the Organization of American States (OAS), the Organization for Security and Co-operation in Europe (OSCE), and the International Institute for Democracy and Electoral Assistance (International IDEA) have all initiated party-related programs.

UNDP's work with parties is part of the broader, very active move into democracy and governance work that UNDP has made around the world since the late 1990s. UNDP's party work includes capacity building for parties both in internal party development as well as governance issues, multiparty dialogue processes, training of parties in parliamentary work, and aid for reform of political party laws and other elements of the legal regulation of parties. These activities have been carried out widely in Asia, Latin America, the Middle East, and sub-Saharan Africa.[6]

The OAS began working on parties at the start of this decade in response to a crystallization of the view among Latin American political leaders that problems with political parties are one of the main obstacles to a successful consolidation of democracy. At the Third Summit of the Americas in Quebec in 2001, the assembled leaders mandated the OAS and the Inter-American Development Bank to convene experts to examine a series of topics relating to the state of political parties in the region, including party financing and the relationship of parties to other sectors of the societies. Later that year an Extraordinary General Assembly of the OAS adopted the Inter-American Democratic Charter, one provision of which highlighted the importance of strengthening political parties for the future of democracy in the region.

In response to these mandates, the OAS created the Inter-American Forum on Political Parties. The forum has met several times, bringing together political experts and aid specialists to analyze and look for solutions to the problems of political parties. The OAS has complemented the work of the forum with some party support activities by the OAS Unit for Democracy Promotion. The largest such undertaking is a substantial party aid program in Guatemala.

The Office for Democratic Institutions and Human Rights (ODIHR) of the OSCE, which carries out democracy assistance through the former communist states in areas such as election observation and rule-of-law development, has entered the field of party work. Its first party project is in Georgia, a multiparty capacity-building program launched in cooperation with NIMD.

International IDEA first became involved in party work in Latin America in the late 1990s. IDEA helped stimulate the growing attention to political parties within the OAS and the Inter-American Development Bank that led to the establishment of the Inter-American Forum on Political Parties. As discussed in more detail in chapter 8, IDEA became involved in the effort to reform Peru's political party law, and is participating in several other party-related projects in the region. Building on these experiences in Latin America, International IDEA has been carrying out work during the past several years on political parties on a global basis. This includes a large-scale, systematic research program to collect information abut the internal functioning of parties and the external regulations that shape party systems in many countries and regions. IDEA has also been sponsoring a series of regional dialogues with party officials to discuss the challenges parties are facing and to help forge agreement on best practices concerning party management and general norms about the role and function of parties in democracies.

Party Internationals

Another set of organizations that are related to and increasingly directly connected to the world of party aid are the party internationals. The four party internationals, Socialist International, Liberal International, the Centrist Democrat International (formerly Christian Democrat International), and the International Democrat Union, are membership organizations of ideologically like-minded parties. Parties join them to gain international recognition, build up contacts, and share information and ideas about party-building methods, ideological issues, and campaign methods. Participation in a party international, aside from payment of a membership fee, primarily involves sending party representatives to the various meetings, congresses, and exchange visits that the international sponsors.

Traditionally the party internationals played only a modest, somewhat indirect role in party strengthening per se. The party internationals have assumed that the many meetings they sponsor will help parties gain ideas from each other about party strengthening. They also believe that the carrot of gaining membership in a party international will encourage some parties in developing or postcommunist countries to professionalize their parties in order to increase their chances of entry. For example, in Mozambique, NDI helped facilitate getting Renamo accepted as a member of Christian Democrat International, and tried to use this entry process as a means of pressuring Renamo's leader to consider undertaking some party reforms, related to internal democratization. NDI believed that this process helped expose Renamo's leader to some useful people and ideas, although it did not lead him to take any significant new reform measures.

In the past several years the party internationals have been examining how they can work more directly on helping parties reform. One area of focus for such work is the articulation of standards for various areas of party organization, on issues such as internal democracy and party financing.

Funding Sources

Almost all funding for international party assistance comes from Western governments, but it reaches the party aid organizations through different governmental channels in different countries. In Germany, for example, the federal budget contains a line for the non-OECD work by the *Stiftungen*. That budget line is administered by the Ministry for Economic Cooperation and Development. The *Stiftungen* receive the funds on the basis of a quota in which their share is determined by their share of seats in parliament. They must submit program requests to the Ministry. Both the Economic Cooperation Ministry and the Foreign Ministry must approve the proposals, although such approval is largely a formality, the *Stiftungen* enjoying a high degree of autonomy.[7] Most of the other European party foundations receive their funds either from the foreign ministry, bilateral aid agency, or national legislature of their country. The four European supraparty organizations—WFD, NIMD, the Norwegian Centre for Democracy Support, and the Finnish Demos—are funded by the foreign ministry of their country.

The U.S. party institutes have three principal funding sources. They receive funds from NED—each institute receives an annual share of NED's core budget, although the funding goes to the institutes through a project-by-project proposal and approval process (NED is primarily congressionally funded but also receives special appropriations from the State Department). In addition, the institutes receive funding from USAID, on a project-by-project basis. In the past approximately ten years, the USAID funding to the institutes has greatly exceeded their NED funding. In recent years the institutes have also received some funding from the State Department.

Each donor country's institutional arrangements for the funding and implementation of party aid has its own strengths and weaknesses; no ideal arrangement exists. In chapter 5, I return to the issue of pluses and minuses of different funding structures. Very generally, the implementers long for independence and flexibility; the funders hunger for accountability, strategic planning, and efficiency. Creating a specialized organization (such as NIMD or WFD) between the governmental funding agency and the party foundations or institutes to help design and oversee party assistance holds out at least the promise of creating a middle level capacity for oversight and expertise without bureaucratizing the assistance.

Aid Amounts

Obtaining hard numbers for the amounts of party aid is very difficult. The larger party aid providers—such as the *Stiftungen* and the U.S. party institutes—engage in many activities of which party aid is only one. Most do not maintain a separate budget line for party-related work and when asked what amounts they devote to party aid, they respond (when they do respond) with rough estimates of the percentage of programmatic spending related to party work. Moreover, the definition of what is party-related work, as opposed to, for example, electoral or legislative assistance, may vary with different organizations. The figures sometimes include all overhead costs and sometimes are simply project costs. The following analysis conveys at least some very approximate idea of the amounts of funding for party programs.

The five largest German *Stiftungen* (all except the Rosa Luxemburg Stiftung) and the U.S. party institutes are by far the largest of party aid actors (along with UNDP, discussed below). In 2004, these *Stiftungen* had a total budget of $418.7 million (Ebert $148.2 million; Adenauer $123.5; Naumann $51.2; Seidel $51.2; Böll $44.6 million). In response to a research survey on party aid carried out by the Netherlands Institute of International Relations ("Clingendael") two of the *Stiftungen* (Adenauer and Böll) reported that 20 percent of their project expenditures are devoted to party work, as opposed to civil society support or other areas.[8] The other *Stiftungen* did not give a breakdown of their project expenditures but the profiles of their activities are fairly similar and thus almost certainly fall in the range of 10 percent to 30 percent for party work. The relationship between project expenditures and overall budget (which includes overhead and other nonproject expenditures) varies among the *Stiftungen* but for the sake of a ballpark figure one can probably assume that as a group in 2004 they spent somewhere between $40 million and $80 million on international party-related activities.

IRI and NDI had overall budgets in 2005 of $75.5 million and $101.7 million respectively. These budgets were swollen over their norm due to the ballooning of Iraq-related work. Excluding Iraq-related work their budgets were $36 and $62.7 million. IRI and NDI estimate that they devote around 43 percent and 35 percent of their work, including their Iraq work, respectively, to party-related activities.[9] Thus in 2005 they probably devoted approximately $68 million combined to party aid.

Four groups are medium-sized next to the large German *Stiftungen* and the U.S. party institutes: the Palme Center (2004 budget of $15 million), the Luxemburg Stiftung ($10.8 million), NIMD ($8.2 million), and WFD ($7.4 million). For the Clingendael study these organizations reported varying percentages of their project expenditures being devoted to party work: Palme, 35 percent; NIMD, 90 percent; and WFD, 65 percent (the Luxemburg Stiftung did not give a breakdown).

The many smaller European party foundations as a group have budgets totaling approximately $20 million to $25 million. These organizations devote all or nearly all of their work to party aid.

Among the multilateral organizations involved in party aid, UNDP devotes by far the greatest resources to the task. In 2005 UNDP spent $1.4 billion, almost half of its overall budget, on activities relating to democratic governance around the world, making it the largest democracy assistance provider in the world. UNDP also does not have a separate budget line for party aid but based on analysis of relevant areas of its budget it might be estimated that party work is somewhere in the $10 million to $30 million range. The OAS's budget for party activities in 2005 was approximately $2.8 million. International IDEA devoted around $1.5 million to party-related programs in 2005.

Thus a very rough estimate of current annual total party aid worldwide would be approximately $200 million. Again, just to give a very rough approximation of scale, with such aid taking place in roughly seventy-five countries, the average amount of party aid is probably between $1 million and $3 million a year per country, with a few places (such as Iraq) receiving much more, and many receiving less. With Western democracy aid probably somewhere between $3 billion and $4 billion per year, party aid is therefore somewhere between 5 percent and 7 percent of democracy aid overall. It is important to emphasize not only the very approximate nature of these figures but also the fact that these expenditures are not transfers to recipient parties but primarily costs associated with carrying out technical assistance, such as training programs, conferences, and exchanges.

A Pattern of Growth

Party aid, broadly defined, is about as old as political parties themselves. In the mid-nineteenth century, European revolutionary movements reached across borders to promote the fortunes of sister groups. The international labor movement became active and contributed to the spread of both socialist and social democratic parties. Across most of the twentieth century, the Soviet Communist Party sought to bolster other communist parties around the world. After World War II, some of the stronger European social democratic parties, such as the Swedish Social Democratic Party, helped social democratic parties rebuild in Germany and other countries.

The contemporary era of international party aid started in the 1970s and has proceeded in several stages, primarily marked by growth both in the range of party aid groups involved and the geographic reach of such work. The larger German *Stiftungen* became heavily involved in party-related work to support the transitions to democracy in Spain and Portugal. Socialist International as well as some other European parties were also involved, but the Germans were the most influential outside actors assisting party development. Spanish and Portuguese politicians later acknowledged the valuable role the German foundations played and this work has since often served as a model of the sort of role that other Western parties or party-related organizations aim to play in democratic transitions. German party aid also spread into the developing world in the 1970s. The Adenauer Stiftung became very active in Latin America, supporting what it hoped would become a network of successful Christian Democratic parties in Central and South America, and working with some ruling parties in Africa.[10] In parallel fashion, the Ebert

Stiftung began establishing relationships with center-left and populist parties in Latin America, and with liberation movements in Southern Africa.

In the 1980s, the U.S. party institutes entered the field. They were small in those years, with annual budgets of less than $10 million each, but they injected new energy into party-building aid and were harbingers of the wider growth of democracy aid that was starting to occur in the world. The U.S. party institutes focused more on electoral work than party aid per se in the 1980s, but the International Republican Institute (which was then called the National Republican Institute for International Affairs) developed some programs to support conservative parties in Latin America. The National Democratic Institute began working with parties in many parts of the world through its activities relating to the promotion of free and fair elections.

Also in that decade, some Swedish and Dutch parties developed or expanded solidarity work with liberation movements in Southern Africa, with the African National Congress above all, but also with groups in Angola, Mozambique, and Namibia. Although this work was more about political struggle than party building per se, it introduced many Northern European parties to the idea and practice of working with parties in Africa, opening the door to what became an active area of party work in the 1990s after transitions to multiparty systems occurred in these countries.

The *Stiftungen* backed away somewhat from party aid in the 1980s. Their initial optimism and idealism about party work in Africa and Latin America cooled off in those years as they discovered that many of the parties or movements they had initially associated themselves with were undemocratic groups that used their support from the *Stiftungen* (which in those years sometimes consisted of direct financial transfers) for their own benefit and not to democratize or otherwise internally reform.

The 1990s saw the significant spread of party aid, with many new party aid actors coming onto the scene, party aid reaching new places, and the quantities of assistance increasing substantially. The growth in party aid in these years was one part of the rapid expansion of democracy aid generally, which was occurring as a response to the dramatic wave of democratic openings in Central and Eastern Europe, the former Soviet Union, sub-Saharan Africa, and Asia.

In the 1990s the U.S. party institutes began to work extensively on party building in many parts of the world. The British government established the WFD. The Swedish parliament established a funding mechanism via the Swedish International Development Cooperation Agency (SIDA) to provide funding for Swedish parties to carry out party aid abroad. Dozens of parties in Europe—in Austria, Greece, the Netherlands, Spain, and elsewhere—established foundations for carrying out party building across borders. The *Stiftungen* continued to stay away from party work in the developing world in the first half of the 1990s (focusing instead on civil society development) but dived into such work in Central and Eastern Europe along with many other party aid groups. During the second half of the 1990s the larger of the *Stiftungen* began moving back into party work in Africa and Latin America, more cautiously than in previous decades but with a slowly growing level of attention and resources.

By far the greatest geographic focus of the burgeoning world of party aid in the 1990s was Central and Eastern Europe and the Baltic states. Although new political parties were emerging in large numbers in many parts of the world in those years, those in Central and Eastern Europe were the dominant magnet for party aid, for several reasons. Parties in the Czech Republic, Hungary, Poland, and elsewhere in the region were more like Western European parties, both organizationally and ideologically, than most parties in other regions. European party aid organizations could easily identify fraternal partners to work with. In fact some of the emergent parties were re-established parties from the pre-World War II era, parties that used to have ties with Western European parties. The geographical proximity of Central and Eastern Europe to Western Europe also contributed to the high level of party aid there. The interchange of people involved in training, consultancies, and study tours is much easier and less expensive than with other regions. Moreover, as the integration of Central European countries into the European Union became a concrete plan, Western European parties gained an additional motivation for establishing ties with sister parties in those countries: Forging relationships with such parties would help them build expanded party blocs in the European Parliament once the Central and Eastern European countries became members of that institution.

The other major area of expansion of party aid in the 1990s came in Southern Africa. As mentioned above, various Northern European parties and aid groups supported liberation movements in Southern Africa in the 1970s and 1980s, above all the African National Congress. As these movements came to power in the 1990s and multiparty systems emerged in Angola, Mozambique, Namibia, and South Africa, the northern European involvement in supporting political actors in these countries evolved into party aid programs. For some Northern European parties and aid groups, this work with parties in Southern Africa stimulated a broader interest in party work in other parts of Africa and in the developing world more generally. The U.S. party institutes also engaged in significant amounts of party work in South Africa in those years, and began working in other African countries as well.

Party aid also increased in other parts of the world. The breakup of the Soviet Union opened the door to party aid in a region previously dominated for seventy years by a single totalitarian party. Party aid providers began working in Georgia, Russia, Ukraine, and other former Soviet republics as part of the opening up of those states. Western party aid also started to reach some countries in Asia, including Bangladesh, Cambodia, Indonesia (after President Suharto's fall from power in 1998), and Nepal. More party aid groups began working in Latin America, although their presence was less extensive than might be expected given the large number of multiparty systems there. A few tentative efforts were initiated in the Middle East.

Still another phase of expansion of party aid is taking place in the current decade. It is marked by the entry into the field of various new actors, including some international organizations (as described previously), and by further geographic extension. Unlike during the 1990s, the expansion of party aid in this decade is not primarily driven by the spread of democratic openings and corresponding increase in democracy aid generally. Instead it is more a reaction to the growing sense in the democracy promotion community that many attempted democratic transitions have moved from the initial phase of excitement to a subsequent phase of sobering challenges. Citizens of fledgling democracies are wondering if their new political institutions can really improve their day-to-day lives, in many cases becoming disillusioned with them as those institutions fall short in many ways. In such contexts, the debilities of political parties stand out as a glaring weakness of the attempted transitions, prompting democracy promoters to give greater attention to party aid than before. An additional factor reinforcing this trend is the cooling off of the enthusiasm for civil society development that swept through the democracy promotion community in the 1990s. Although civil society support remains an integral part of democracy aid almost everywhere, democracy promoters have become more conscious of the limits of such assistance, especially the fact that NGOs, despite their value on many fronts, are not capable of taking the place of weak political parties. That is to say, the advocacy or service NGOs that Western donors typically support are rarely broadly representative organizations capable of (or interested in) fulfilling the political roles that democracy promoters hope parties will fulfill such as aggregating and articulating the political interests of the citizenry.

In this decade, party aid has decreased in the region where it used to be most extensive—Central and Eastern Europe—as many of these countries have joined the European Union or are on the path to doing so and have been "graduated" from many democracy aid programs. Party aid has been increasing almost everywhere else. The widespread sense in Latin America of a crisis of representation rooted in a crisis of political parties has stimulated Western party aid providers to give more attention to that region. The greatly heightened U.S. and European emphasis on democracy promotion in the Middle East is leading to more democracy aid there, with party programs one part of that increased flow. Although party aid groups have encountered frustration and resistance in Russia, they have been active in other former Soviet republics such as Azerbaijan, Kyrgyzstan, Georgia, and Ukraine. Party aid is spreading in sub-Saharan Africa as countries there continue to struggle to make multipartyism meaningful. As corruption continues to bedevil many Asian societies, party programs are finding an entry point on party finance issues in a region that was traditionally seen as less welcoming of Western party assistance.

What Is Party Aid?

Indirect versus Direct Aid

Describing and categorizing the main types of party aid is difficult not only because it is a large and growing domain, but also because its borders are fuzzy. Many democracy aid programs other than ones explicitly aimed at strengthening or reforming parties have effects on parties. They are best understood, however, as indirect rather than direct party aid, because their primary objective is something other than party strengthening; whatever effects they have on parties are essentially side benefits.

Elections aid is a major area of indirect party aid. The many things that democracy aid providers do to help promote free and fair elections in other countries—such as providing technical assistance to electoral commissions, fostering domestic election monitoring capabilities, and sending international election observers—benefit political parties because freer, fairer electoral processes facilitate political party development. In addition, some specific types of elections assistance directly involve parties. For example democracy promoters sometimes organize activities during a pre-electoral period to help parties negotiate as a group with an electoral commission over electoral rules—both to encourage the commission to take on board the point of view of the parties and to help the parties to engage in and better understand the rules and the rulemaking process. Or electoral aid groups sometimes train parties in how to conduct electoral monitoring. The primary goal of most electoral aid is to increase the odds of a fair election, but the parties experience some capacity-building as well.

Civil society aid also sometimes benefits parties. Some civil society programs aim to help advocacy NGOs connect more effectively to the political process as part of the search for a better realization of their advocacy aims. Such efforts may steer NGOs to have more direct contacts both with political institutions, such as legislatures and executive branch agencies, and also parties. In so doing it can help parties open up better communication with civil society. Similarly, civil society aid that seeks to render the government more accountable and responsive to citizens' interests (through monitoring, anticorruption legislation, or other measures) may indirectly benefit parties by reducing some of the causes of low public regard for the government and the parties.

Legislative strengthening is another area overlapping with party development. Given the central role of parties in legislatures, programs that seek to help develop a legislature as an institution—through training of parliamentarians and their staff, technical assistance on procedural reforms, and help for setting up information centers and outreach offices—have spillover benefits to the parties. As discussed below, some party aid is specifically designed to help parties perform their legislative role more effectively.

Although these are probably the major types of indirect party aid, other elements of the standard democracy aid portfolio also may at times benefit parties. A program to train investigative journalists may indirectly help reduce corruption in parties. Civic education programs may increase citizens' understanding of the role of parties, thereby facilitating parties' grassroots membership drives or campaign efforts. Parties are so central to a democratic political process that at least some intersections occur between parties and almost all areas of democracy aid.

The primary focus here, however, is direct aid—assistance efforts whose primary objective is party strengthening or reform. Direct party aid can in theory be directed primarily at institutions other than parties, such as civil society groups, as a way of producing positive changes in parties. Almost all direct party aid, however, is targeted at parties. Two types are by far the most common: first, aid before or during an electoral period to help one or more parties learn how to mount an effective electoral campaign; and second, aid outside of an electoral period that aims to help one or more parties develop their overall organizational capacity as a party. A third type of direct party aid also turns up somewhat around the edges of the two main categories: aid to help parties better fulfill their governance role, above all as members of legislatures. In addition, a growing set of party aid programs (discussed in chapter 8), often developed by some of the newer actors in the party aid field, do not seek to help individual parties through party-to-party training and advice. They attempt to promote positive party change by bolstering the overall party system in a country. They may do this by stimulating and facilitating the reform of the underlying laws and regulations that govern the operation of parties. Or they may create multiparty dialogue processes that encourage parties to communicate with each other better and to work together on systemic reform issues of common concern.

Strengthening Electoral Campaigns

Party aid often focuses on the role of parties in campaigns for several reasons. To start with, campaigning is central to a party's existence, and so aid providers turn to it as a natural area of attention—help a party learn to campaign and you have helped strengthen a central muscle in the party anatomy. Democracy aid providers often make a big push to help a fledging democracy get through a first or second time election, mounting huge, multifaceted electoral aid efforts. The bulk of such aid usually goes to electoral administration and civic education but the aid providers often recognize parties as a necessary element of a successful election and therefore include some party aid in the mix. Parties come alive in electoral periods and thus become receptive to receiving help from the outside, hoping it will improve their showing in the election. Campaign-related aid is also a common type of party assistance because the elements of successful campaigning are a well-defined body of knowledge, one that lends itself well to technical assistance.

In some cases, campaign-related aid entails just glancing involvement on a few issues by party aid providers. Other times it takes the form of large programs in which all the main parties in a country receive help with the whole gamut of campaign tasks, over the entire electoral period.

Campaign-related aid may start in the preparatory phase of an electoral campaign, usually eight to twelve months before an election. Party aid groups work with recipient parties on the recruitment, selection, and training of candidates and with the development of a strategic plan or approach for the campaign overall. Coalition-building is often an issue in the preparatory phase, and party aid providers sometimes get involved in trying to foster or facilitate it, especially among disparate opposition parties. They may cajole opposition party leaders on the subject and bring them together to hear about the value of coalitions and experience from other countries, or to be shown the results of polls commissioned by the party aid providers that highlight the potential advantages of coalition formation.

As parties move ahead in the campaign period, party aid may cover the whole variety of challenges they face in preparing to reach the voters: fundraising, platform development, message development, polling, and recruitment and training of staff and volunteers. Then when the campaign becomes active, the assistance turns to the actual methods of campaigning—door-to-door outreach, media relations, ad writing and placement, public speaking for candidates, and get-out-the-vote campaigns. Party aid may follow the electoral process all the way through election day, helping parties learn to organize and carry out pollwatching, which often involves fielding thousands of party representatives at polling stations around the country.

The goal of campaign-related aid is of course to help parties mount effective campaigns—campaigns that skillfully target likely voters, reaching them with persuasive messages. Such aid often seeks to promote effective campaigns not just in the narrow, results-oriented sense but also in the broader sense of a good campaign from the point of view of what aid providers think would be good for democracy-building more generally. Thus, for example, when aid providers work with parties on message development, they often urge parties to adopt issue-based, positive messages rather than personality-based, negative ones. They recommend fundraising strategies to produce broad-based, transparent funding rather than what parties may see as the easier path of lining up a few wealthy, secretive backers. They may push parties to develop well-elaborated party platforms even if the parties have little interest in doing so and it appears that the voters are unlikely to give them much attention. They advocate candidate selection methods that will produce meritocratic candidates rather than just pretty faces, or wealthy well-connected pols. In other words, when party aid providers focus on campaigns, as they often do, they promote effective, vote-getting campaigns but also campaign methods that they hope may boost citizens' belief in parties and in the political system, and produce better qualified elected representatives and parties better prepared for governing.

Party aid providers normally hope that their campaign-related aid, although primarily directed at helping parties campaign more effectively, will also contribute to the parties' long-term organizational development. Many of the elements of a campaign, from platform and message development to fundraising and staff recruitment, are part and parcel of party building between elections. Thus the line between campaign-related aid and the second main category of party aid—party organizational development—is not sharp.

The fact that much of the campaign-related aid is value-oriented rather than just results-oriented underscores some of the differences between such assistance and what for-hire political consultants do. The last twenty years have seen an explosion of political consulting work across borders. More and more candidates and parties in developing and postcommunist countries are using the services of political consultants (often U.S. consultants, but increasingly from other countries) in their campaigns.[11] In many ways, the advice these hard-charging consultants offer resembles the help that party foundations and institutes provide—how to craft effective campaign messages, how to deal effectively with the media, how to carry out and use polls, and so forth. One can ask, therefore, given that campaign expertise is widely available for hire, and a growing number of candidates and parties, including many that plead poverty to donors, are making use of it, why should Western party aid organizations provide it for free? In Romania in 2004, for example, the ruling party turned down an offer of campaign-related aid from NDI (NDI offered the assistance to all major parties), telling NDI that it preferred to make use of the services of some prominent for-hire American political consultants.

Looked at more closely, the overlap between what for-hire political consultants and Western party aid programs offer is actually only very partial. Within the extensive menu of campaign-related issues, paid consultants focus on a limited set—those issues having to do with campaign message development and delivery, media relations, polling, and outreach strategy. They are much less involved in party structural issues, such as candidate selection procedures, staff recruitment, internal training methods, and communication between party branches and the party leadership. As a result the work that consultants do is less likely than party aid to contribute to the long-term organizational development of the party. The fact that paid consultants communicate directly and often almost exclusively with the party leadership, whereas party aid activities often involve contacts with many different levels of the party, is a related point of difference.

Additionally, the work that for-hire consultants do on campaigns is entirely results-oriented in the narrow sense of electoral performance. It is not value-oriented in a prodemocratic direction. Nor is it aimed at the party's long-term health and viability. They are hired to help candidates or parties win elections, pure and simple. As such their campaign advice is not mixed with any ideas about what would be good for democracy overall. If negative campaigning appears likely to be effective, they will likely recommend it. If voters want personalities, not issues, they will help parties give them personalities. This, too, constitutes a significant difference from the work of party aid providers.

Organizational Development

The other main type of party aid—activities to help parties with their long-term organizational development—generally takes place in between electoral campaigns. In such periods, parties are not caught up with the near-term pressures of a campaign and thus have more time and flexibility, if they choose to use it, to devote to longer-term, broader party building.

Such assistance falls roughly into two interconnected halves. One part of it focuses on helping parties build (if they are new) or strengthen (if they have already been in existence for some time) their organizational structure. This usually consists of training and advice on various interrelated elements—management methods for senior party leadership, recruitment and training of party cadres, establishing and strengthening local party branches, developing systems for staff evaluations and promotions, and so forth. The goal of this kind of support is to help parties become coherent, well-administered organizations with clear lines of authority, the ability to engage in strategic planning, effective internal communication, and other attributes of a well-run organization. The goal is usually, however, more than just organizational strength and capacity. Perhaps the single most common objective party aid groups talk about when they discuss their work is helping or pushing parties to become more internally democratic. This objective cuts across all party aid organizations, and is pursued in all regions where they work.

The core of the sought-after internal democracy is the establishment of democratic selection procedures for choosing the party leader and for nominating candidates. Party aid providers pursue this in multiple ways. They jawbone stubborn, entrenched party leaders on the importance and potential value of internal democracy, offer comparative experience from other countries, hold training seminars for party cadres on the subject, and support and sometimes even underwrite party congresses at which new democratic procedures are to be tried out. The emphasis on internal democracy goes beyond just urging the establishment of democratic selection procedures. It usually also includes recommendations for a fuller set of reforms aimed at decentralizing power within the party, such as greater transparency and rationalization of the handling of party finances, enhanced communications between the party leadership and the rest of the party apparatus, and greater autonomy for party branches.

The other half of assistance for the organizational development of parties is directed at the outreach activities of parties. Aid providers assist parties with the entire array of tasks involved in connecting to the public and representing citizens' interests—expanding party membership, building a stable constituency, forging ties to social organizations, developing a capacity to carry out policy analysis and to create a well-elaborated party platform, and learning new fundraising techniques. The aim of this bundle of activities is to fortify the representational side of parties that are often weakly rooted in the society and preoccupied with the immediate interests and ambitions of their leaders.

In addition to the aforementioned areas, party aid frequently emphasizes two special themes relating to organizational development: greater incorporation of women and youth. Regarding women, party aid providers encourage parties to fill more places in the top circles of the party with women, to recruit and train more women as cadres in the central structure, to identify and nurture women leaders at the grassroots level and bring them into the party, to nominate more women candidates, to incorporate women's issues into the party platform, and to undertake more efforts to build a greater constituency among women voters. A similar cluster of priorities surrounds the push for parties to incorporate youth more actively, with particular attention to the establishment or reinforcing of youth wings in the parties and creating outreach methods that will appeal to youth. The common emphasis on women in party aid reflects the fact that women are poorly represented in the political life of most new or struggling democracies and that democracy suffers as a result. Of course this is true in many established democracies as well. Chapter 8 explores the issue of women in parties more fully. The stress on youth derives from the fact that in many developing and postcommunist countries young people are alienated from politics and perceive parties as the vehicles of older generations of elites who are uninterested in their views or concerns.

Strengthening Parties in Legislatures

Alongside the two main categories of party aid is a third type, much less developed than the others, although becoming more common. This is aid that seeks to bolster parties' capacity to function in legislatures. In many new or struggling democracies, parties that make it into the parliament often have little to no experience in such a role. Where parties do have considerable parliamentary experience, the process of democratic transition may open up the possibility for reforms in the parliament, reforms that imply changes in how the parties operate in the legislative body.

Such aid usually focuses on a well-defined battery of skills: analyzing and drafting legislation, structuring and managing a party caucus, legislative coalition-building, fostering parliamentary ethics, and other issues pertaining to the basic role of parties in parliaments. An additional major focus of such work is usually developing constituent relations—helping parliamentarians learn how to communicate more effectively with their constituents, including setting up and running constituent outreach offices, and sometimes organizing fora for parliamentarians and citizens to meet. The aim of this sort of assistance is both technical capability on the part of the parties about legislative work, as well as a better grasp of the representational side of parliamentary life.

Programs designed to help parties to perform their legislative role more effectively are both a type of party aid of legislative assistance. That is to say, its purpose is both to strengthen parties and legislatures. Much legislative assistance, however, does not deal with parties per se, despite their central role in legislatures. Instead it focuses on legislatures as self-standing institutions and parliamentarians as members of the legislature rather than as party actors. Much of the substance of such assistance is rather similar in content to the party aid that works with legislatures—such as methods of legislative analysis and drafting—but it is carried out with primary attention to what is good for the legislature itself rather than the parties.

What Party Aid Seeks

If you ask representatives of party aid organizations to describe the goal of their work with parties in any particular country, they will likely respond in very general, often abbreviated terms, saying they seek to help build stronger or more capable parties. If you press them on what would constitute stronger or more capable parties, they will usually come forward with a set of criteria that may vary a bit from program to program, country to country, but are a notably consistent list even among party aid organizations from very different aid-providing countries with very different types of parties. By extracting the various specific goals from the three main types of party aid we can come up with an integrated list of what party aid providers are trying to achieve overall with parties, a list that effectively represents what party aid providers mean when they say that they would like to help build stronger, more capable parties. Figure 4.1 sets out this list. Stated briefly, Western party aid seeks to help build parties that are competently managed, internally democratic, well-rooted in society, law-abiding, financially transparent and adequately funded, ideologically defined, inclusive of women and youth, effective at campaigning (especially grassroots campaigning), and capable of governing effectively. Obviously party aid providers know that this set of goals, taken together,

---

Figure 4.1. Overall Objectives of Party Aid

Party aid providers seek to help parties in new or struggling democracies to have:

- A strong central party organization with competent, rational, and transparent management structures, well-trained cadres, and meritocratic systems of personnel selection, training, and promotion;
- Processes of internal democracy for choosing the party leader and other senior party management, as well as candidates;
- A well-elaborated party platform and the capacity to engage in serious policy analysis;
- A clear ideological self-definition that also avoids any ideological extremes;
- Transparent, broad-based, and adequate funding;
- Capacity to campaign effectively, including a strong grassroots outreach;
- Capacity to govern effectively in the executive and legislative branches;
- A substantial presence around the country via a network of local branches that enjoy significant responsibility and autonomy;
- A well-defined membership base and regular contacts between the party and the membership;
- Cooperative, productive relations with civil society organizations;
- A strong role for women in the party as candidates, party leaders and managers, and members; and
- A good youth program that brings youth into the party, trains them, and makes use of their energy and talents.

---

represent an ideal. They do not expect the parties they work with to achieve it overnight. It is an endpoint that defines the path along which they hope to get parties to move. In the next chapter I consider whether this is a realistic set of goals.

These three main types of party aid focus on parties one by one. Implicit in them, however, are ideas not just about what is a good party but what is a good party system. In a very general sense, of course, party aid providers seek to encourage party systems made up of strong, capable parties—parties with the characteristics listed in figure 4.1. By examining their programs and talking with them about their approaches, one can deduce that party aid organizations operate from a number of more specific ideas of what is a desirable party system: (1) political power within the system should be distributed among at least a few parties and not held primarily by just one party; (2) at the same time, the system should not be fragmented among a large number of parties; (3) the system should be relatively stable but not so much that it prevents the entry of new parties; (4) the system should embody a fair amount of ideological diversity yet not be polarized around extremes. In short, a moderate vision prevails, one in which the party system is balanced between ideological polarization and homogeneity and between fragmentation and centralization.

As mentioned previously, in recent years some party aid providers are also undertaking efforts specifically designed to develop the overall party system of a country rather than individual parties. Chapter 8 examines these programs.

Case Studies of Party Aid[12]

Romania: From Partisanship to Normalization

Western party aid to Romania, which started in 1990, has followed a path similar to Western party aid throughout much of Central and Eastern Europe: an initial partisan orientation favoring the newly emergent reform-oriented parties against the successor postcommunist forces, with very rapid engagement by the United States and somewhat slower but ultimately more extensive involvement of European party aid groups; and then a fading of the partisan orientation over time as Romanian politics followed a path of what can be considered political normalization in pursuit of European integration.

Western party aid to Romania began with an intensive burst of U.S. support for the nascent Romanian opposition parties immediately after the fall of President Nicolae Ceauşescu in December, 1989. IRI rapidly mounted an effort in the early months of 1990 to assist the newly formed (or re-formed from pre-World War II roots) opposition parties as they struggled to get ready to compete with the National Salvation Front in the May 1990 elections. That effort expanded over the next two years as IRI deepened its involvement, helping what was still a very shaky set of opposition parties prepare to compete in the next set of national elections in 1992.

In these years IRI flew in a regular stream of U.S. political consultants to train the opposition parties in campaign methods and basic party building. IRI representatives also labored to encourage the fractious opposition parties to form an electoral coalition. Once a coalition was formed, the Democratic Convention, IRI provided material support for it, including underwriting the cost of a set of field offices around the country. As the 1992 elections neared, IRI's Bucharest office went into full campaign mode, providing strategic advice for the Convention, stepping up campaign workshops, and sending its main political consultant around the country to exhort opposition party branches to work harder.

IRI's pointedly partisan approach in Romania in those years was based on the view that Romanian politics were starkly divided between a neocommunist, antidemocratic ruling elite and a set of fledgling democratic forces. In this view, if the United States and other prodemocratic outside actors did not help level the political playing field, Romanian democracy risked being stillborn. The U.S. government was divided both over its assessment of the political intentions of President Ion Iliescu and his National Salvation Front and over the wisdom of the United States backing the opposition. IRI's view struck enough of a responsive chord in the U.S. policy bureaucracy that it received funding and political support for its pro-opposition activities. NDI decided not to get involved in party work in the country, devoting its efforts instead to building up a domestic election monitoring organization. European parties and party foundations did not move quickly into Romania (with the exception of the British Conservative Party, which worked alongside IRI), taking their time about setting up there.

After the 1992 elections, which were a disappointment for the Democratic Convention, Western party aid took on a longer-term character. The first two years of post-Ceauşescu politics had made clear that it would take years for the opposition parties to build themselves into a well-organized, strong political force. IRI continued its support for them, although at a reduced pace and with a focus on long-term party building. European parties and party foundations from Austria, Britain, France, Germany, and elsewhere began developing ties with individual Romanian parties, on a fraternal party basis. Although the European party aid groups were less overtly pro-opposition, most of their aid went to the opposition parties (which, after the victory of the Democratic Convention in the 1996 elections, entered the government and were no longer opposition parties). This was due to the fact that European center-left parties (which would have been the balancers to the aid from European center-right parties going to the Romanian opposition parties) were uncertain about the wisdom of working with the ruling party. They doubted the democratic bona fides of President Iliescu's party (then known as the Romanian Social Democratic Party, or PDSR) and either stayed away from the country or instead aided the Democratic Party, a center-left party that had split off from President Iliescu's party and migrated toward the opposition. The only significant inclusion of the PDSR in the Western party aid programs in the 1990s was in a leadership training program for young activists in all the main parties, sponsored by a Romanian NGO, with NED funding.

After the 2000 elections, which brought Ion Iliescu and his party, now called the Social Democratic Party (PSD), back to power, Western party aid changed gears, moving away from its partisan orientation. As one part of President Iliescu's effort to position himself as a pro-Europe leader, the PSD undertook a persistent and successful effort to gain European acceptance as a "normal" center-left party. The PSD gained admission to Socialist International. Cooperation between the PSD and many European center-left parties or party foundations followed as the British Labour Party, the Palme Center, the Alfred Mozer Foundation (Dutch Labor Party), the Friedrich Ebert Stiftung, the French Socialist Party, and the Austrian Social Democratic Party all set up joint seminars or training activities with the PSD.

At the same time that Western party cooperation with the PSD was rising, it was declining with the opposition parties. The National Peasant Party, formerly the largest party in the Democratic Convention and the largest recipient of Western party aid, was dying after its extremely poor showing in 2000 and thus no longer the object of much Western attention. The other two main opposition parties, the Liberals and the Democratic Party, had fewer ties with Western parties or party foundations. The Liberals' many years of severe fractionalism had impeded the establishment of strong ties with external groups and the Democratic Party no longer had obvious fraternal partners since the PSD had gained the mantle of the main center-left party. The U.S. party institutes launched a new party program after the 2000 elections, a multipartisan program to strengthen ties between all the main parties and civil society organizations at the local level.

Thus, in the early years of this decade a surprising turnaround had occurred in the pattern of Western party aid to Romania compared to that of the 1990s. President Iliescu's party appeared to be close to achieving a secure place as a dominant party, through co-option and corruption, with the opposition parties in danger of declining into a semipermanent state of debilitated opposition. Yet Western party aid was increasing to Iliescu's party and shrinking to the opposition. This pattern was partly altered in 2004 when NDI carried out a program of campaign assistance. Although the program was multipartisan, it primarily benefited the main opposition parties because the PSD decided not to take part in most of it. The surprise victory of the opposition in the 2004 elections, which appears to have been due to voter anger over perceived high levels of state corruption and general fatigue with the PSD leaders, gave a much-needed round of further alternation of power to the Romanian system.

Russia: A Narrow, Rocky Road

Western party aid in Russia followed a consistent line from the early 1990s on: supporting the two main pro-Western reform-oriented parties in their (ultimately unsuccessful) struggle to become significant forces in Russian politics.

After the breakup of the Soviet Union in 1991, the U.S. party institutes and the German party foundations (especially the Adenauer and the Naumann Stiftungs) began working with emergent Russian political activists and groups to help them form parties and compete in the first post-Soviet elections in Russia, the legislative elections of 1993. As in other parts of the postcommunist world, Western party aid providers working in Russia, especially the U.S. party institutes, were infused with a sense of urgency, believing that rapid, decisive assistance was vital to making sure that a historic political opening would allow Russia to move toward democracy.

This early assistance aimed to identify and support persons and groups that the Western party organizations believed to be democrats, in a political scene crowded with actors whom the Western organizations believed to be undemocratic or merely opportunistic at best. As the party aid continued and became more institutionalized after the 1993 elections, this early emphasis on helping a narrow band of "reformers" or "democrats" solidified into a primary focus on the two Western-oriented, liberal reformist parties or groupings—the newly formed Yabloko party, led by the outspoken liberal Gregor Yavlinksy, and the political forces led by Yegor Gaidar, which initially took form as a party known as Russia's Choice, expanded, and then evolved into the Union of Right Forces (SPS).

For the next ten years after those first legislative elections, the U.S. institutes and German foundations, together with smaller but similar efforts by the British Conservative Party and a few other European parties, provided extensive training and advice to these two Russian parties on every possible element of campaigning and party building. The assistance was fairly continuous throughout the decade, although it intensified around each of the legislative elections, in 1995, 1999, and 2003. Representatives of the Western party aid organizations also frequently jawboned the leaders of these Russian parties, usually in vain, about the value of opposition unity and of a possible alliance or merger. NDI gave particular attention to Yabloko, as did the Adenauer Stiftung. The Naumann Stiftung favored Gaidar and his organization. IRI initially did not direct its aid at any one party, although most of the participants in IRI training seminars were from the two reformist parties. Over time, however, IRI concentrated its aid somewhat more narrowly and in the lead-up to the 2003 elections worked primarily with SPS.

The concentration of Western party aid on these two small parties reflected the view of the party aid organizations that these were the only two democratic parties in the country. The larger parties such as the Communist Party, Unity, and Vladimir Zhirinovsky's Liberal Democratic Party appeared to them as unsuitable partners for Western aid. The many very small parties around the edges of the political landscape seemed too marginal to bother aiding. When the U.S. party institutes were pushed on the issue of inclusivity, as they were at times by USAID (which was funding their work) as well as by others in both the United States and Russia, they responded that their training seminars were often open to and attended by people from other parties, although it was apparent that their main partners were the two pro-Western, reformist parties.

Both IRI and NDI devoted substantial attention to local level training for Yabloko and SPS, with each institute concentrating on approximately a half dozen provinces in addition to their work in Moscow and St. Petersburg. Their strong investment in provincial level work reflected both the importance the U.S. institutes attached to Yabloko and SPS becoming truly national parties with a presence throughout the country rather than elite capital-centric clubs, and the institutes' frustration with the difficulty of making much headway in changing the top-down central structures of both parties. The German party foundations focused less on campaign training and more on ideological formation and policy capacity-building; they carried out most of their work with the parties' central structures.

Unlike in many other countries, Western party aid in Russia gave little attention to the presidential elections, focusing almost entirely on the parties' role in legislative elections. This was a result of the disconnect in Russian politics between the electoral competition in the legislative campaigns (where the parties were active) and the electoral competition in the presidential campaigns, which were conducted on a nonparty basis (the Russian Constitution prohibits the president from being a member of a political party). The partisan nature of the aid nevertheless provoked controversy at various times and Yabloko and SPS found themselves accused of being Western lackeys by Russian politicians or political commentators. This issue reached a head in 2003 when six months before the December 2003 legislative elections Yabloko stopped working with the U.S. party institutes, saying that new restrictions on party financing made it too risky for continued collaboration. SPS continued participating actively in the U.S. and German-sponsored campaign training until close before the elections.

The failure of both Yabloko and SPS to make the threshold for parliamentary representation in the December 2003 elections badly hurt those parties and marked the end of the more than ten-year chapter of Western efforts to support them. The U.S. party institutes and the German foundations have since 2003 maintained some contacts with those parties but are no longer carrying out training programs for them and have been exploring other types of work to support at least some continued pluralism in Russia. With President Vladimir Putin's ongoing offensive against politically oriented Western aid to Russia, it is unlikely that the sorts of party aid that were carried out in the 1990s would be allowed in the country today.

Guatemala: A Crowded Field

Party aid in Guatemala has followed a very different trajectory than in Romania, Russia, or the other postcommunist states. Party aid did not surge after the country's democratic opening in 1985, has followed a largely nonpartisan orientation, and has increased over time, with substantial new efforts unfolding only relatively late in the process. Although party aid has not followed any one particular pattern in Latin America, the contours of party aid in Guatemala largely track those elsewhere in the region where party aid providers have been active (primarily Central America and the Andean region).

The Adenauer Stiftung supported the Guatemalan Christian Democratic Party during the 1970s and 1980s, as part of its broad support for Christian Democratic parties in Latin America. No other outside groups found an entry point for party aid during these years in which Guatemala was convulsed by a bitter, bloody civil war and massive, harsh repression.

Guatemala's transition to elected civilian rule in 1985 opened the door to Western democracy aid. For many years after that opening, however, European and U.S. democracy aid providers concentrated on civil society support, rule of law aid, legislative strengthening, civic education, and media assistance. The Adenauer Stiftung remained involved with party work but in a reduced way after the Christian Democratic Party lost power in the wake of the unsuccessful presidency of Vinicio Cerezo from 1986 to 1990 and shrank to a party that received less than a 5 percent share of the vote during the 1990s. Adenauer funded ongoing training seminars for party activists from multiple parties through a Guatemalan policy institute.

As the peace process took hold in the mid-1990s, the Ebert Stiftung began working with the Guatemalan National Revolutionary Unity (URNG), the party newly formed by the former leftist guerilla movement, to help it make the transition from armed struggle to multiparty politics. Few other Western groups worked with the many Guatemalan parties in the 1990s. IRI did some work training civic and political leaders at the local level; NDI was not substantially engaged in the country. The absence of the U.S. institutes from the party domain related to USAID's lack of interest in sponsoring such work in most of Latin America. It also reflected the party institutes' view that

Guatemala's turbulent, unstable party scene represented problematic terrain for the sorts of aid they had to offer.

This picture changed sharply after 1999. The election to the presidency of Alfonso Portillo Cabrera, the candidate of the right-wing party founded by General Ríos Montt (who had been president briefly during the years of military rule) crystallized the growing perception among many observers that Guatemala's attempted democratic transition was at risk of collapsing, and that the weak, unstable nature of Guatemala's parties was a primary cause of this looming failure. In response, a host of Western organizations initiated party strengthening programs. IRI launched a multiyear effort to provide training in party building to a wide range of party activists. Spanish party foundations began offering seminars and workshops on party building. NIMD made available funds to support internal reform initiatives by parties. The Swedish party institutes, in their first-ever joint undertaking, established a long-term educational program to train several hundred young, local-level political activists to enable them to work for change from within parties. The Adenauer and Ebert foundations continued their work.

These various programs were largely multipartisan (the German and Spanish party foundations focused somewhat on selected parts of the ideological spectrum, but not narrowly on one party). The Guatemalan party scene lacked (and continues to lack) the sort of clear or stable ideological definition that would permit fraternal party partnerships. Most of the external party organizations proceeded from the idea that Guatemala's party system was still in a state of formation that did not lend itself to fixed partnerships. The issue of inclusion or exclusion did arise at times regarding whether Ríos Montt's party, which many observers viewed as a nondemocratic party, should be allowed to take part in training exercises. Most, although not all, of the external party institutes or foundations opted for inclusion, not wanting to exclude and therefore possibly antagonize the governing party of the country and hoping that participation in training programs might increase understanding of democratic norms and practices among activists from Montt's party.

Not only party institutes and foundations entered the Guatemalan party scene after 1999. The Organization of American States, with Nordic government funding, launched a substantial party aid program consisting of the sponsorship of a consultative forum for political parties as well as training and other activities for parties. The United Nations Development Programme, with NIMD support, organized a multiparty dialogue mechanism that led to the development of a cross-party shared national agenda, presented to the national legislature after the 2003 elections. Unlike the work of party institutes or foundations, the party programs by these two multilateral institutions focused not on strengthening individual parties but instead on improving lines of communication among the parties. This emphasis arose from the conflict resolution perspective of the main multilateral institutions in the country and the view that lack of cooperative dialogue among the parties was a leading cause of the poor performance of the successive Guatemalan governments. For the OAS and UNDP, their party work in Guatemala was their first or nearly their first substantial party program in the region and opened the door to the development of other such programs in other countries.

By the middle of this decade, the Guatemalan party scene had gone from being only very lightly touched by external party aid to one crowded with Dutch, German, OAS, Spanish, Swedish, UNDP, and U.S. training workshops, seminars, study tours, dialogues, and similar activities for the Guatemalan parties.

Mozambique: From Peace Building to Normalization

Western assistance for political party development in Mozambique began in the early 1990s as one part of the intensive international effort, coordinated by the United Nations, to help end the country's extremely long, destructive civil war. As part of a conflict resolution process, the aid had a different character (consisting primarily of large amounts of direct cash infusions into the parties) than Western party aid in most other contexts. As Mozambique's political life settled down at the end of the 1990s into more normalized multiparty competition, the external party aid normalized as well.

The party aid related to the conflict resolution process began in the early 1990s. In 1992, after the signing of the General Peace Accords between Frelimo, the governing party, and Renamo, Frelimo's long-term adversary, Afonso Dhlakama, Renamo's leader, requested $10 million to $12 million from the United Nations. This money was necessary, Dhlakama asserted, to make possible the transformation of Renamo from a guerilla movement to a political party capable of competing in the elections that would seal the Peace Accords. In December of that year, Renamo signed an agreement with Frelimo according to which Renamo would receive $15 million from the UN (to be principally supplied by Italy, which was playing a key role in the peace process) and all the other opposition parties would receive $17 million. Between then and the elections (held in 1994) Renamo received periodic, substantial injections of UN funds while continually complaining that the Western governments involved in the peace process were not living up to their promises and threatening to pull out of the elections if it did not get what it was promised. Renamo's threats were effective and it ended up receiving $17 million, which it used to purchase office space, housing for party activists, vehicles, office equipment, and to pay staff salaries and office expenses. During one four-month period in 1994, Dhlakama personally received $300,000 a month in cash to use however he wanted to support his party.[13] The UN also established a separate fund to support other new parties. Although the fund was smaller than Renamo's fund, it was of considerable utility to these many fledgling groups. They enjoyed what one observer described as "a real feast," buying houses, cars, and equipment that they are still making use of today.[14]

The next national elections, held in 1999, saw a repeat, albeit on a smaller scale, of the international support for Mozambique's parties. Although the peace process was advancing reasonably well, there were still fears about the solidity of the political consensus over the electoral process and an inclination to use party aid to help hold it together. Under Mozambique's electoral law, the government is supposed to create a fund to support the parties' electoral campaigns. In the year before the 1999 elections, some Western governments became concerned that the Frelimo government would fail to fulfill its obligation, either due to a shortage of funds or reluctance to do anything that would help Renamo. USAID and some European donors decided to help underwrite the fund and contributed most of what would eventually become a $1.4 million fund. The money was distributed to Frelimo, Renamo, and the main smaller parties according to a formula agreed upon by the parties.[15] For Renamo and the smaller parties it was a useful boost to their campaigns, although they complained that it came late in the electoral process. For the much better-funded Frelimo the fund was less significant.

The unusual willingness of the western donors to provide significant amounts of money to Mozambique's parties in the 1990s (through the UN and the government campaign fund facility) reflected the nature of the international community's involvement in conflict resolution and postconflict situations. When the international community does decide to get substantially involved in trying to help end a civil war and then keep the peace afterward, it often devotes very substantial funds to the task, in effect paying for the whole initial phase of the political reconstruction process, no matter how great the costs. Once Mozambique was seen as having passed out of this conflict resolution process and into a normalization phase of its democratic life, which occurred at the end of the 1990s, that international support for the political reconstruction process dropped away, although Mozambique continued to receive large amounts of development aid.

As part of that normalization process, more conventional Western party aid (modest amounts of training and technical assistance rather than large cash transfers) got under way around the 1999 elections. Frelimo had previously received some such support from some European center-left parties or party foundations, including the Portuguese Socialist Party and the Ebert Stiftung. In 1999, NDI initiated what became a five-year party building program primarily directed at Frelimo and Renamo. USAID funded the program in the hope that it would help Renamo begin to play a more effective role as an opposition party and that a multiparty program would improve communication between Frelimo and Renamo, thereby reducing the frequent unproductive standoffs between them. NIMD started up work in Mozambique soon after, helping to organize some multiparty dialogue activities and offering grants to all registered parties for training or other organizational development activities. The European Parliamentarians for Africa (AWEPA), a left-of-center European parliamentary group that did party work in South Africa in the 1990s, began offering training programs to parties on a multiparty basis.

In addition to those multiparty efforts, some European party groups established fraternally based assistance programs as well. The left-right ideological divide was present enough in Mozambique to allow European foundations to pursue the fraternal method more easily than in many other parts of Africa. The Adenauer Stiftung set up an office in Maputo in 2002 and began giving support to Renamo. The British Conservative Party also backed Renamo, offering both some modest material aid and technical assistance. The Ebert Stiftung reinvigorated its work with Frelimo, giving advice and training aimed to help the long-time governing party get back in better touch with its constituents. By the middle of the decade the party aid scene in Mozambique was moderately active, although it was only a small part of the very large, and growing, donor commitment to the country.

Morocco: Tentative Steps

Western aid for political parties is relatively scarce in the Middle East, reflecting the generally low level of democracy assistance in the region. U.S. and European aid organizations undertook some modest efforts to start up democracy aid projects in the Middle East during the 1990s. They were limited by the lack of political space and readily identifiable opportunities and partners for such work, as well as by their own governments' lack of real interest in promoting democracy in a region where authoritarian stability served Western interests. With the shift in this decade toward a more prodemocratic stance by both the United States and Europe, democracy aid to the region is increasing. Part of this new wave of aid is more party work, although it remains modest and rather scattered in a region where open and fair multiparty competition is the exception. Morocco (along with Lebanon) has the most developed multiparty political life in the Arab world, and thus has attracted somewhat more party aid than other Arab countries, although still only relatively small programs.

The Ebert Stiftung has worked in Morocco since 1984, although its work with parties was limited in the 1980s and 1990s to off-and-on contacts with the Socialist Party (Socialist Union of Populist Forces), the party it identified as its natural fraternal counterpart. In the last several years, however, it has developed closer, more regular ties with the party, including a series of meetings on developing a social democratic party agenda. Ebert has also started sponsoring seminars for the youth wings of all the identifiable center-left and left-wing parties in Morocco. The Naumann Stiftung has also increased its party work in Morocco in the past five years, supporting a new liberal party (the Alliance of Liberties), which grew out of a business-based policy NGO that Naumann and some other Western organizations previously supported.

Both NDI and IRI are engaged in some party work in Morocco as one element of a broader set of activities relating to elections and also parliamentary strengthening. As in many other countries, while the *Stiftungen* are working primarily on a fraternal party basis, the U.S. party institutes are following a multiparty approach. The International Republican Institute carried out some training for the main Moroccan parties in the late 1990s. IRI found the overall political environment unconducive to party change, however, and shifted within two years to work with NGOs and polling firms aimed at raising public awareness about democratic political values and political attitudes of the society. As the political reform process advanced under Morocco's new king in the early years of this decade, IRI returned to political party work. IRI began carrying out a series of discussions with the leaders of the main political parties, encouraging them to undertake party reforms, providing them with the results of polls to make them more aware of citizens' priorities and concerns, and offering seminars on internal party democracy and other reform issues. IRI also provided training to local level activists of the main parties in basic elements of campaigning, especially message development and grassroots organizing to help them prepare for the next national elections.

NDI began offering training to parties in the early years of this decade, with a focus on encouraging greater inclusion of women and youth in the parties. NDI also established a focus group center at which political party representatives are invited to observe (from behind a one-way mirror) ordinary citizens discussing their views of political parties, to help parties concretely understand the low regard most Moroccan citizens have for their political parties. As NDI has developed its relationship with party leaders and other senior party figures it has sought to use those relationships to informally encourage parties to participate effectively in the debates and negotiations over issues of structural reform of the political system, such as the enactment of a new law on political parties and the crucial question of possible constitutional reform relating to the king's political powers.

By the middle of this decade party aid in Morocco had become moderately active with both the German and U.S. party foundations or institutes looking for ways to get more involved with parties to take advantage and further stimulate the general process of political reform.

Indonesia: A Late Start

As in most Asian countries, Western party aid is only lightly present in Indonesia, although it has increased markedly in this decade. Some political parties were allowed to exist during the Suharto years in Indonesia, but political life was strictly controlled and there was no space for Western cooperation in this domain. After Suharto fell in 1998 and the country moved quickly to prepare for national elections, the door for external party aid opened. The U.S. party institutes quickly set up programs before the 1999 elections to help Indonesia's mushrooming parties prepare for the country's first open electoral campaign since the 1950s. IRI and NDI both worked on a broadly multipartisan basis, offering parties a full range of campaign-related training.

After the elections, the U.S. party institutes moved out of campaign mode and shifted to longer-term party-building work, with particular focus on internal and external communication and increasing the incorporation of women and youth into the parties. Both institutes concentrated the bulk of their attention on party-building work at the provincial level with each selecting a set of major provincial cities and doing much of their training in those places. Their decentralized approach reflected both the country's unusually large size and geographical diversity (hence a particularly strong need to help parties develop organizations with a genuinely national reach) and their perception that the main parties, which have existed for decades and are strongly run from the top down, might be more open to reforms at the provincial level than the national level.

NDI also ran what it called a political leadership academy in Jakarta—a more sustained (ten-day) course on core political skills for young political activists in the parties. The aim of the academy, which graduated close to 150 people, was to seed the parties with well-trained young cadres who, with exposure to significant knowledge about party-building methods, might over time become agents of reform in their parties. The academy also sought to create a cross-party network of young party activists that might facilitate better communication over the long term among a set of often fractious parties.

The Naumann Stiftung also entered the party field in Indonesia in the late 1990s, developing various seminars and other training activities for local level party activists and providing books, papers, and other such material for some parties. Naumann has been following a modified multiparty approach. It offers its local level training and books and papers to all parties, but carries out training activities for national level party officials only with a few parties that it considers closer friends due to a general sense of ideological compatibility. Naumann is unusual among the German *Stiftungen* and other European party foundations in its involvement in Indonesia. The other *Stiftungen* and other European party foundations have not developed party work in Indonesia since its democratic opening, both because of their general lack of interest in such work in Asia and the more specific problem of their not being able to find fraternal party counterparts in a country whose political spectrum is not organized at all around a Western left-right polarity.

As the 2004 elections drew near, the U.S. party institutes moved back into campaign mode, orienting their activities toward campaign-related training. Several electoral reforms that were put into place before those elections changed some elements of political competition, including the introduction of direct presidential elections as well as direct elections for district and provincial legislatures and a provision allowing voters in national legislative elections to select individual candidates in addition to parties on the ballot. The reforms created new campaign opportunities both for parties and candidates and the U.S. party institutes sought to help parties and candidates take advantage of them, through a strong emphasis on training in grassroots campaign methods.

CHAPTER FIVE

The Standard Method
and Beyond

A s I have argued in previous writings, most democracy assistance operates using a method I call "institutional modeling."[1] Democracy promoters embrace a set of institutions as the key features of democracy.
Their usual list includes free and fair elections; an independent, efficient judiciary; a representative, effective parliament; an active, independent civil society; and other familiar elements of the democracy promotion template. When
they go to another society to promote democracy, they compare the state of
the counterpart institutions there to what they believe such institutions should
look like (based on real or idealized models from established democracies).
They almost always find the local institutions wanting, and they design assistance programs for each institution to close the gap between the local reality
and the envisioned ideal. These programs rely heavily on the transfer of
knowledge, especially through training.

Political parties are on the democracy promotion template and political
party aid largely follows the approach of institutional modeling. This chapter
describes how this approach works in practice, analyzing what I call the standard method of party aid, its major variants, and its strengths and weaknesses. Some party aid providers are attempting innovations and
improvements on the standard method. The chapter also explores these developments. The search for better ways to aid parties raises issues about optimal
funding mechanisms and other institutional arrangements. The final section
of the chapter examines these questions.

The Standard Method

The standard method of party aid is straightforward: party aid providers get to know the parties in a new or struggling democracy, find that they do not conform to the ideas that the aid providers have about what constitutes a good political party, and design assistance programs to try to reshape them along those lines primarily, although not exclusively, through the transfer of knowledge. Training is by far the most common element in this standard method. Party aid is a sea of training activities, large and small, formal and informal, long and short, as party aid organizations train representatives of recipient or target parties in the wide array of elements of campaigning, party building, and legislative work. Training methods are diversifying over time, but for years party aid providers have relied on very conventional, even ritualized methods of training with the archetypical training event being a two- or three-day workshop, seminar, or conference led by a few experts from the sponsoring country who fly in to instruct several dozen party cadres from one or more parties in the recipient country about party building or electoral campaigning. These training programs are often repeated for years in a country with little variation.

Party aid providers also frequently sponsor and organize exchange visits and study tours. They typically involve a group of representatives of one or several parties in the aid-receiving country traveling for a week or two to the aid-providing country to visit with a range of people in political life. The general purpose is to let the participants see first hand how parties in established democracies are organized or other elements of democratic politics. The exchange visit may go in the other direction, with a delegation of party representatives, often parliamentarians, traveling from the aid-providing to the aid-receiving country to establish contact with representatives of a counterpart party or parties, learn more about that country's struggle with democratization, and perhaps some training.

In addition, party aid often includes extensive advice and counsel, provided to party leaders or activists by representatives of Western party foundations or institutes. Such advice and counsel might be on any area of party building or party activity—Western party aid representatives might cajole a party leader to delegate power to his subordinates or form a coalition with another party, urge a party's executive committee to adopt a new method of candidate selection, or persuade a party to carry out some polls to gain a realistic idea of citizens' regard for it. Some party aid representatives, especially heads of in-country field offices who stay in aid-receiving countries for several years and get to know some of the party leaders and activists fairly well, put a high value on such informal advice and counsel, believing it to be very influential if delivered to the right persons in the right way at the right time.

Some party aid organizations also offer material assistance to parties they seek to help. This usually does not consist of direct, general financial support to parties.[2] Instead, party aid providers may underwrite the cost of training seminars or conferences that recipient parties organize themselves or of party activities, like party congresses, that aid providers want to encourage. Western party foundations or institutes often supply books, training manuals, or other written material containing information about party building, the role of parties in democracy, party ideologies, or related topics. They sometimes pay for some computers, copy machines, fax machines, or other small-scale material goods for parties, in the belief that even modest gestures of this sort will build goodwill with counterpart parties.

One party aid group, NIMD, has tried giving direct monetary grants to parties in some countries, such as Guatemala, Mozambique, and Tanzania. These are grants to cover activities by the parties (such as meetings and workshops) that foster organizational capacity-building, especially for example, greater communication between the party's central leadership structures and the rest of the party. Under this approach NIMD establishes an overall amount it will make available to the parties in a country (for example, it has made approximately $500,000 per year available in some African countries)—parties are assigned a portion of this as "drawing rights" in accordance with a formula relating to their share of votes in recent elections. Parties then apply to the local office of NIMD to access their drawing rights, submitting proposals for seminars, workshops, or other party-building activities.

Although the many different organizations involved in party aid draw from the same toolbox of methods, they have different styles of configuring their aid role. Three different ways party aid providers operate can be identified:

1. *Flexible party resource.* Some party aid providers, especially the larger German party foundations, like to conceive of their role in a country where they have decided to support parties as that of a resource center for the party or parties they seek to help. The head of their local office (or, if they do not have an office in the country, their representative who travels periodically to the country) offers to the recipient party or parties a flexible mix of assistance—workshops and seminars, some material aid, occasional exchange visits or study tours, books and other publications, and frequent advice. An ongoing relationship is estab-

lished with the party leadership and the party aid group encourages the leadership to make use of the assistance as it chooses and to view the aid relationship as a sort of partnership. In the case of the *Stiftungen*, which often stay in countries for a long time, these aid relationships are sometimes built up over many years with specific aid activities coming and going in service of a long-term fraternal party relationship.

2. *Concentrated training.* Other party aid providers, most notably the U.S. party institutes, emphasize training in their work with foreign parties, defining their goals more in terms of helping achieve certain defined capabilities and characteristics in the parties they work with rather than a long-term, multifaceted partnership. Campaign-related training is often the entry point, evolving over time into a broader focus on party organizational development and an attempt to bolster the role of parties in the legislature. The training often concentrates first on party cadres and activists in the party's central organization (although in some larger countries the aid providers may concentrate first on training at the provincial level, in the belief that more interest in change exists there). In some cases, the training becomes very extensive and simultaneously reaches all three levels of the aided party or parties—the party leadership, the mid-level cadres, and the local branches. Other elements from the aid toolbox—such as exchange visits or material aid—are less important in the training-centered approach, being used usually only as supplements to the main training activities.

3. *Exchange relations.* A less intensive mode of party aid, but a very common one, especially among the smaller European party foundations, is one that primarily features exchanges. This method is mainly used in one-on-one assistance relationships where the aid-giving party concentrates on one recipient party in a particular country. The aid-giving party sends regular delegations to the recipient party, both to build contacts and provide some training, and it sponsors a regular flow of visiting delegations from the recipient party, again for contacts and some knowledge transfer. The relationship advances as the exchanges proceed, with a wider range of people in the parties on both sides taking part, friendships being established, and trust developing. To supplement the exchanges, the party aid organization may underwrite some conferences and seminars that the recipient party wishes to hold on themes congruent with the overall party-building enterprise. This mode of party aid is often pursued when the aid organization has no field offices and is operating from a distance.

The Fraternal Method versus the Multiparty Method

These variations of the standard approach to party aid are pursued using either the fraternal party method or the multiparty method (although the latter of the three approaches—exchange relations—is almost exclusively carried out by groups that follow the fraternal party method). Under the fraternal method, when a Western party aid organization decides to work in a particular country it seeks out an ideologically like-minded counterpart. Thus a Western conservative party looks to find a conservative party, a Western social democratic party seeks a social democratic partner, and so forth. Usually it is an exclusive relationship; the Western party aid organization chooses just one party to work with in any one country.

The fraternal method is the backbone of European party aid. It connects to the long-standing European traditions of political movements reaching across borders and forming fraternal networks, such as the Socialist International. A common assumption (although one that, as discussed in the next chapter, is of debatable validity) among practitioners of party aid is that although the method is openly partisan (in the sense that any one party aid provider works only with one other party, on an ideological basis), overall the application of the method will be multipartisan and balanced. This is based on the idea that the different parties or party foundations from any one aid-providing country will each develop their own relationships with a counterpart party in the recipient country, thereby ensuring a multipartisan balance of aid.

The primary advantage of the fraternal method is that the common ideological link between the provider party institute and receiver political party may be the basis for a bond that will make cooperation more effective. Party organizations that use the fraternal method insist that their partner parties in new or struggling democracies believe that they can trust them more because they know it is a potential long-term partnership rooted in ideological fraternity, or what some of the German foundations call a values-based relationship. This trust, they say, is essential to gaining access and influence within the parties they are trying to help. Furthermore, party organizations using the fraternal method also believe they can be more effective helping parties with a similar ideological orientation because they will understand their particular challenges. For example, a right-of-center party institute may have special experience helping parties build ties to business constituencies while a left-of-center party institute may be similarly expert in cultivating relations with trade unions. In this way, fraternally based party programs, unlike standardized multiparty programs that offer the same things to all parties, may contribute to the greater or clearer differentiation of parties within any one country context, which can be useful given that a common problem of parties in many new or struggling democracies is a lack of distinctive identity.

A major disadvantage of the fraternal party method is the difficulty of finding ideological partners in countries where the European left-right spectrum does not define party life. In some countries, finding an ideologically like-minded partner is relatively easy. In Central and Eastern Europe and Latin America, for example, the traditional right-left spectrum of party politics exists in many places and Western European parties can often find ideological counterparts. Even in those regions, however, the ideological landscape is in some places quite hazy. In Argentina, pinpointing the place of the two largest parties of the past twenty years, the Peronists and the Radicals, on a left-right axis is challenging. In Serbia the crowded, jostling post-Milosevic party landscape is rife with ideological posturing but does not present a well-defined array of choices lining up from left to right. In both regions, parties toward either edges of the ideological spectrum mix together rightist and leftist tendencies and parties in between gravitate toward a technocratic, reformist centrism, rendering the ideological spectrum rather confused in conventional terms.

In other parts of the world, especially Africa, East Asia, and the Middle East, the left-right spectrum often has little relevance at all. The party scene is instead divided up along other lines, such as religion, ethnicity, and regionalism, or is simply a mix of parties with few clear differences beyond the contending personalities and ambitions of their leaders. In South Africa, for example, politics do not fall along a left-right axis—the African National Congress, the Nationalist Party, and the Inkatha Party, do not base their identity on a place on the left-right spectrum. In Indonesia, the major parties draw their identity from diverse sources, including religious leanings, association with prominent personalities, and certain social affiliations, none of which is tied closely to a traditional ideological grouping.

In such places, Western party aid organizations used to operating under the fraternal party method have a hard time finding ideological soul mates. Sometimes they forge ahead, doing their best to identify whatever ideological leanings exist and to make attachments accordingly. In other cases they decide not to work with parties and they focus instead on civil society assistance. In a small number of cases, such as with the *Stiftungen* in some African countries or the Swedish party foundations in Guatemala, they diverge from their usual fraternal approach and try multiparty work. This challenge of matching the fraternal approach with party context where the left-right spectrum does not define party life is only growing as party aid diminishes in Central and Eastern Europe and reaches more widely in the non-Western world.

Under the multiparty method, the aid provider offers assistance to all of the main political parties in a country. This is the principal method of the U.S. party institutes and NIMD, and of the party work carried out by multilateral institutions such as UNDP and the OAS. Although in this method multiple parties are reached, the training and advice is often carried out with each party separately. This is done because aid providers have discovered that, not surprisingly, parties generally prefer not to be together with rival parties in training seminars because they are inhibited about discussing their internal workings and problems with competitors present. There are some exceptions to this pattern. The "party schools" and study tours that aid providers sponsor often involve participants from different parties at once, part of the purpose of such exercises being precisely to create better lines of communication among parties. Some issues, such as pollwatching methods, are often dealt with in multiparty training sessions because they involve technocratic knowledge that is not related to a party electoral style or capacity, and participating in such trainings does not require parties to share any sensitive information about their internal conditions or tactics.

A critical issue in the multiparty method is which parties get included and which are excluded. Although party aid organizations using a multiparty method generally intend to reach all the parties in the country, choices about inclusion and exclusion do have to be made, for two reasons. First, party aid providers are uncomfortable assisting nondemocratic parties or parties that advocate violence, and so they exclude parties they determine to fit those criteria. The determination of what is a nondemocratic party is sometimes clear-cut and sometimes not. It can be based on a party's stated ideology or its political actions. Far-right nationalist parties, such as Vladimir Zhirinovsky's Liberal Democratic Party in Russia or Corneliu Vadim Tudor's Greater Romania Party are usually excluded from Western aid programs as nondemocratic parties. As discussed in chapter 6, in some cases the decision about which parties are nondemocratic is made in a way that gives the impression that the party aid organization in question is basically just choosing to assist parties it likes and exclude parties it dislikes. In Russia in the 1990s for example, the U.S. party institutes worked primarily with two main pro-Western, proreform parties, asserting that those were the only real democratic parties in Russia, working much less or not at all with some other parties that accepted the democratic rules of the game, but were much less pro-Western.

Party aid providers also sometimes have to limit the number of parties they work with in a multiparty program because there are just too many parties. In some countries that have experienced a mushrooming of parties after a democratic opening, there are dozens of parties, or even more than one hundred. More than about ten parties presents a challenge for aid providers, who are usually operating with very limited funds and are generally loath to disperse their efforts among very small parties. Thus aid providers often limit most of their work to a compact circle of larger parties, while perhaps opening up some training events to representatives of smaller parties. Or they decide to work only with parties that have gained a place in parliament. This winnowing is a logical response to the problem of very large numbers of small parties. It carries with it the danger that party aid will end up helping to lock in the existing parties and miss the opportunity to support emergent new parties. A partial exception in this regard is NIMD, which in some countries, such as Guatemala and Mozambique, has opened up its assistance to all the parties in the country, well beyond the parliamentary parties. In the case of Mozambique for example, this led to party building support for more than twenty parties. With such large numbers of parties participating, not very much assistance can usually be offered to the many very small parties, but being very small, they do not have absorptive capacity for more than modest amounts of outside help.

In addition to entailing less risk of accusations of partisanship, the multiparty method has another significant advantage. It facilitates efforts by the aid provider to think about the overall problems of parties in the country as a whole. This can be useful to help stimulate the external aid actors to confront all factors shaping the evolution of parties in the country rather than to continue training one party at a time under the assumption that the main obstacles and solutions to party development lie only within the parties themselves. In this way, the multiparty method can advance the development of new types of efforts aimed at strengthening the overall party system in a country rather than just the individual parties.

The main disadvantage of the multiparty method is the greater difficulty of creating a very close party-to-party relationship between the provider and recipient. The value of such relationships is open to debate but, as noted previously, adherents of the fraternal method (who are often quite critical of the multiparty method) believe that such relationships are crucial to gaining real influence inside the party to push for important internal reforms.

To alleviate this disadvantage, party groups using the multiparty method often try to provide training and advice separately to each party they work with, as noted above. In some cases they take this separation very far in order to build trust with the individual parties. In Kosovo for example, the National Democratic Institute designed its three-party training program so that a different local staff person and different external consultants were assigned to each party. In this way each party had its own assistance team—a sort of fraternal party method carried out within the larger framework of a multiparty program.

Weaknesses of the Standard Method

A Troubled Toolbox

The standard method of party aid has a few clear strengths. It allows aid providers to go to almost any other country, no matter how unfamiliar the political life and murky the underlying sociopolitical structures and settle quickly on a party strengthening program that at least has a clear sense of both purpose and method. Its consistency across highly varied contexts allows for a certain ease and economy of execution. It plays to the strengths of the parties involved on the aid-providing side, drawing on some of the things they do well, such as campaigning and managing large party organizations.

At the same time, however, the standard method has some serious weaknesses. In fact, in carrying out the research for this book I was struck that not only does one hear a standard lament about political parties in new or struggling democracies, one also hears a fairly standard lament among people in recipient parties about Western political party aid. This is not to say that party assistance programs are never appreciated or valued. In some cases they are; occasionally very much. Even where recipients praise party aid organizations they have worked with or cite benefits of participating in particular assistance programs, they still frequently criticize certain common features of the assistance. Above all, they point to what they view as preset, standardized designs not well-adapted to their particular context and mechanistic methods of implementation. Looking at each of the three main variations of the standard method that aid providers use—the flexible party resource approach, the training-centered approach, and the exchange relations approach—certain characteristic shortcomings of each can be identified.

The appeal of the flexible resource approach is clear—a Western party foundation serves as a multifaceted partner over a sustained period to a counterpart party, supplying it with varied doses of training, material aid, study tours and the like as the need arises, and backing this up with bits of advice and counsel. In practice, however, these relationships, although certainly not unwelcome, are usually much less valuable than the providers hope. The aid provided often ends up being a nonstrategic scattering of activities over time based on no serious underlying research or analysis of what impulses for positive change actually exist within the party, whether the political context is favorable for such changes, and how limited amounts of occasional technical assistance might facilitate a deep-reaching process of internal party reform. None of the specific elements of the assistance is problematic in and of itself but taken together they end up not contributing to any real change in the basic organization or operational methods of the recipient party.

A particularly wide gap between the perceptions of the providers and the recipients occurs regarding the advice and counsel that the field representatives of the Western party foundations give. In my interviews, such representatives often reported having a direct influential line to the leader and other key figures in the recipient party. Yet when I asked senior people in the parties in question about these same field representatives, they tended to describe them as pleasant friends of the parties but distant outsiders to the real internal workings of the party. In short, these long-term flexible resource provider relationships are certainly a good way of building and maintaining party-to-party friendships; their utility as a method for stimulating and supporting fundamental party reforms is less certain.

Regarding party aid efforts centered around training, several significant weaknesses are apparent. The high level of "workshop fatigue" among persons in parties on the receiving end of political party training programs is very striking. The complaints about the training are pervasive and highly consistent among parties in all different parts of the world:

- Training workshops are often short, one-off events with no real follow-up and thus participants are unable to incorporate into their party work or build on what they were exposed to in the workshops.
- Party aid groups let the leaders of the recipient parties choose the participants for training workshops, and party leaders frequently choose the wrong sort of people. They use the workshops as a reward for cronies who have no real interest in being trained, or as a dumping ground for marginal persons who will not be able to effect change in the party.
- The trainers are often "fly-in" experts—political consultants, parliamentarians, or professors from the aid-providing country who fly in for the workshop and fly out immediately afterwards. Such trainers usually lack substantial knowledge of the local scene and teach from a set script

based on political practices in their own country that may not be applicable in the recipient country. The short duration of their stay also means that they are not available to plan or carry out any follow-up activities. As one Guatemalan parliamentarian, a veteran of the recent wave of Western-sponsored training workshops, said to me in an interview, "If I have to sit through one more workshop and listen to one more European or North American tell me how great parties in his country are, I will scream."[3]

- The topics covered in the workshops are often chosen by the aid providers, reflecting what they believe the recipient parties need rather than what those parties actually have an interest in.
- The training programs are repetitive. They repeat the same materials many times without going deeper into the subjects.

Shortcomings of exchange relations as a method of party aid are also manifest. Study tours and exchange visits are useful for building goodwill and personal ties between parties but they are generally a poor method for supporting party reform. If a study tour is very carefully designed and planned, the participants rigorously and thoughtfully chosen, and the tour closely integrated with other training activities that will provide reinforcement and follow-up opportunities, it can be useful. Most study tours, however, do not have these characteristics and they serve little purpose beyond relationship building. In far too many cases, the wrong participants are selected (because they speak English, or because the party leader owes them a favor), the tour is a grab-bag of superficial meetings in which people in the host country who know little about the visitors' specific political context give generic presentations on "how things work here," and the participants devote their primary attention to meals and finding opportunities to shop using their travel per diem.

Exchange visits in the other direction are often of similarly low value in terms of actual training or stimulation of reform processes. A delegation of parliamentarians affiliated with the aid-sponsoring party spends several days in the capital of the aid-receiving country, meeting with counterparts, giving a few talks to party cadres about how parties or democracy are supposed to work, sharing some meals and drinks, and expressing sympathy for the difficulties that their counterparts face and solidarity in the common ideological struggle. Such study tours and return visits continue back and forth, solidifying party-to-party friendship but doing little to facilitate actual processes of internal party change.

The Mythic Model

The standard method of party aid is problematic not just because of its reliance on stale techniques of institutional modeling. It grows out of what could be described as a mythic model of parties in established democracies. All areas of democracy aid suffer to some degree from a gap between idealized models that aid providers hold out to people in the countries where they work—whether it is of efficient, noncorrupt legislatures; swift, highly competent, and politically disinterested judiciaries; vigorous, diverse independent media; nonpartisan, self-sustaining, powerful NGO sectors; or engaged, well-informed citizenries—and the realities of most such institutions or sectors in established democracies. Yet this problem is particularly acute when it comes to political party work. Perhaps a few parties in the established democracies have the main characteristics that party aid seeks to produce in parties in new or struggling democracies. That is to say, perhaps a few parties are internally democratic, financially transparent, managed in a rational, nonpersonalistic fashion, highly inclusive of women at all levels, ideologically coherent, committed to issue-based, grassroots work (rather than negative, personality-oriented television campaigning), and driven by ethical and policy principles rather than opportunism. Many, or most, however, fall quite short of this ideal.

A gap between prescriptions dispensed abroad and realities at home hits U.S. political party aid especially hard. Political scientists continue to debate the best way to characterize the main U.S. political parties but almost all would agree the Republican and Democratic parties scarcely resemble the "normal" model—the European model of a political party with a strong central organization that serves a well-defined party membership base and exerts control over candidate selection and candidate platforms. U.S. political parties have hollowed out steadily in the last fifty years to the point where they are highly candidate-centric organizations whose main role arguably is to organize party primaries and structure the electoral choice process. Thus it is striking to see U.S. democracy promoters going to other countries to push for the development of a type of political party that does not really exist in the United States. It is interesting that although in most areas of democracy aid U.S. democracy promoters consciously or unconsciously support the reproduction of U.S.-style institutions, in the party domain, U.S. aid providers are working to spread what is essentially a northern European model (or an idealized version of such) of political parties.

Western party aid appears to be based on a model of parties that is not just unusually virtuous compared to reality but also somewhat dislocated in time.

Many of the organizational features that party aid programs emphasize hark back to an earlier age, sometimes in the first half of the twentieth century, before the rise of television-driven, image-oriented campaigning, the diminution of direct links between parties and voters, the blurring and fading of traditional ideological orientations, the widespread cynicism about politics, and the rise of individualism. Some party aid practitioners seem to believe that fledgling parties in new or struggling democracies can first evolve as parties did in the days of traditional politics in the established democracies (although fully inclusive of women in accordance with contemporary Western values) and then at some later stage deal with the exigencies of sociopolitical postmodernism. As discussed in chapter 3, however, new or struggling democracies face the challenge of democratic compression—they do not have the luxury of passing slowly through the various evolutionary stages of European political development, and they are pushed both by their own citizens and the international community to move quickly ahead on all elements of democratization at the same time. For many parties this means plunging directly into the age of media-saturated, hyperindividualistic politics without a century or so of prior gradual, grassroots-oriented development.

Problematic Persistence

The chronic weaknesses of the standard method are, generally speaking, recognizable symptoms of technical assistance that is supply-driven, externally designed, and externally implemented (in the sense of being implemented by persons not from the recipient society). As has been experienced in many other domains where technical assistance follows this model, such efforts usually fail to penetrate the sociopolitical fabric of the recipient society, to identify and nurture local processes of change, and to generate much real ownership among the intended beneficiaries.

As examined later in this chapter, some party aid organizations are trying to improve on the standard method, yet it is still widely used. Given its fairly obvious shortcomings, and the consistency of critiques about it that emerge from recipient parties, why does this method show such persistence?

Two reasons are immediately apparent. First, as noted above, the standard method is simple and straightforward. Party foundations and institutes face the daunting challenge of trying to work in numerous countries around the world without their funders giving them either adequate time or resources to get to know the local scene before plunging in or the flexibility to experiment with different approaches. The standard method can be plugged into place anywhere quickly, and it always makes a certain sense based on the ubiquitous aid logic of institutional modeling. Second, as discussed in the next chapter, some share of party aid, at least European party aid, is much more about relationship-building for various political purposes than about actually trying to stimulate and support reform in the counterpart parties. Some elements of the standard method, especially study tours and exchange visits, are quite well-suited to relationship-building, regardless of their value, or lack of value, as methods of producing party change.

The standard method also persists for other reasons. Most people who staff party aid organizations are political people of one type or another—former party activists, political consultants, legislative aides, and politically oriented lawyers. Their expertise is parties and politics. Sometimes for better and sometimes for worse, they are not imbued with nor even often much exposed to the world of development aid. Thus they are often unfamiliar with its accumulated ideas among developmentalists about how to try to produce or support change in other societies, such as the need to nurture local processes of change rather than trying to be the actual agent of change. In fact, party aid representatives often pride themselves on not being part of the traditional developmentalist community. They view themselves as a different type of aid actor—more political, direct, and action-oriented. They believe that they, not developmentalists, know about political parties and therefore they should not have to be told by developmentalists how to go about aiding parties.

The instinctive methodological inclination of this mind-set is straight institutional modeling. Stated in crude terms it is, "we the Westerners know how parties are supposed to work and we will teach you, the representatives of parties that are not working as parties should, to learn to make your parties work correctly." This outlook sees political parties everywhere as being basically similar in essential ways (organizations that seek power through elections) and needing the same sort of help. It does not give much attention to underlying questions about whether parties in some societies should be understood as being quite different sorts of organizations and dealt with in fundamentally different ways.

Another important reason for the persistence of the flawed standard method is that most party aid organizations rarely engage or are required to take part in rigorous, independent evaluations of their work. They are rarely confronted with challenging, in-depth assessments of what they do that might push them to question their existing methods and try something different. In interviewing representatives of European party foundations, I have been struck by how little attention their organizations seem to give the question of evaluation. They will often work for many years in a country without stopping to engage in any serious review of what they have done, what has been accomplished, and what they might do differently in the future. They seem willing to operate indefinitely from a simple, central idea that they represent well-developed political parties and are going to keep sharing their knowledge with less well-developed parties in other parts of the world.

In his pathbreaking study of the work of the German *Stiftungen* in Africa, Gero Erdmann underlines this weakness of evaluation and reflection on methods and results of party assistance.[4] He points out that none of the *Stiftungen* has a policy or strategy paper that deals with party assistance. None of the *Stiftungen*, he asserts, "has systematically appraised their particular collaboration with, and assistance to, political parties, either internally or by external experts" and "all acknowledge the lack of systematic knowledge about their work with political parties." Erdmann concludes that despite decades of work by the *Stiftungen* on party strengthening around the world, "the foundations appear not to be in a position to address the particular challenges of party promotion adequately.... The parties are certainly not distinguished in party promotion."

With the growing focus on the continuing problems of parties in developing democracies, this traditional nonevaluative approach of the European party foundations is showing a few signs of change. The Ebert Stiftung carried out in 2005–2006 an internal study of its party aid work and incorporated findings from the study into training sessions with field representatives. The Palme Center has also begun carrying out some country evaluations of its party programs and to reflect internally in a more systematic way about its party work.

The party aid programs of the U.S. party institutes are sometimes subjected to external evaluations, usually imposed by USAID, their largest funder. These evaluations are typically carried out by one of the all-purpose development consulting firms that have ongoing relationships with USAID. These evaluations rarely are a very happy experience for the party institutes and they usually do not seem to produce much learning. The evaluations typically focus on whether promised activity outcomes were fulfilled and, in some cases, whether relatively superficial indicators of party reform (for example, was a party congress held or a youth league established) were met. They do not entail any significant analysis of the parties being aided and do not go deeply into the question of how the program actually affected the recipient parties. They do not examine the basic assumptions that underlie the core methodology that the institutes use. The party institutes, like most evaluees in these sorts of exercises, often do not believe that the evaluations give them proper credit for what they have accomplished, and, privately at least, question the value of evaluations carried out by development generalists rather than experts in parties and party aid. When the evaluations are critical, the party institutes push back and the criticisms end up more as matters of dispute than as opportunities for learning or improvement.

One noteworthy exception to the prevailing nonevaluative landscape is NIMD. From the start of its operations NIMD has commissioned an outside evaluation of each of its party programs and in 2005 commissioned an overall institutional evaluation of itself. The outside evaluations are sometimes somewhat critical although so far at least they have focused on more middle-level issues of program design and administration than on deeper issues of actual effects.

Improving the Standard Model

The standard method persists, for all the reasons elaborated above. Nevertheless, some party aid organizations, or at least some experienced practitioners within them, are making efforts to broaden it and correct some of its deficiencies. None of these attempts or initiatives represent a dramatic breakthrough or sharp change of course. They are worth noting as possible building blocks to a better overall approach going forward.

Better Training

Party training, a domain beset with ritualized and often problematic practices, is ripe for improvement. In the field, one can observe some efforts to do better. A key weakness of traditional party training seminars are the trainers. Although fly-in trainers with little knowledge of the local scene remain dispiritingly common, some organizations are trying to find better solutions. Some have accumulated a roster of more experienced outside trainers, persons who have logged numerous trips to new or struggling democracies and developed expertise in specific regions or countries or at least some real familiarity with the kinds of problems that parties in these countries face. A few organizations, notably for example NDI, are increasing the use of "third-country" trainers— that is, sending experienced experts from one new or struggling democracy to do training in another where their experience is relevant, such as sending a South African to do training in Mozambique or a Chilean to assist in Peru. Although there is no guarantee that a third-country trainer's national experience will apply easily in a different national context, often the greater similarity of the political changes they have lived and worked through gives them a credibility and allows them to create a kind of bond that a trainer from the United States or Europe will not easily be able to establish.

At least in a limited number of cases, party aid groups are employing trainer-of-trainer methods in which they identify and extensively train a group of talented, energetic young activists who then carry out trainings within their parties. Considering how widespread and popular the training-of-trainers methodology is in other areas of foreign aid, such as community development work, it is striking how slowly and only very partially party aid organizations have taken it up. IRI and NDI, for example, were essentially obliged to give it a try in Serbia in the late 1990s. They were intent on providing training to the Serbian opposition parties but were not permitted to maintain offices in the country (due to the hostile state of U.S.-Serbian relations) or send in U.S. trainers. As a result they tried bringing a select group of young Serbian political activists to Hungary for an intensive dose of training and having them return to Serbia to carry out training within the opposition parties. The program worked well, the Serbian trainers got high marks from the parties, which encouraged the U.S. party institutes to try the approach more widely.

Beyond just improving the trainers, some aid providers are starting to eschew the short-term, no follow-up nature of conventional party aid workshops or seminars and instead create more sustained learning opportunities. In some cases these are a series of connected training events across time for the same participants, with structured follow-up in which the participants carry out reform initiatives in their parties to build on what they learned in the trainings. In other cases they are an intensive set of trainings, a sort of compressed course, sometimes billed as a "leadership academy," usually offered to promising young activists, in the hope that substantial investment in training dynamic young party cadres will create "change agents" within the parties. The long-term educational program for young Guatemalan party activists organized by the Swedish party foundations, for example, which was mentioned in chapter 4, is an example of a more sustained training experience. Since 1999, NDI has been running a training program for young Latin American political party activists. Participants start the year-long program with an extended seminar on party development issues, then spend most of the year designing and implementing an internal reform project within their party, with continued technical support from the outside. Approximately 200 students have passed through the program.

Some efforts are also being made to use new learning methods such as distance learning. IRI for example has developed a partnership with a Colombian online governance training institute, the *Escuela de Gobierno Tomás Moro* (Thomas More School of Government) to offer an in-depth virtual political training diploma course. In the first two years of the program, 2004 and 2005, IRI underwrote the costs for more than 300 young (under 40 years old) political leaders and civil society activists to complete the course (which requires approximately a half-time commitment over three months). The Hanns Seidel Stiftung has also begun sponsoring party representatives to do the course. The course is more detailed than the usual sorts of workshops and seminars that party aid groups offer and entails a substantial amount of practical exercises and applications. IRI is working to develop postcourse follow-up, such as including course alumni in further events, to integrate the experience of doing the course with being part of a wider network of trained young political activists in the region.

Looking Before You Leap

Party aid organizations have traditionally not spent significant amounts of time and energy studying a country's political party scene, or political landscape more generally, before starting to work there. Their funders generally do not support in-depth background research, being oriented toward direct action and quick impact. Because many party aid groups have relied on preset notions of what party-building work is, they have often not felt a strong need to do extensive studies to pave the way for it. A few groups, however, in the past several years have begun experimenting with ways to assess a political party scene in more depth as a way of preparing a deeper analytic foundation for a new program or revising an existing one.

For example, NDI, working with support from the British Department for International Development, has carried out in-depth political economy studies of the party landscape in Bolivia and Peru.[5] These studies focus on issues that party aid groups have traditionally not given much attention to, like the sociological roots of the parties and the incentive structures that shape their behavior, especially on the socioeconomic front. The aim of these studies is to provide a deeper basis of knowledge for designing party aid programs in countries where the very place of political parties is uncertain or in flux, and where it is obvious that conventional methods of party building have proved inadequate.

Several organizations are carrying out extensive information-gathering exercises based on direct participation by the parties themselves, through self-reporting or other similar methods. NIMD, for example, has initiated its work in Georgia (in the program it is running together with the OSCE) with an in-depth self-evaluation in which Georgian parties analyze their own strengths and weaknesses and suggest possible types of reform.[6] In Latin America, International IDEA, in cooperation with the OAS and other regional partners, is engaged in a large-scale effort to have parties report on many aspects of their internal organization and functioning. IDEA is expanding this information collection effort to other regions as well, with the aim of establishing a wide and deep collection of information about the state of political parties around the world.

All of these new efforts to obtain more information about and a deeper understanding of parties are in the testing stage. It is not clear yet whether and how they will translate into aid programs that differ from conventional approaches. Nevertheless, they reflect a growing awareness that to go deeper and have greater effects, party aid providers need to know more about the parties and overall political contexts of the places where they work.

Tougher Love and Better Timing

A central weakness of some party aid efforts, particularly those carried out via what I called in chapter 4 the "flexible party resource mode" (a long-term, multifaceted cooperative relationship between a party aid organization and a counterpart party), is the tendency of the party aid provider to slip into an uncritical, autopilot pattern of assistance. The assistance goes on and on, uninformed by any strategic conception about how to produce change in the other party, as the counterpart party gradually learns that it can basically do anything it wants and still have access to the study tours, exchange visits, material aid, conferences, and all the rest.

Some representatives of the *Stiftungen* (which with their long-term field offices and their orientation in some countries toward forming long-term ideologically based partnership relationships make the greatest use of the flexible party resource mode) are trying to inject some elements of challenge into these relationships. In Guatemala, for example, the representative of one of the *Stiftungen* working there tried to stir up the party with which it had the closest relationship—a party that was not showing any real interest in reform—by opening up its offer of assistance to other parties and requiring parties to compete for aid by setting out strategies for reform and plans for how aid would be used. In Morocco, one of the *Stiftungen* present in the country came to realize that the rather standardized meetings on party ideology that it was sponsoring for its counterpart party were not actually of great interest to the party. The Stiftung replaced that series with a set of meetings at which local party officials were asked to define what they believed were the top priorities for party reform and how external aid might help advance the process. In Mozambique, one of the *Stiftungen* recently tried to shake up the cozy, forgive-all nature of its organization's long-term relationship with one of the main Mozambican parties by stressing that it wanted to focus its aid on the problem of party corruption and neglect of the party's voter base. These are only very mild attempts at change, basic efforts to break out of the trap of supply-driven assistance. They are at least positive examples of innovation within a mode of party aid long characterized by stasis.

Much party aid has traditionally not been based on strategic thinking about the context for aid, for example trying to determine when is a favorable time to try to support processes of change in parties. Party aid providers have operated in accordance with a very basic framework regarding timing: when parties are preparing for a campaign is the time to work on campaign-related aid; in between elections is the time for party organizational work; and when parties first get into national legislatures is a natural time for legislative capacity work. Those party foundations that seek to build long-term relationships with parties view party aid as a continual process, often carrying on such relationships for many years with little thought to the underlying context for change.

Some party aid providers, however, in confronting the fact that parties they work with often resist changes they push for, are giving more attention to what contexts are favorable for change and to stepping up aid decisively at favorable moments.

The most obvious ripe moment for pushing a party to reform is immediately after it performs poorly in an election. A bad electoral performance is not an automatic stimulus for party reform. A blinkered party leader may blame defeat on factors other than party shortcomings, ranging from real or imagined electoral fraud to ignorant voters. Even if the leader does decide that changes are called for, he or she may pursue different ones than the prodemocratic reforms that party aid providers will be recommending. For example, rather than delegating more autonomy to the provincial branches in the hope they will be motivated to try new organizational methods, the leader may further tighten his or her grip on power. Nevertheless, disappointing electoral performance sometimes creates a stimulus for positive change in a party.

A party may also enter a period of openness to change when a generational shift occurs within a party, creating the possibility of leadership renewal. Many parties in new or struggling democracies have a founders' generation that has long dominated the party leadership and is impervious to change until the moment comes when that generation loses its hold. Such moments often take much longer to arrive than the rising generation hopes but when they do arrive, they constitute important opportunities for change.

Parties sometimes also open up to internal reforms as a result of larger changes in the overall political environment. A liberalizing moment can stimulate or at least increase the chances of party reforms. In Morocco, for example, the recent declarations by King Mohamed VI that he would like to see stronger political parties may represent an opportunity for Morocco's traditionally emasculated parties to assert themselves more vigorously and gain some power. In Indonesia, the various prodemocratic constitutional reforms enacted in the first half of this decade created new rules of the political game that represented stimuli for party reform, such as party decentralization to match the new process of direct elections for provincial and local legislatures.

Giving more attention to identifying and taking advantage of favorable contexts for party change does not mean that party aid programs should therefore often be short-term opportunistic efforts. Usually, a party aid organization will be able to take advantage most effectively of a positive juncture if it has been working in the country for some time, building relationships, and thus already well in place when the fortuitous moment occurs. What this implies for programming is the need to combine a sustained aid presence with a flexible design that allows the aid provider to change the scale of the effort quickly to respond to opportunities that arise. Some of the larger party aid providers, which have the possibility of combining a long-term presence with the ability to launch a sizeable initiative when a favorable moment arises, are starting to show a greater interest in operating in this more strategic manner. The U.S. party institutes' work with Moroccan parties, for example, has evolved in tandem with the changing context for party reform in that country. They have adapted their work to take on issues such as party law reform and possible constitutional reform that have arisen along the way, while attempting to build the long-term relationships necessary to take advantage of larger opportunities that may arise if the Moroccan king makes good on his stated intention to allow a general strengthening of a traditionally emasculated party domain. Some smaller party aid providers are also showing a heightened focus on political opportunity in order to find pivotal moments. Some of the Swedish foundations operating in authoritarian environments such as Belarus and Cuba, for example, engage in fine-grained efforts to calibrate their work to the harsh, shifting political environments in those countries, to exploit small openings, and lower their profile when necessary as well.

Horizontal Learning and Normative Development

The past five years have seen a surge of efforts by different party aid groups to convene large meetings of representatives of parties from new or struggling democracies, usually on a broad regional basis (and not on the basis of shared ideology), at which the representatives discuss common concerns about the state of parties generally in their country or region and their own parties specifically. One central purpose of such meetings is to provide representatives from a broad swath of parties an opportunity to learn about the common problems and challenges that they face. The organizers usually hope that party representatives will be able to share approaches they have used in addressing problems and learn from each other. Another main purpose of such activities is to promote the idea of norms or standards for how parties should operate. The agenda of such meetings usually emphasizes the sorts of topics that the sponsoring organizations wish to stress, such as achieving more internal democracy, promoting greater inclusion of women, and increasing financial transparency. Through such agenda-setting, party aid providers are seeking to spread their ideas about what good parties are, in the explicit or implicit hope that such ideas will gain traction as norms or standards among party elites and citizens generally in all new or struggling democracies.

The most developed series of regional party meetings are those taking place in Latin America under the aegis of the OAS's Inter-American Forum on Political Parties, mentioned in chapter 4. The forum has convened numerous region-wide, broad-ranging gatherings of party leaders and party activists as well as more specialized subregional or thematically focused meetings. International IDEA, for example, started in 2005 holding a series of regional party workshops of this type in various parts of the world. In the first half of this decade, NDI sponsored a series of meeting for Asian party leaders focused on the problem of party corruption, with an added innovative element. In addition to analyzing the problems of party corruption, the Asian party participants formulated a plan to carry out party-to-party observation of the behavior of Asian parties in electoral campaigns. A cross-national group of the representatives visited four Asian countries during electoral campaigns and wrote reports assessing the legality and cleanliness of the campaigns.[7] The reports were disseminated in the countries in question and also among the overall group of Asian party representatives. Having some parties in a region (rather than international observers or domestic civil society representatives) observe and critique other parties in the same region is a novel step, and the Asian-to-Asian character of the observation was useful given the sensitivity of the corruption issues involved.

Bridging the Civil Society Gap

As party aid organizations seek to go deeper into the question of how parties in target countries can be strengthened or reformed, they frequently confront the fact that parties in many new or struggling democracies lack much connection to civil society. More strongly, many representatives of civil society organizations in developing or former communist countries express a strong aversion to parties and to having any contact with them. Conventional party building programs that aim to foster party outreach to the public are usually focused either on attracting votes in a campaign or party adherents in between campaigns. They are more individually oriented than directed at civil society groups.

Some party aid providers have begun to initiate aid activities specifically designed to build ties between parties and civil society. Such programs typically consist of roundtable meetings or workshops that bring together representatives of political parties with representatives of civil society organizations. The idea behind the meetings is that if the two sides get to know each other better and learn about each other's interests and outlooks they will better understand the importance of working with each other and perhaps initiate new efforts to do so.

These party–civil society connection activities are based on an important idea—that the lack of societal rootedness of parties in new or struggling democracies is a core problem. They have not yet gained much traction where they have been tried in recent years, such as in Guatemala (by the OAS) and Romania (by the U.S. party institutes). Civil society representatives who attend such meetings often come out of them complaining that the political parties have no interest in real partnership and just want to dominate civil society groups and use them for their own purposes. The political party people, in turn, complain that the civil society activists are only interested in their own issues and look down on political parties.

Some of the problem with the attempts so far to help forge stronger ties between political parties and civil society comes from the narrow definition of civil society that democracy promoters use. They are in the habit of essentially equating civil society with NGOs, especially the rather specialized world of public interest advocacy and service NGOs that are close to the donor world. These NGOs are only one part of civil society and they are one of the parts that is least likely to want to work closely with parties. They are usually led and peopled by activists who entered the NGO sector as an alternative to a political sector they view as corrupt and unproductive. Their interests in policy advocacy and service delivery lead them to be deeply wary of close association with any party or group of parties. Such an association can hurt their ability to obtain needed access or cooperation with the government if the other party comes to power. These NGOs, very much at the donors' urging, have cultivated the ideal of nonpartisanship and a certain technocratic distance from the swamp of politics. They are surprised, and rather confused, when they hear from some Western democracy promoters that they should in fact now be building ties to parties.[8]

For assistance work on this issue to advance, aid providers will have to broaden their scope to take on board a much wider conception of civil society. It is precisely the types of civil society groups that are often not part of donor-funded civil society development programs—groups oriented toward mobilization and wide membership, such as teachers' organizations, indigenous persons' groups, informal ethnic associations, professional associations, and trade unions—that are more likely to have the sort of political interests and orientation that would lead them to want to work closely with political parties. Several of the European party foundations linked to social democratic parties, for example, notably the Palme Center and the Ebert Stiftung, have done some useful work in many countries by attempting to help center-left parties connect more effectively to labor unions. Party aid groups will need to abandon the idea of party–civil society relationships as a kind of policy-oriented partnership and instead figure out how to support the kinds of deeply strategic (and, for better or worse, opportunistic) party–civil society relationships that actually exist in established democracies, such as those between many different German social organizations and the German parties and between many interest group organizations and the U.S. parties. In short, meaningful efforts to connect parties to civil society require giving up the mythic donor idea of civil society as a virtuous realm free of partisanship and of civil society engagement in the public sphere as consisting primarily of nonpartisan advocacy.

New Forms of Political Representation

Programs to connect parties to civil society represent one approach to the broad problem of parties in many new or struggling democracies not being rooted in their own societies. Given that most of the civil society actors involved in such programs are the more formalized NGO-type organizations, which are often as elite-based as the parties themselves, such programs can be considered a horizontal approach to party rootedness. Other aid actors are trying to come at this problem more from the bottom up, based on the assumption that parties are so cut off from their own societies because they are elite-focused organizations that are not trying or do not know how to be useful to ordinary citizens. Their operative question is either how to get parties interested in serving ordinary citizens, or how to connect citizens to the political process in societies where politics are formally democratic but not really responsive to ordinary citizens.

Many donors have been pursuing a whole host of programs over the past several decades aimed at making governments more responsive to citizens at the local level. These often entail efforts to connect local governments to local level NGOs, such as community development organizations, that help citizens identify and assert their needs. Such efforts, although frequently valuable in terms of bettering the lives of local communities and individuals, are usually not focused on the problem of political representation per se. They proceed more from the idea of deliberative civil society action—dialogue, advocacy, and often partnership with local governments—than from the issues of political identification, mobilization, and association. Political parties are rarely much of a focus in such initiatives. If they are brought in, they are just considered an additional partner to the local civil society groups.

A small but distinctive example of an effort to connect citizens to parties (rather than to networks of local NGOs and local government organizations) are some recent activities in the Andean region carried out by International IDEA and the Peruvian civic group Transparencia, in conjunction with the United Nations Children's Fund (UNICEF), and also in Peru with NDI. These activities entail offering political and civic education to various groups of citizens who have little contact with the formal political process to raise their awareness about how parties and politicians can (and should) address social issues such as poverty reduction and child welfare. At the same time, the program offers training to parties on how to formulate effective platforms and policies on these various issues. The idea is to encourage citizens both to see parties as organizations that should take responsibility for improving their daily lives and to demand that from parties. Simultaneously the program seeks to help parties become capable of meeting that demand.

As with the work on party–civil society relations, this is an interesting line of work, yet also one that has yet to show it can effect substantial changes in how parties relate (or do not relate) to their societies. It is difficult to change the incentive structures that shape parties' behavior just by changing some of the attitudes of citizens about parties (to whatever extent civic education can do that). Parties' problematic relationship to citizens has many entrenched causes, from patronage structures to sociocultural hierarchies, none of which can be easily changed by some mild attitudinal shifts on the part of some citizens. Establishing clear, rational linkages between the policy performance of parties and the actual preferences and choices of voters is something that takes place only very imperfectly, even in established democracies. In the United States, for example, many voters make notably irrational (viewed strictly in terms of economic causality) judgments about the responsibility of the president for economic trends, simplistically assuming the macroeconomic cycles are the direct results of specific presidential actions. Their voting choices rest on personalistic, and sometimes quixotic, factors rather than any serious assessment of their economic self-interest and the policy platforms or policy records of competing candidates or parties.

A group of primarily Nordic political researchers (the Network on Contextual Politics in Developing Countries) is attempting to find entry points for pursuing this problem of political representation, which they define as a gap between traditional elitist politics on the one hand and depoliticized local civil society activism on the other. In Indonesia, one of the countries that some of these researchers are following, they had some hopes for what looked like a popular prodemocratic movement that contributed to the downfall of President Suharto in the late 1990s but was not tied to the traditional political parties. As happened to the once leading civil society activists in post-1989 Central and Eastern Europe, however, the Indonesian prodemocracy activists were quickly pushed aside by hard-charging political parties once elections got under way. The civil society actors showed little real stomach or talent for constructing political institutions and engaging in day-to-day politics once the struggle against the dictator was won. The Nordic researchers are only at the exploratory stage but are at least pushing hard on a problem that merits attention.[9] Some observers hope that populist figures and movements such as President Evo Morales and his indigenous movement in Bolivia can forge new connections between alienated citizens and their political systems. The history of populist parties in Latin America and elsewhere, such as Africa, is a sobering one, however, because of both the poor performance of such movements once in power and their tendency to lapse into undemocratic methods of rule. The space between elitist parties and civic activism in many new or struggling democracies is evident; what might fill it is not.

Encouraging Innovation and Excellence

Funding Mechanisms

In looking at some of the innovations emerging in party aid, it is logical to ask how positive processes of change can be stimulated. What kinds of funding mechanisms and institutional arrangements encourage innovations and improvements in party aid?

Regarding funding, a look at the pluses and minuses of each of the three main sources of party aid money—bilateral aid agencies, foreign ministries, and national legislatures—highlights the fact that no one funding source is ideal. Funding party aid from a bilateral aid agency (as the United States and Sweden do) has some at least potential advantages. Such agencies are repositories of useful knowledge about development work that should have at least some applicability to party programs. There is however a basic problem of fit. Western bilateral aid agencies are primarily devoted to socioeconomic work. Although many Western bilateral aid agencies sponsor some democracy programs, they remain organizations primarily focused on socioeconomic aid. They are almost congenitally uncomfortable with political work. Party aid, being perhaps the most overtly political type of democracy aid, sits especially poorly with them. In addition, good party aid—which often necessarily involves close, flexible relationships between party aid groups on the one hand and colorful politicians and their often corrupt, nontransparent parties on the other—is far from the model of technocratic, rapid-impact, project-focused assistance that bilateral aid organizations strive for. Measuring progress in the ways that bilateral aid agencies like to do—through precisely defined, often quantitative indicators—is rather elusive in the party domain. It is easy enough to chart a party's electoral progress, but this is a poor measurement of the effects of party aid given both that the causal factors behind a party's electoral performance are a complex stew and that party aid usually aims at a much wider array of goals, such as internal democracy and societal rootedness, than just vote-getting. Arriving at highly precise measurements of performance on the wider set of goals is difficult. Some institutional steps can be fairly specifically defined and measured. Yet party leaders are often masters at carrying out reform after apparent reform in the party while actually keeping intact the core problematic features of the institution.

Funding for party programs from foreign ministries has various possible advantages. Politics is the lifeblood of foreign ministries and so the political nature of party aid is likely to be less problematic for them than for aid agencies. Foreign ministries also have a more flexible, less project-focused approach to aid giving, which can work well for party programs. At the same time there are possible pitfalls. One is that the foreign ministry may not have any real interest in supporting political party development for prodemocratic reasons and instead want to use the party aid to curry favor with particular politicians or influence near-term electoral outcomes for the sake of security or economic interests. Another is that foreign ministries will instinctively prefer short-term approaches and not support sustained assistance efforts. In the diplomatic mind-set, aid is often a short-term lever rather than a long-term investment.

Party aid foundations or institutes that receive funding from national legislatures (such as the German *Stiftungen*) favor the relative independence that such funding usually brings them. The danger of too much independence is that the party foundations will not be held closely accountable for what they do and that they may not be sufficiently challenged to assess and improve their overall methods and strategies over time. In some cases where legislative funding is used for party aid, intermediate mechanisms of review and approval are set up to avoid that danger. The National Endowment for Democracy represents such a gateway between the congressional funds that it receives and the party institutes to which some of those funds go. NED program officers review and approve proposals from the party institutes and constitute a layer of outside review and accountability. The other danger of legislative funding for party aid is that it is often apportioned on the basis of different parties' performance in the last elections. Variations in that performance can lead to abrupt, sizeable increases or decreases in the funds available to party foundations, forcing them either to very rapidly close down or open up programs, which is not necessarily a route to good programmatic design and implementation.

In short there is no one funding mechanism or source for party aid that is best. Each of the main governmental sources (which constitute the sources of most existing party aid) has its pluses and minuses. The same is true with respect to institutional forms. Each of the different types of organizations involved in party aid—party foundations or institutes, multiparty organizations (like NIMD or WFD), and multilateral organizations—has different strengths. Party foundations and institutes have direct access to party expertise and the possibility of bonding at a party-to-party level with foreign counterparts. Multiparty organizations can operate one level above the specific party-to-party relationships both to extract lessons from those experiences and attempt more systemic interventions. Multilateral organizations have a political neutrality that can give them greater political access in sensitive situations. All have a place and it is good that the monopoly party foundations and institutes long had on party aid is being replaced by a wider array of actors.

Operational Lessons

Although no single funding mechanism or institutional form for party aid is necessarily best, it is possible to identify certain operational arrangements or patterns that seem to ensure more innovative and effective programs. To start with, carrying out party aid from a field office rather than from a donor capital is a major plus. A field office makes possible, among other things, a qualitatively higher level of knowledge about the local political and party scenes, and much more regular and extensive contacts with relevant actors. A field office may bring with it, as some party foundations that do not have field offices say, the danger of "local capture," that is, coming too closely under the influence of particular local political actors, but that danger is greatly outweighed by the benefits.

As is the case with almost all development aid programs, party programs that invest seriously in capacitating persons from the recipient country (rather than relying on the importation of external expertise) and giving some real responsibility to local actors for project design and implementation are more likely to have lasting positive effects. This is the most obvious sort of aid-related "lesson learned" but one that has been slow to penetrate the party aid world. One can still observe party aid organizations operating for years in a country but then when they do eventually depart, leaving behind almost no local institutional trace and no cadre of people of the country trained and prepared to carry on the work.

Although sustained commitments are no guarantee of success, they have a much better chance of producing meaningful results than short-term, putatively quick impact interventions. Given the resistance that most parties have to change, the complexities of how parties fit into the sociopolitical life, and the natural wariness in most political contexts to outside assistance in this area, only long-term efforts are likely to clear all of these hurdles. Staying for a long time raises the danger of falling into the cozy, tractionless relationships discussed previously, yet the solution is not to avoid long-term efforts but rather to ensure that they avoid that trap.

A key way to do that is through periodic, searching evaluations, preferably by outside experts (including from the recipient country). Such evaluations need to go beyond charting outputs to assess how such aid is actually experienced and viewed by people on the recipient side, whether its underlying assumptions about how to stimulate and support change are correct, and what effects, intended and unintended, it is having over a period of years, not just months. In addition to taking evaluations seriously, party aid providers would be well-advised to find ways to invest in research efforts that parallel their programming and provide answers to questions that may be otherwise assumed away. Examples of relevant questions include whether attempts at grassroots campaigning in a country are actually helping change citizens' perceptions of parties, what effects party finance legal reforms are actually having on party behavior, and whether persons being trained within parties are able over the medium term to make use of what they have learned to effect changes in the party, and if not why not.

Excellence and innovation will also be encouraged if party aid groups have at least some political latitude from their funders. They need some breathing space between them and the state institutions that fund them. This is needed so that they can make programmatic choices based on a genuine interest in facilitating party development and on the knowledge they have about party work, not on the near-term foreign policy interests of the funder state. At the same time, funders need to maintain some oversight and control over the party work they fund to ensure that party aid groups do not use the political latitude they have to pursue their private foreign policy agendas. Achieving the right balance between political flexibility and control in this domain is a constant challenge.

Finally, good party aid clearly requires considerable flexibility. To get beyond cookie-cutter approaches, party aid groups have to be allowed by their funders to spend significant time getting to know a local political scene before designing an aid program there, to experiment with different methods that may or may not pan out, and to stay at least minimally involved in a country for years to be positioned to take advantage of positive junctures when they do occur. On the other hand, unlimited flexibility can be problematic. The funding should entail some qualitative goal-setting, programmatic oversight, and periodic strategic review to ensure that party aid providers do have a clear idea of what they are doing and do not fall into stale, repetitive types of aid that accomplish little but keep being justified as worthwhile under a hazy rationale of "relationship-building."

CHAPTER SIX

Interests and Partisanship

Although the current wave of democracy aid has been going on for more than 20 years and has grown into an extremely active, multifaceted domain populated by a wide array of organizations, it is still often questioned, doubted, or challenged in countries where it takes place. People in countries on the receiving end of democracy aid often ask, "What are the real objectives and intentions of these foreign organizations involving themselves in our political affairs?" Many people assume, quite naturally and understandably, that these foreign organizations have underlying interests different from their professed prodemocratic aims, above all to manipulate or control political outcomes for their own benefit. Democracy promoters sometimes overlook or ignore such views, assuming that their own prodemocratic values should speak for themselves and that the doubters in any particular setting are an anti-Western fringe.

Doubts and suspicions about underlying objectives and intentions are particularly acute regarding party aid. Although all areas of democracy aid, and in fact many areas of socioeconomic aid also, affect a country's political life, party aid is especially politically sensitive. It directly touches the key political actors vying for power and has the clear potential to affect a society's core political choices. The legacy of covert party assistance during the Cold War—when the United States and the Soviet Union funneled money to ideologically friendly parties in Europe and many developing countries to bolster allies, undermine enemies, and tilt elections—still weighs on the world of party aid.

There is clearly the possibility that covert forms of party aid continue today, whether from the United States, Russia, or other countries. There were credible reports after the 2004 Ukrainian elections, for example, that the Russian government had given large amounts of money to the campaign of Prime Minister Viktor Yanukovych, its preferred candidate.[1] Thus more than any other area of democracy aid, party aid starts with a very high burden in terms of establishing its credibility with local audiences.

This chapter explores the underlying objectives and interests of party aid and takes up the question of partisanship—whether party assistance is used to favor particular parties and, in so doing, to affect electoral outcomes. Clearly practices vary among aid actors and in different countries. Accurate generalizations are elusive. Nevertheless some patterns emerge, especially contrasting European and U.S. approaches. Some of the forms of partisanship that occur in party aid raise significant questions about the legitimacy of such work. These questions are all the more pressing in the current context of heightened debate and controversy over the legitimacy of democracy promotion generally stemming from the George W. Bush administration's pointed use of the concept to justify the Iraq War and its embrace more generally of the idea that democratic regime change may be the best way to deal with certain unfriendly governments.

No Easy Answers

The official answer usually offered by party aid organizations and the governmental bodies that fund them to questions about the objectives and interests underlying party aid is straightforward: party aid does not seek to influence the outcome of elections but rather to help build strong, effective, parties around the world capable of fulfilling the main prodemocratic roles that parties should perform in a democracy. This official explanation is partially or even significantly true in many cases. The reality, however, is not always quite so simple.

A Varied European Menu

In some cases party aid has purposes other than democracy promotion. Some portion of European party assistance—especially that part of it that is less about training or other types of technical assistance and more about exchanges and visits between parties—has diplomatic rather than prodemocratic aims. European parties use their international outreach work, whether conducted through party foundations or an international office within the party, to develop useful contacts and nurture channels of influence and friendship with foreign political actors. When the aid-giving party is in power it may use these personal contacts and channels to supplement its regular diplomatic channels and contacts in pursuit of various foreign policy goals. If it is out of power, it seeks to build contacts that may be useful when it does get into power.

In Central and Eastern Europe, some Western European parties discovered a particular additional purpose for their party outreach work—building up party partners that would eventually join their blocs in the European Parliament once the country being aided joined the European Union. In Romania for example this was made clear to me by the office director of one of the German *Stiftungen* working there. When I asked him how the programs they were doing with their Romanian party counterpart contributed to democracy building, he admonished me for the phrasing of my question. His purpose in Romania, he said, was not to promote democracy. It was to support a Romanian fraternal counterpart to his party so that his party would have a Romanian partner to join its European Parliament bloc when Romania joins the European Union.[2]

This bloc-building focus of some of the German *Stiftungen* and other West European party groups is not simply different from democracy building, but sometimes at odds with it. One of the problems the Romanian opposition faced in the early years of this decade, before their victory in the 2004 elections, was achieving unity and avoiding fractionation in the center-right part of the political spectrum. The National Peasant Party was dying and had broken into several remnant parties, which some observers felt would soon pass from the scene, allowing the center-right to unify around other larger parties. Because Germany has three *Stiftungen* representing center-right parties (associated with the Liberals, the Christian Democrats, and the Bavarian Christian Social Union), German party-building work with the center-right forces in Romania was oriented in those years toward keeping alive at least three separate parties, a Liberal party, a Christian Democratic party, and an alternative Christian Democratic party. Each of the three *Stiftungen* wanted its own party partner, even if this was harmful to the larger cause of oppositional coherence (and thus to the chance of a democratic alternation of power) in the country.

It would be very difficult to assess what proportion of the international work by European party foundations and European parties is primarily aimed at serving diplomatic or other interests and what proportion seeks to advance the broader goal of democracy building. In some cases the same activity (such as a series of study tours by top cadres of a fraternal party to the host's capital) may serve both ends simultaneously. In other cases, party work that is pursued for diplomatic purposes is distinctly disconnected from prodemocratic goals, such as relationship building with ruling parties in nondemocratic countries for the sake of furthering economic or security relationships. Arriving at an assessment about the relative priority of their different goals in different countries is made even harder by the fact that party foundations are not very forthcoming about the various purposes of the work they do. They usually rest on very broad concepts like "international outreach" and generalized assertions of prodemocratic intent to cover a gamut of aims and activities.

American Interests

The U.S. party institutes do much less of this sort of party-to-party diplomatic facilitation than the European party foundations. They are less close to their "mother" parties than are the European foundations. U.S. parties are much less involved generally in the world of fraternal party-to-party contacts. The party institutes sometimes sponsor visits to Washington by leaders or other senior representatives of parties they have worked with, opening doors for them and generally helping ensure they have a productive visit. Sometimes these visits have a political purpose, such as helping an opposition leader in a democratically besieged country gain support in Washington. Other times they are just a way of maintaining good relations with parties they are working with.

Although the U.S. party institutes are less involved than their European counterparts in building and using party-to-party contacts for the sake of diplomatic relations, the question often arises of whose interests the party institutes represent when they work in another country. The institutes are largely funded with money coming from the U.S. government and are tied to the two parties that occupy the U.S. executive and legislative branches. Not surprisingly therefore many people who encounter them abroad assume that they are representatives of the U.S. government and interpret their actions as the direct expressions of U.S. foreign policy. Thus if one of the institutes decides to work with one party but not another, some people in the country will interpret this as evidence that the White House or the State Department favors that party. Yet the institutes usually stress their nongovernmental nature, telling people where they work that although they are U.S. government-funded, they are not governmental organizations and their decisions about what to do and whom to work with are their own, not the U.S. government's.

In fact, the relationship between the U.S. party institutes and U.S. foreign policy is complicated and not easy to characterize. Being U.S. government-funded, they are part of U.S. foreign policy in a broad sense, in the same way that all organizations whose international work is funded by the U.S. government can be considered to be part of U.S. foreign policy. From the point of view of their governmental funders, primarily USAID, Congress, and the State Department, the party institutes, although not part of the policy-making process, are part of the implementation of policy. If USAID decides it wants to strengthen democracy in a country and believes that supporting party development is a way to do that, it can give the institutes funds to do such work. If a U.S. ambassador in a country wants to help bolster the government's democratic legitimacy, he or she can push to get the party institutes involved in supporting party development as part of a broader elections support effort. Although the ambassador cannot direct the party institutes to do what he or she wants, he or she can likely have some influence, especially via USAID funding.

The party institutes see their relationship to U.S. policy a bit differently. They view themselves as autonomous actors that, unlike the U.S. government, have only democracy promotion as their mandate. They believe that their actions are consistent with U.S. policy, but are their own. That is, they generally initiate and make their own decisions about what countries to work in and what to do therein, based on their own assessments of what is an important and viable opportunity for democracy promotion. They deemphasize the idea that they follow and implement USAID's priorities. Instead they highlight the idea that they often have to persuade USAID to fund them to do what they believe would be best to build democracy generally. When they cannot convince USAID (or the State Department) to fund a project they want to do, they can fall back on their lesser but more flexible NED funds and do it anyway.

Although the work of the institutes is broadly part of U.S. foreign policy, their partial autonomy results in frequent cases of their leaning one way or the other to push U.S. policy a bit more in what they view as a prodemocratic direction (such as to be more supportive of an opposition coalition challenging a strongman regime). A couple of examples highlight the fact that their programs are sometimes mildly or even moderately divergent from the main policy line.

In the lead-up to Kenya's 2002 presidential elections, for example, NDI perceived an opportunity to work with Kenyan political parties to help them compete more vigorously and effectively in what NDI believed could be decisive elections. President Daniel Arap Moi, Kenya's strongman president, was finally stepping down and there was a chance an opposition coalition could win and Kenya would thereby experience a valuable (from the point of view of democratization) alternation of power. USAID was dubious about the potential value of working with political parties that were on the whole highly troubled organizations. The State Department was not very interested in any political aid work that might rock the boat of the fairly productive overall U.S. relationship with the Kenyan government. Rather than trying to obtain USAID funds for a Kenya program, NDI drew on its more flexible NED funds and carried out a training program for both opposition and progovernment parties. NDI's work did not run contrary to U.S. policy in Kenya, but neither did it grow out of or fit comfortably with it. NDI's own views and interests drove it.

In Haiti in the second half of the 1990s, after the U.S. invasion to restore President Jean-Bertrand Aristide to power, IRI carried out political party strengthening work there. IRI was dubious about whether President Aristide and his political party, Lavalas, were prodemocratic and thus chose to work primarily with the main opposition parties, believing them to be the only real democratic parties in the country. This approach did not reflect the main line of U.S. policy in Haiti, which was largely supportive of Aristide. The gap between IRI's approach and the U.S. policy line was evident in the aftermath to Haiti's 1995 national elections that resulted in the victory of René Préval, a close associate of Aristide's. The official U.S. observer delegation to the elections led by the head of USAID described the elections as "a very significant breakthrough for democracy."[3] On the very same day, IRI issued a "Haiti Election Alert" calling attention to "the nationwide breakdown of the electoral process."[4]

The relationship between IRI's party work and U.S. policy in Haiti in the first half of this decade became an issue of public controversy in 2006. A lengthy *New York Times* article reported that the U.S. ambassador to Haiti from 2001 to 2003 had accused IRI of undermining or at least working at odds with U.S. policy in the country by supporting opposition figures who opposed compromise with the Haitian government.[5] IRI defended itself, pointing out that its work (which was funded by USAID) had been well-known to the State Department and USAID, and arguing it was fully consistent with U.S. policy.[6] It appears that in the first administration of President George W. Bush there were divisions within the U.S. policy bureaucracy over Haiti, with some persons favoring a tougher line toward Lavalas than others. IRI's approach fit with one side of the divided policy camp, but was at odds with the other camp.

A Development Rationale

Finally regarding underlying intentions and objectives of party work, some of the multilateral organizations that have recently started doing party aid, as well as some of the European bilateral aid agencies or parliaments that fund party work, view party programs as part of their development agenda. Democracy for them may be a goal, but as a means to an end, with that end being development. They support party work in the hope or belief that stronger, more capable, democratic parties will contribute to development—by ensuring that citizens' economic interests (especially the interests of the poor) will be better represented, and by helping parties develop a greater capacity for formulating and implementing effective socioeconomic policies. It is not yet clear whether a development lens will lead to different approaches to party work than a democracy lens (the more developmentally oriented aid actors engaged in party work are still new to the domain). In other areas, such as civil society promotion and state reform, a development rather than democracy-building focus has often led to different partners and programs, and so the same may arise in the realm of party aid.

Partisanship

The fact that party aid providers sometimes work with parties in other countries for purposes other than party building, such as cultivating useful relations with key politicians, causes some people in recipient countries to question the prodemocratic character of party aid generally. The issue that most frequently causes controversy and concern about party aid in recipient countries is partisanship or political interventionism. Yes, party aid providers may actually be aiming to strengthen parties, not just building useful contacts, political observers concede, but aren't they playing favorites—helping certain parties over others—to influence the outcomes of elections in ways favorable to their own political agendas and interests?

Providers of party aid usually downplay the notion that their work might be partisan (in the sense of favoring one party over others) and deny that they might be seeking to influence electoral outcomes. USAID for example has specific written policy on the issue, which states that "USAID programs must make a good faith effort to assist *all democratic* parties with equitable levels of assistance."[7] In fact, however, partisanship is common in both European and U.S. party aid, although in different ways. Understanding the role partisanship plays in party aid requires careful analysis of what party aid providers do rather than what they say they do. Partisanship in party aid raises some basic questions. Above all, is partisan assistance legitimate given the norm of political sovereignty?

European Fraternal Partisanship

As discussed in chapter 5, most European party aid follows the fraternal party approach (the largest exception is work by the NIMD, which is primarily multipartisan). Fraternal party assistance appears inherently partisan—a party foundation directs its party-related work in a country toward supporting and strengthening just one party. Yet European party foundations and parties often insist that their international work is not really partisan and has nothing to do with influencing electoral outcomes. They argue that although they may work only with one counterpart party in a particular country, the other parties or party foundations from their country will work with the other main parties there, ensuring an ideological balance in the assistance. Also, they contend, the thrust of most of their work is long-term party building rather than campaign-related and therefore such aid does not seek to influence a party's performance in any specific election. They add, if they do happen to work with a party in the lead-up to an election, they stop their assistance activities some time before the election (typically one month before), to ensure they do not interfere during the heart of the electoral process.

These arguments, which surface often in interviews or conversations with representatives of European party aid providers when the issue of partisanship is raised, are not very persuasive if one looks closely at the realities of such programs. The idea that an ideological balance will be achieved due to the ideological diversity of the party foundations in the aid-providing country is flawed, for several reasons. First, aid-providing governments usually apportion funds for international party aid to their own parties or party foundations in accordance with the parties' share of votes in the most recent parliamentary election. In some situations this will result in a party foundation of one or another political stripe receiving much greater funding than the others. That country's overall international party aid will therefore reflect that weighting, not a neutral ideological balance. In Sweden, for example, the Social Democratic Party's long domination of the electoral scene means that the party foundation tied to the Social Democratic Party has long received much more money than the country's other party foundations. Given that the Swedish foundations usually follow the fraternal party method, this means that on the whole, Swedish party aid has been distinctly weighted toward supporting center-left parties around the world.

Even if the main parties of an aid-providing country are balanced across the left-right divide in terms of size, this will not necessarily translate into balanced party aid in any one country. The country's right-of-center party foun-

dation might decide to work actively on party building in a particular country while the country's left-of-center foundation, for whatever reason, might
decide not to work with parties there (working instead for example with civil
society groups or choosing not to work at all in the country). Thus a country's
fraternal party aid, even if balanced overall, may often be unbalanced in any
one recipient country. In Russia, for example, during the 1990s, Germany's
largest right-of-center party foundation (the Adenauer Stiftung) was actively
involved in party aid whereas the largest left-of-center foundation (the Ebert
Stiftung) did not engage much in party work. In Morocco, the reverse has
been true in this decade. Many other such examples from different European
aid providers could be cited.

Taking this argument one step further, even if an aid-providing country's
main party foundations are similar in size and they do all engage in party support in a particular country, the country's party aid may still not be ideologically balanced. The parties of the aid-receiving country may not fall clearly
along a left-right spectrum—they may be divided more along religious,
regional, or ethnic lines, or not have clearly identifiable distinguishing lines
among them at all. Thus while some of the parties in the country may match
up with European party foundations on the basis of shared ideology, others
may not. Those that do will be candidates for European party aid; those that
do not, will not be. For example, in Morocco, the Socialist Party has a
European-style ideological identity and is therefore a natural partner for European center-left party foundations that choose to work in the country. Some
of Morocco's other principal parties, such as its main Islamist party, the Justice and Development Party, do not have such a European ideology and therefore are not chosen as partners by European party foundations. In Indonesia,
the one German party foundation active in party work in the first half of this
decade (the Naumann Stiftung) offered some assistance to all the parties. It
had a closer relationship with the two parties whose ideological outlooks it
found more compatible with European-style ideologies generally. Thus the
dissimilarity between Indonesia's ideological spectrum and the European left-
right one results in some Indonesian parties receiving more external aid than
others.

The argument that European fraternal party aid does not seek to have any
effect on electoral outcomes because it is usually aimed at long-term party
building rather than at bolstering parties' participation in an upcoming election is also problematic. In the first place, some European party aid is very
much campaign-focused. The international work of the British parties, for
example, often consists of training in campaign methods. In their work in the

postcommunist countries, the German *Stiftungen* often helped parties with campaign-related issues, from the development of party platforms to strategies for public outreach. To take just one example, in Russia the Adenauer Stiftung partnered with IRI in the year leading up to the December 2003 Duma elections on a campaign-focused training program for Yabloko and SPS.

Moreover, the idea that a sharp line can be drawn between aid for party building and for campaigning is illusory. If basic party organizational work— such as membership development, cadre training, fundraising, and strengthening of local branches—is effective, it will undoubtedly help a party campaign better and therefore do better electorally. The notion that stopping party aid a month before an election somehow immunizes an aid provider from the charge that it may be affecting the outcome of the election has a completely unpersuasive "recovered virginity" quality. Training and other activities that help a party prepare for a campaign presumably produce effects that last all the way through the campaign to the election—stopping the assistance a month before the election does not stop the benefits of that assistance from having effects on the performance of the parties in the election.

If pressed on these points, representatives of European party foundations sometimes acknowledge that their work might possibly be seen as partisan involvement in other countries' politics. Even if they do acknowledge this, however, they do not seem very concerned about it. In part this is because they distinguish their countries from what they consider interventionist powers (above all the United States and also Russia, at least in its "near abroad"). Thus the fact that their country's party programs might end up helping one party more than another in any particular country does not strike them as especially significant or sensitive.

Their lack of concern about partisanship also reflects the fact that most people who work in Western party aid groups are political people (party activists, former political consultants, former legislative staff members) rather than developmentalists. As such they generally do not share the reluctance of developmentalists to act politically in other countries. They think that the main ideological "families" of political parties are universalistic categories— that every country should have a center-left social-democratic type party, a center-right conservative party, or whichever party ideology they subscribe to. When in an interview I asked the representative of a European conservative party engaged in international party support about the goals of the party's work abroad, the answer was simple: the aim is to strengthen conservative parties in as many countries throughout the world as possible. When I asked whether they had any hesitation about taking sides in other countries' political life, the answer was equally straightforward: every country needs a strong conservative party. When I inquired how it is possible to transport their very specific social and economic ideas about what constitutes conservatism to such different societies, the response was still simple: all societies have "real conservatives," you just have to find them.[8]

This universalistic instinct among representatives of the main European party families is noteworthy. U.S. democracy promoters are often infused with a heady universalistic conviction about the possibility and value of democracy as a general political ideal. Speaking very generally, Europeans, at least Western Europeans, are much less inclined to such an outlook, and are sometimes disdainful of it as a naïve American enthusiasm. Yet Europeans active in party aid turn out to harbor surprisingly universalistic ideas about the viability and applicability of the main nineteenth and twentieth century European ideologies, especially social democracy and European liberalism.

Although European party foundations tend not to see the partisan nature of their party work in other countries as a concern, such assistance sometimes roils the local political waters. The partisan quality of fraternal aid may not be evident or important to those providing it, but people within the recipient country may have a different view. If they hear that organizations from wealthy Western countries are aiding parties in their country, few people will know that such assistance consists primarily of modest training programs, not large amounts of cash passed in envelopes behind closed doors to pliant party leaders. They will often naturally assume the aid is connected to larger political or other interests of the aid-providing country. In many developing countries, especially aid-dependent ones, political life is laced with constant speculation, sometimes unfounded, sometimes not, about which party or which political figures are favored by various powerful foreign countries (or, in aid-dependent countries, by the major donor organizations). People commonly assume that the outside powers will do any number of things to produce the political outcomes they want, including using aid directly or indirectly to influence elections. Party aid fits naturally into this unhelpful world of speculation and accusation.

In Mozambique, for example, there was intense speculation during the 1999 and 2004 elections about whether the donors (who together, contribute approximately half of the country's budget) favored Frelimo or Renamo. Some senior Frelimo politicians were convinced that some donors wanted Renamo to win and were using various tactics, including aid to Renamo, for that end. Some senior Renamo representatives were convinced of the reverse. In this way, party aid, especially when it has an openly partisan nature, can contribute to the syndrome of disempowerment that is so common, and so destructive, in new or struggling democracies. In this syndrome, ordinary citizens come to believe that although they may have gained the right to vote, and participate politically in other ways, it is not worth doing so because the important decisions in the country remain in the hands of powerful, behind-the-scenes actors, especially foreign ones.

Taking Sides, U.S.-Style

Most U.S. party aid is multipartisan. It is offered to all the main parties in a country (either all the parties represented in the national legislature or all the parties above a certain size) on a roughly equal basis. Of course multipartisan programs do still sometimes exclude parties—either because they appear too small to be significant or they are judged (by the aid provider) to be antidemocratic. Multipartisan programs of the U.S. party institutes are usually broadly inclusive and the exclusion of parties on political grounds is limited to fairly obvious cases of antidemocratic parties, such as extreme nationalist parties, not parties that are critical of U.S. policy or the United States generally. For example, in various Muslim countries, such as Indonesia, Morocco, and Yemen, IRI and NDI have included in their party programs Islamic parties that are sometimes sharply or even stridently critical of the U.S. government.

Sometimes, however, U.S. party aid is partisan. Partisanship appears (or has appeared) in two types of cases: one that occurred in the first half of the 1990s and has largely faded away, and another that occurred occasionally in the 1980s and 1990s and has become more common this decade. The first type of case occurred in Central and Eastern Europe after the fall of the Berlin Wall. In most countries of the region, including Albania, Bulgaria, Hungary, Poland, and Romania, one or both of the U.S. party institutes supported new prodemocratic, usually center-right or centrist parties that emerged in the transitions and were engaged in electoral struggles with the left-leaning successor parties of the defunct Communist parties. Although both party institutes engaged in this sort of partisan work in this region, IRI did so more extensively and more pointedly, with NDI usually preferring a multipartisan approach.

IRI's rationale for its partisan approach in postcommunist Europe—which often had a very sharp political edge, with highly focused campaign aid designed to help IRI's partner parties win specific elections—was straightforward. IRI viewed the political life of these transitional countries as a black-and-white struggle between emergent democratic parties and holdover postcommunist or neocommunist forces with an uncertain commitment to democracy. IRI believed that because many of the successor postcommunist parties enjoyed significant advantages over their challengers (due to inherited resources, political experience, and in some cases, a continuing ability to use state levers of influence and control), aid to the other parties was necessary to level the playing field. In short, promoting democracy meant helping the new parties of the center and center-right. In IRI's view, partisan aid did not risk unbalancing nascent multiparty systems in postcommunist countries; rather it was a way to balance them.

The much more partisan nature of U.S. party assistance in the postcommunist world of the 1990s compared with other regions reflected a lowered psychological barrier on the part of the U.S. policy community about political intervention in the postcommunist world. During the last two decades of the Cold War, the U.S. government and various democracy promotion groups had become increasingly involved in supporting prodemocratic movements and groups in Eastern Europe and the Soviet Union. Unlike U.S. Cold War political intervention in Latin America or other parts of the developing world, which often consisted of U.S. support for friendly anticommunist tyrants, the U.S. political pressure aimed at the Soviet Union and Eastern Europe was prodemocratic, including support to Poland's Solidarity, Czechoslovakia's Charter 77, and Soviet dissidents.

While U.S. democracy aid providers in the 1990s were generally (although not always) rather cautious about openly partisan involvement in the developing world, they were much less inhibited in this regard in Central and Eastern Europe. For some U.S. democracy promoters, working to counteract the strength of former communists seemed a natural extension of the earlier cause of fighting communism. Many ordinary citizens of these countries were less wary of U.S. involvement in their political life than were people in most of the developing world, due to the differing legacies of U.S. Cold War interventionism. This extension of the Cold War framework of partisan engagement into the postcommunist Central and Eastern Europe faded as the 1990s unfolded, former Communists became social democrats, and politics normalized in most of the region.

The other type of case where U.S. party aid sometimes takes a partisan line is in situations where an entrenched semiauthoritarian regime is holding elections (to try to legitimate its continued rule) but has a clear record of circumscribing or manipulating electoral processes (through measures such as harassing opposition opponents, blocking opposition access to media, or tampering with the voting process). In some such situations, the U.S. party institutes support the main opposition parties. They may offer campaign and party building training as well as strategic advice and arm-twisting to encourage opposition unity. In a small number of cases they have also provided modest material support for the opposition parties, for purchasing office equipment and supplies, renting offices, and paying for other basic operating costs. Faced as they often are in such contexts with accusations of partisan political interference, IRI and NDI invariably insist that they are not trying to affect the outcome of the elections—to produce an opposition victory—but are merely seeking to level a manifestly unlevel electoral playing field.

Three early cases of such partisan work were the efforts to help the Chilean opposition parties in their "Campaign for the No" against Chilean president Augusto Pinochet in 1987–1988, U.S. support for the political opposition to General Manuel Noriega in the 1989 Panamanian elections, and U.S. support for the Nicaraguan parties competing against the ruling Sandinista Party in Nicaragua's 1990 elections. More recent cases, from the mid-1990s on, include support by one or other or both of the party institutes to opposition parties or groups competing against the following leaders: Cambodian Prime Minister Hun Sen; Haitian Presidents Jean-Bertrand Aristide and René Préval; Croatian President Franjo Tudjman, Serbian President Slobodan Milosevic; Belarusan President Alexander Lukashenko, Azeri President Ilham Aliyev; and Ukrainian President Leonid Kuchma.

In some cases, such as in Haiti in the second half of the 1990s and Cambodia from the mid-1990s to the present, this partisan party aid is something one or both of the party institutes do largely on their own, not as part of a broader U.S.-sponsored set of activities to support groups and persons interested in challenging the regime. In these cases the work is usually low-key and long-term, accepting repeated opposition defeats as part of a hoped-for building process over time. In other cases, this opposition-focused party work is part of a larger set of U.S. (and sometime also European) assistance programs and diplomatic activities and economic measures (such as sanctions) to support a wide array of groups and forces—including not just opposition parties but student protest groups, civic education organizations, human rights groups, independent media, and domestic election monitors—that are working together to challenge an incumbent regime in a specific election. Such wider campaigns embody a multifaceted strategy to increase the chances of a free and fair election, or failing that, to empower the society to protest against a manipulated one, and perhaps cause the ouster of the regime through widespread peaceful popular protest in what has come to be known as an "electoral revolution." These campaigns consist of several interrelated parts: (1) building up the capacity of independent civil society to foster citizen belief in the possibility of political change and broad engagement in the electoral process;

(2) helping opposition parties overcome the obstacles put up by the regime and to make their best showing possible; (3) ensuring a local capacity for domestic election monitoring including for a parallel vote count, to ensure that citizens will be able to learn the true results of the election; and (4) exerting diplomatic pressure on the regime not to manipulate the elections (or at least raising the political costs to the regime of such manipulation).

The U.S. and European effort in Serbia in the late 1990s to support the opposition and exert diplomatic and economic pressure against President Slobodan Milosevic was a leading example of this multifaceted approach.[9] All the elements of the strategy fell into place and Milosevic's efforts to override a negative result were massively rejected by a mobilized citizenry that drove him from power. The United States and some European actors have mounted a similar, but less successful, effort in Belarus for both the 2001 and 2006 presidential elections.[10] Significant Western aid also went to a wide range of civic and political groups fighting for free and fair elections, and political change, in Georgia prior to the 2003 Rose Revolution and Ukraine prior to the 2004 Orange Revolution.[11]

The Question of Legitimacy

Many types of democracy aid face questions about whether they can be reconciled with the norm of political sovereignty. Pointed questions especially arise about the sorts of partisan party aid described previously in which serious, sustained efforts are made to bolster the performance of the political opposition in a national election. What right do outside actors, particularly ones financed by a powerful, wealthy government with myriad economic and strategic interests around the world, have to help some political parties challenge the sitting government? What gives U.S. party institutes the right to carry out activities, such as material assistance to parties and highly directed campaign training for parties, that would almost certainly not be permitted by a foreign actor in their own country?

These are not academic questions or debates. In most of the places where the U.S. party institutes carry out partisan work, controversies occur. The opposition forces that are recipients of such aid view it as perfectly legitimate and, in fact, their due. From their perspective, given that the government is harassing them, restricting their political and civil rights, using state resources for its own benefit, and limiting their access to media, foreign support is more than justified to redress the imbalance. The target government and its supporters in turn view Western support for the opposition (and the government usually lumps together most civil society assistance with party aid, seeing any support for independent groups as oppositional work) as illegitimate interference in their country's political life. Sometimes they put up with it. They may do so because they do not take the opposition very seriously and doubt that external aid to it will make any difference. Or they may judge that the likely cost to their international reputation (many semiauthoritarian regimes labor assiduously to try to gain international credibility as democrats) of chasing out the foreign groups will exceed the political benefits of getting rid of them. Often, however, they do not put up with it, pushing back against it with various formal and informal measures, from restrictive laws on foreign aid to the expulsion of Western aid groups, and the aid providers end up in complex struggles and byzantine arrangements (such as carrying out training in semisecrecy in neighboring countries or slipping cash in across the border in the hands of trusted local activists) to carry out the work they want to do.[12]

These controversies sometimes spill back into the United States and other aid-providing countries as well. As mentioned previously, IRI's work to support opposition parties in Haiti in the early years of this decade, for example, recently provoked controversy in the United States. U.S. efforts to support civic opposition to President Hugo Chávez have also sparked debates not only in Venezuela but also the United States about the appropriate political boundaries of democracy aid. The U.S. role in supporting political and civil groups that contributed to the color revolutions in Georgia and Ukraine prompted some European commentators to decry what they called "made-in-America revolutions."[13]

The landscape of opinion in the United States about such activities divides into several camps. Conservatives and some moderate Democrats defend such work as justified interventionism and ask what is wrong with helping besieged prodemocratic groups challenge strongman regimes that abridge human rights and manipulate elections. Some realist conservatives are more wary about such efforts, as part of their general doubts about the wisdom of the United States expending political and financial capital striving to promote democracy abroad rather than concentrating on "hard" economic and strategic interests. Many on the left in the United States (and Europe) are skeptical about an assertive U.S. role in supporting opposition groups in other countries. They doubt that the United States government is primarily motivated by a concern for democracy, as opposed to getting rid of troublesome governments, and they are bothered by the inconsistency of the larger policy picture—the U.S. (and other) governments standing up for democracy in some places while maintaining cozy relations with useful autocrats in others. They are prone to see pointed prodemocratic assistance as one more chapter in a long history of U.S. efforts to undercut governments that do not go along with U.S. interests. The ideological nature of these debates and divisions in the United States and other Western countries is underlined by the fact that when certain widely unpopular leaders are the target of broad assistance campaigns, such as Pinochet or Milosevic, the debates are much more muted than when a left-of-center government is involved, such as Aristide in Haiti or Chávez in Venezuela.

Pro-oppositional assistance in semiauthoritarian contexts presents a genuinely hard question about legitimacy. The idea of aiding prodemocratic groups struggling against the undemocratic practices of a regime determined to maintain power at any cost is an appealing one. Yet at the same time, for a government-funded organization from one country to carry out extensive, pointed efforts to bolster a set of opposition parties in another country that are challenging the incumbent government clearly crosses a sovereignty line. The U.S. party institutes insist that they are not trying to shape electoral outcomes, but just to level the playing field. Yet it seems clear in most cases of such aid that their staff working on the programs are hoping very much for a victory by the side they are aiding and that the U.S. government has funded the program precisely in the hope of such an outcome. Even if their goal is just to level the playing field, some serious questions can be raised.

First, where is it established that one country has the right to involve itself as a direct political actor in another country's political affairs to try to compel a free and fair election? The U.S. party institutes justify their partisan involvement in semiauthoritarian electoral contexts by arguing that they are just trying to hold those other governments to democratic standards they have committed to (through adherence to regional agreements or charters on democracy, such as those promulgated by the OSCE and the OAS, or just through leaders' declarations of democratic intent). Yet this line of argument, which implies that governments that fall short on democracy forfeit their right to sovereignty, finds little support in international norms or practice. In the human rights domain, for example, many standards are well-established and there is a wide activist body of activity aimed at getting governments to obey the standards. Yet falling short on some human rights standards does not give external actors the right to intervene to compel adherence to them, except in extreme cases, like genocide, that trigger a right of humanitarian intervention.

Second, what would be the threshold for nondemocratic behavior that would result in the forfeiting of sovereignty? Many, or arguably most, governments have some undemocratic features or failings. Dozens of countries are in a gray zone between good compliance with democratic norms and outright authoritarianism. How would a clear line be defined and established to separate those whose behavior disqualifies them from international legal protection against well-financed external actors bent on influencing their political life and those that still enjoy such protection?

Third, if there were to be such a threshold, who should have the right to make the decisions about it? Stated differently, how could such decisions be made by governments or government-funded organizations without other interests or motivations other than a principled concern for democracy coming into play? The U.S. party institutes and other U.S. democracy promotion groups that carry out these pro-oppositional campaigns insist, and sincerely believe, that they are primarily or even exclusively motivated by the concern for democracy. The decisions they make about whether a particular leader is so undemocratic as to justify partisan support of the opposition to him—whether it is President Jean-Bertrand Aristide in the 1990s, Venezuelan President Hugo Chávez now, or an Iranian president in the future—are subjective decisions that will reflect their own ideological outlook and not necessarily command agreement from others on the international stage. Moreover, their main funder, the U.S. government, clearly decides in which countries it will support major pro-oppositional campaigns not simply on the basis of the nondemocratic character of the government but also its antagonism to U.S. economic and security interests. If democracy were the principal concern, why would the U.S. government be making available substantial funds for explicitly pro-oppositional work in Belarus and Iran, but not Kazakhstan and Tunisia?

This concern about "who decides?" is alleviated somewhat when more than just U.S. organizations are involved in a particular pro-oppositional campaign. One of the strengths of the Western support for the Serbian opposition in the late 1990s was that a wide range of actors, U.S. and European, public and private, were involved. When such campaigns also include multilateral organizations, such as the OSCE, and rely on their judgments about the validity of the elections in question, the case for such campaigns is further strengthened.

Nevertheless, even multilateral pro-oppositional campaigns still ignite controversies both in the target countries and many other places as well given the continued concerns many developing and postcommunist countries have about foreign interventionism. Western democracy groups will continue asserting a right to do so on the basis of prodemocratic principle and resistant semiauthoritarian governments will claim a right to block such efforts on the basis of sovereignty. Each side will assert that the other's claims to principle are just poorly disguised political arguments cloaking other, less savory interests. Given the current aggravated state of international perceptions about democracy promotion—due to the association of the term with the Iraq War and with a U.S. war on terror that has provoked distrust in many quarters—it is unlikely that any broader evolution of international norms on democracy promotion will occur that might create ground for wider agreement on the sensitive issue of partisan political aid.

CHAPTER SEVEN

The Question of Effects

In studying and observing democracy promotion policies and programs over the years, I have often noticed that expectations or beliefs about the effects of such efforts fall into two quite divergent modes. On the one side, many people within the democracy promotion community believe that democracy-building activities can have significant, even transformative or catalytic effects if given sufficient financial and diplomatic support. Optimistic views of the effects of democracy building are especially common among U.S. democracy promoters.

On the other side, many people involved in international affairs but outside the democracy promotion community have skeptical views. They operate from a blanket assumption that "democracy cannot be exported" and assume that external efforts to influence the political evolution of other societies are likely to be of little significance.

In fact, the truth about the effects of democracy promotion generally, and political party assistance in particular, usually lies in between these two outlooks. The vast majority of democracy promotion efforts do not produce transformative or catalytic effects on the political life of other societies. That is to say they are not primary agents of change that shift the direction of national politics. Yet at the same time, some democracy promotion initiatives facilitate positive changes that are already occurring or help increase the chances of new prodemocratic developments where none have yet flourished. In probably several dozen countries in the world in the past twenty years where Western and multilateral organizations have concentrated sizeable resources and energy on democracy promotion, one could not adequately explain the political development of the country without reference to these activities, even if they were not, in and of themselves, decisive or determinative.

The question of the effects of party aid falls into this framework. Providers of party aid talk about the goals of their efforts in broad terms. They seek to help parties overcome what the aid providers regard as fundamental deficiencies, from the lack of internal democracy to the absence of clear ideologies and platforms. Although party aid providers are rarely specific about exactly when these goals will be achieved or to what degree they will be achieved, the promise of transformative effects is implicit. Like many other practitioners of democracy aid, representatives of party foundations and institutes evince a strong optimism about their work, rooted in an instinctive faith that they know what is good for parties in other countries and how to help bring those changes about.

Outside of party foundations and party institutes, widespread skepticism prevails. Aid agency development specialists, diplomats, political observers, and in fact most people in the broader foreign policy community are dubious about the likely value and effects of party aid. Many such people hold parties in new or struggling democracies in very low regard and are skeptical about trying to help what they view as deeply corrupt, self-serving, and ineffective organizations. In the case of U.S.-sponsored party assistance, serious skepticism about the value of such work sometimes exists even within the U.S. embassy of a country (including the USAID mission) where such aid is being carried out and where the U.S. government is funding it.

These sharply discordant estimations of the effects and value of party aid have coexisted for years. There has been no resolution of the gap between them because there has been little solid information available about what party aid is actually accomplishing. As discussed in chapter 5, party aid programs are rarely subjected to independent evaluations and party aid organizations have engaged in notably few efforts to examine the results of their own efforts and generate a written base of knowledge about the likely effects of party aid in different circumstances.

In this chapter I analyze the effects of party aid. In my view, the effects of party aid generally correspond to the effects of most other types of democracy assistance. It rarely has transformative impact, despite the hopes and sometimes beliefs of its providers. This is true both because of the difficulty of the task and the inadequacies of much of the assistance. Neither, however, is it a futile enterprise. It sometimes has modest but real positive effects. When aid providers take seriously the challenge of improving their work, as some are doing, it can make a contribution to party development, both regarding the capacity of parties to campaign and their overall organizational strength.

Absence of Transformative Impact

A party aid program directed at one party can be said to have a transformative impact if it helps the recipient party substantially ameliorate the central organizational or functional characteristics that the aid providers seek to address. In other words, aid is transformative if it helps a leader-centric, structurally debilitated, ideologically incoherent, weakly rooted party establish genuine internal party democracy, build a strong organizational structure, embrace and embody a clear ideologically rooted platform, and develop an extensive social base. If a party aid program is directed at all of the main parties in a country, it would be transformative if it produces such substantial effects in at least several of the most important parties. If aid providers seek to change how the parties in a country interrelate with each other, their work would be transformative if it were able to change a pattern of confrontational, zero-sum party relations into a situation in which the parties are able to communicate regularly and work together productively on issues of national importance.

Very broadly speaking, there is an absence of evidence of transformative effects of party aid. This is clear from the sobering fact that almost everywhere party aid providers are working in the developing and postcommunist worlds, and often have been working for many years, the political parties today embody most or all of the shortcomings that party aid seeks to overcome. To put it simply, if party aid were having transformative effects, parties would not be in such a profoundly troubled state all over the world. This conclusion comes quickly enough to anyone attending for example one of the various workshops or conferences in Latin America in recent years on "the crisis of Latin American political parties." Listening to the participants bewail the profoundly troubled state of parties in that region one cannot help thinking about the fact that Western party aid has been active in the region for decades, and wonder about the effects of that assistance.

This does not mean that party assistance never has positive effects. As discussed later in this chapter, it sometimes does and many parties have benefited at least somewhat from it. It is, however, very difficult to come up with many or even any cases where it appears to have had major or decisive effects. When one asks representatives of party aid providers where they believe their work is making a major difference in the state of political parties, the response is usually a cautious silence followed by a few examples of promising but still small signs of progress in a few countries. When the question is broadened to include cases from the past, three cases are often mentioned: South Africa and the end of apartheid, Chile and the termination of Pinochet's rule, and Serbia and the ouster of Milosevic. Arguably, external aid (by a mix of European and U.S. actors) played an important role in these three transitions, although it was a helping hand to valiant, skillful domestic actors, not the principal source of change. As examples of party aid effectiveness, however, these cases are only of limited applicability.

Party aid was only one small part of a much larger, wider package of aid that contributed to the process of change in these countries, with civil society aid, economic sanctions, and diplomatic pressure critical to the overall picture. Also, the party aid that went to these countries included direct financial assistance to the parties in question, which is exceptional compared with most party aid. The success in each was more about helping a wide range of domestic forces bring about a change of regime than it was about transforming the parties per se. In the case of the Serbian parties for example, the aid bolstered their effort to oust Milosevic but did little to transform them into effective, well-run, internally democratic parties over the long term.

Underlining this basic conclusion about party aid's scarcity of transformative effects is the fact that even some of its largest, most concentrated undertakings have failed to produce many lasting positive results. For example as mentioned in chapter 4, the Adenauer and Ebert Stiftungs made major efforts in the 1970s and 1980s to build up center-right and center-left parties in Latin America. The Adenauer Stiftung invested substantial resources (including direct financial transfers to parties) in trying to build a network of thriving Christian Democratic parties in the region. The flagship party in that effort, Venezuela's Christian Democratic party, COPEI, collapsed from the weight of its own accumulated strategic and tactical blunders in the early 1990s. Other Christian Democratic parties, such as in El Salvador and Guatemala, also nosedived in that period. Today, with the lone exception of the Chilean Christian Democratic Party, Christian Democracy is largely finished as a political movement in Latin America.

Similarly, the Ebert Stiftung befriended numerous left-leaning Latin American parties in those years, such as Alan García's Alianza Popular Revolucionaria Americana (APRA) in Peru, the Peronist Party in Argentina, and Democratic Action in Venezuela, in the hope of helping them evolve into democratic, well-run parties. The fortunes of these parties have varied over time, but to put it mildly, none has evolved into an internally democratic, law-based, well-managed organization. One Ebert Stiftung representative I interviewed who worked in Latin America in the 1980s now shakes his head at the "grand, romantic illusions" that animated Ebert's Latin American work of that period and regrets the too-cozy embrace that Ebert gave to parties of flawed democratic character.[1]

Another, more recent example of the limited impact of major concentrations of party aid is that of European and U.S. support for center-right parties in Central and Eastern Europe in the 1990s. Such assistance represents the largest concentration of party aid of the post–Cold War period, with many Western party foundations and institutes taking part, driven by a strong sense of mission about helping cement in place center-right parties capable of leading the way in the historic transition away from Communism. Yet fifteen years later, center-right parties are at best a very mixed bag in the region. In Poland, which some Western democracy promoters think of as a leading example of successful democracy aid overall, center-right parties have fragmented and turned illiberal, despite significant Western party aid on their behalf. In Hungary the center-right party that attracted most of the early attention of the Western aid providers (the Hungarian Democratic Forum) has shrunk to a minor party and the center-right party that now dominates that side of the political spectrum, Fidesz, has worrisome nationalistic tendencies. In the Czech Republic the main center-right party has endured but is hardly a model of internal democracy. In Romania the main recipient of party aid among centrist and center-right parties, the National Peasant Party, collapsed after the 2000 national elections. In Bulgaria, the center-right coalition group (the United Democratic Forces) that attracted considerable outside help across the 1990s has fragmented and done poorly in the past two national elections.

The difficult experience Western party aid providers have had supporting center-right parties in Central and Eastern Europe is one part of an important larger story: Western party aid had very limited effects generally in this region, the region toward which more party aid was directed (in the 1990s) than any other region and in which the underlying structural conditions for party development were more favorable than anywhere else party aid providers operated. Western aid was certainly able to help Central and Eastern Europeans improve their campaign skills and make some organizational reforms. As Attila Ágh has argued, at most these parties may have achieved "external Europeanization," an elite-based process of establishing contacts with international party organizations and Western parties and aligning programs, values, and public discourse with them. However, they have only just started the process of "internal Europeanization," transforming their membership, organization, and constituencies in a mass-based way.[2]

A Return to the Case Study Countries

A look at the effects of party aid in the six case study countries reinforces this general conclusion about the absence of transformative effects, and, as discussed later in this chapter, also highlights the presence of some modest positive effects. The case studies also shed light on the different reasons party aid is generally not transformative.

Romania

Despite relatively substantial European and American assistance to most of the main Romanian political parties since 1989, especially on the center and center-right of the political spectrum, the Romanian party scene today is highly troubled. To start with, the principal target or recipient of Western party aid to Romania—the National Peasant Party—ended up as the most visible failure on the post–Cold War Romanian political stage. Across the 1990s, it failed to renovate its aging top leadership circle or to strengthen significantly its basic internal organization. After its defeat in the 2000 national elections, it fell apart and has now disappeared altogether.

The main parties competing for power today are an uneven collection of organizations, each exhibiting some or most of the problematic characteristics making up the standard lament about parties. There are two elite-oriented, leader-centric, internally weak parties (center-right and centrist) leading a governing coalition; a profoundly corrupt former governing party of the center-left, now in a state of deep leadership crisis and internal division; an extreme nationalist party that is the personalistic vehicle of a demagogic populist; and an ethnic Hungarian party that enjoys an almost guaranteed share of the vote but nonetheless faces serious internal tensions and leadership stagnation. The near constant emphasis over fifteen years by Western party aid providers on competent party management, organizational rationalization and management decentralization, well-defined ideological platforms, anti-corruption, and other elements of party development is little reflected in the actual state of Romanian parties. Thanks in some significant part to the positive pull of European integration, Romania is moving ahead economically, and to some extent politically, but political parties are clearly at the trailing edge of this movement.

Given the centrality of the National Peasant Party in Western party aid to Romania of the past fifteen years, it is interesting to ask why this extensive aid was not able to help the party thrive, or at least avoid extinction. There is no single explanation. Representatives of European and U.S. aid groups that assisted the party tell one story. In their view, the post-1989 Peasant Party was a fundamentally troubled organization from the start. It was an awkward ghost from the past, saddled with stubborn, old leaders who were unable to adapt to the new political context, bereft of any real policy ideas and governance capabilities, and lacking any real ties to a broad constituency.

These representatives convey a tale of sustained frustration about trying to help the Peasant Party. In their view (a view shared by mainstream Romanian political analysts) the party leadership was uninterested in building a strong national party organization. Party leaders were convinced that the party had a moral right to voter support (derived from their historical anticommunist stance) and did not actually have to work for it. The leadership persistently stifled the rising next generation of party leaders, blocking the ideas for party renewal that these younger activists had and creating debilitating internal rifts. The party leadership jealously held onto all important decision-making powers and prevented local branches from gaining a useful amount of autonomy. These and other problems dogged the party while it was in opposition. Then once the party made it into power in 1997 (thanks to voter fatigue with Ion Iliescu's party) they contributed to the party's disastrous turn in power, one marked by corruption, infighting, and fecklessness.

From within the middle ranks of the Peasant Party—the persons who most actively took part in the Western-sponsored training programs—explanations for the weak effects of external assistance are different. These former party activists acknowledge the serious shortcomings of the party leadership. Some of them also believe that the Western aid was not up to the task. To start with, like recipients of party assistance in many countries, they were disappointed that U.S. and European party groups did not offer direct financial support, which is what many Peasant Party activists thought was the party's greatest need. Regarding what aid they did receive, some are quite critical. They found the Europeans and those from the United States who came offering to help them were often condescending, poorly informed about Romanian realities, given to repeating the same trainings over and over again, and insistent on following their own agendas rather than tailoring their work to what people within the party felt was most needed. These shortcomings, they say, led to weak, often unproductive partnerships between the party and the outside groups trying to help it.

Peasant Party activists certainly acknowledge that the party had serious internal shortcomings but they argue that its poor performance overall was due in significant part to external factors. The Romanian electorate, they argued, was profoundly alienated from parties and politics generally throughout the 1990s, due to the devastating legacy of the Ceauşescu years. The country's halting progress on economic reform post-1989 stifled the emergence of a dynamic new class of independent businessmen, thereby undercutting a critical source of support for a center-right party. The party's main rival, the successor party to the Communist party, enjoyed weighty structural advantages, above all inherited material resources and a generation of talented, well-trained technocrats and party cadres. All these factors were real, but it must be noted that other parties challenged Iliescu's party in the same years and did at least somewhat better than the Peasant Party in building party organizations and a stable voter base. The Peasant Party's internal pathologies, above all its entrenched, dysfunctional leadership, were clearly a dominant factor in its failure, and one that Western party aid was unable to do much about.

Russia

Western party aid in Russia from the early 1990s to the early years of this decade produced no major positive effects. The two parties that were the primary recipients of Western attention, Yabloko and SPS (and its forerunners), failed in these years to increase their combined vote share beyond 15 percent. After falling short of the 5 percent parliamentary threshold in the 2003 parliamentary elections they slid even further to the margins of Russian political life and today are struggling to avoid irrelevance. Their lack of development as parties has been reflected not only in their poor vote-getting but in the frustrating persistence of the basic problems that have afflicted these two parties since their formation, above all their "large head, small body" nature and their associated top-down managerial style and lack of commitment and follow-through in developing a truly national organization.

Why was ten years of extensive, focused external aid to these parties unable to help them overcome the core challenges of party development? The answer echoes the one for Romania. As representatives of the Western party aid organizations that have worked in Russia are quick to point out, Yabloko and SPS proved resistant to external pushes for reform. From their inception they were highly personalistic organizations led by charismatic, ambitious men, primarily interested in their own political fortunes rather than in broader party building (in the perception of Western party aid representatives). At times these leaders got caught up with their own personal relationships to the

Kremlin, showing only patchy interest in their party's challenges. It some-times seemed that as long as their parties made it into Parliament they were satisfied, as this ensured them and their closest associates the benefits of parliamentary membership, above all a voice in national politics and parliamentary immunity.

The U.S. and German party organizations that worked extensively with Yabloko and SPS (and its predecessors) encountered much frustration. Yabloko and SPS often did not act on the endless stream of advice and cajoling coming from the aid groups about the need to devote more time and attention to building local party branches, the importance of decentralizing party management, the value of opposition unity, and so forth. As one representative of a German party foundation put it, his organization found Yabloko "immune to counsel."[3] The Western party aid providers found some responsive people within the parties, especially at the provincial level. These people were typically unable to achieve broader changes in the party due to disinterest or resistance from the party's leadership.

As in Romania, there exists a parallel narrative of frustration about party aid in Russia on the side of the recipients. In interviews, representatives of Yabloko and SPS articulate a series of criticisms about the Western aid directed at their parties:

- The Western party aid groups focused too much of the training on campaign methods rather than on broader issues of party development.
- The training seminars were both too simple and highly repetitive, which was numbing and demoralizing for the participants.
- The training did not often enough incorporate persons in the senior leadership circles of the parties, even though it was the lack of knowledge on the part of those people that especially impeded party reform.
- The reputational damage to the parties in the Russian electorate of being tagged as recipients of Western support was significant and outweighed the value of the assistance.

Although resistance to reform within the parties and shortcomings in the party aid undoubtedly contributed to the weak effects of that aid, the broader unfavorable conditions in Russia for party development were also a factor. Since 1991, the development of political parties in Russia has been hampered by a powerful set of interrelated factors. Russia has a superpresidential system in which the main center of power (the president and the apparat around him) is separate from party politics. By law the president cannot belong to a political party. The main legislative organ is quite weak. The citizenry is deeply antipolitical and profoundly distrustful of party politics. A centralized system of control over the country's governors stifles party development at the local level. This profoundly unfavorable context for party development has been made even more problematic by President Putin's authoritarian nature. He has further undercut the country's already weak pluralism through his low tolerance for opposition and systematic efforts to undercut any and all independent political actors. Again, as with Romania, these structural factors overwhelmed and undermined the Western party aid.

Guatemala

Despite quite diverse, active Western assistance programs aimed at Guatemalan political parties since approximately the late 1990s, the overall state of parties in the country remains deeply problematic. Countless seminars and workshops have been convened by outside aid providers on all the main elements of party building, but parties continue to be highly personalistic entities constantly merging or splitting off from one another, lacking stable or well-defined constituencies, standing for little other than the personal ambitions of their leaders, and commanding scant respect from the public. Guatemala has for more than five years received more external party aid per capita than other country in Latin America (and the vast majority of countries in the rest of the world). Yet talk of a crisis of political parties remains a common theme of national political life and there is little sense that the parties are evolving in a positive direction.

Most party aid providers working in Guatemala believe that it is too early to reach any definitive conclusions about the effects of their work. When pressed, however, they acknowledge that their efforts to encourage internal party reforms have often been frustrated by the relentless personalism and instability of Guatemalan parties. In Guatemala's presidential, highly centralized political system, party life is dominated by ambitious political figures maneuvering for a run at the presidency and treating the parties as little more than potential vehicles for that purpose. The one-term rule of the presidency (presidents serve for one four-year term and cannot be reelected) increases the tendency of presidential candidates to think of parties in a very short-term, single-use way as electoral vehicles. As a result, although the various party aid initiatives find and assist people in the middle levels of the parties who are sincerely interested in long-term party building, it is usually hard for those persons to have significant effects on the way parties are run at the top.

The experience of the 2003 presidential election underscored the entrenched personalism of Guatemalan politics. Before that election, the main center-right party, the National Advancement Party (PAN), experienced a split. Oscar Berger, who had won the party's nomination, broke away from the party. Needing a party as his formal electoral mechanism, he hastily associated himself with a loose alliance of three small parties and became their candidate. Despite the relative inconsequentiality of these parties, he won the presidency, thanks to his personal popularity (he had earlier been a popular mayor of the capital city) and the fact that he had prised away from PAN financial support coming from significant parts of the main business elite. His victory made clear how little role parties actually play in the main arena of competition in Guatemalan politics, twenty years after the return to civilian rule and regular elections.

The two most concentrated efforts by Western party aid organizations to help specific Guatemalan parties have not been able to overcome chronic internal weaknesses and lack of uptake within the parties. Various conservative Western party aid groups for years saw in PAN the potential to become a broad-based, well-rooted, competent center-right party and furnished aid to help support PAN's internal development. A series of destructive leadership battles in the party starting in 1999 and continuing through the departure of Berger in 2003, however, undermined any progress achieved through training and other technical assistance to the party ranks.

The URNG, the party of the former leftist guerilla movement, also received special attention by some external aid providers, at least in the years immediately following the signing of the peace accords and the entry of the URNG into Guatemalan party life. Many European center-left party foundations and NGOs were eager to help build a successful center-left or left-leaning political party capable of representing Guatemala's many poor and marginalized citizens. Some of them provided assistance to help the URNG make the transition from armed movement to political party. This effort, however, proved largely futile. The URNG has failed to make any real progress as a party, polling just 4.2 percent in the 2003 congressional elections. Representatives of European party foundations that have worked with the URNG complain that the party leadership was stuck in unrealistic, unproductive modes of thinking about politics, and unwilling to take seriously the task of party building.

The weak apparent impact so far of Western aid on Guatemala's political parties is due not just to the persistent personalism of those parties and a one-term presidential system that militates against party development. The chronic weakness of the country's parties also reflects underlying structural factors. The transition to civilian rule in the mid-1980s and the subsequent end of the civil war have allowed a modicum of democracy to emerge. The main centers of power in the country, the small, very wealthy business elite rooted in the coffee industry and the largely unrepentant, unreconstructed military and intelligence services, remain unbounded by or unincorporated into the formal political system. They stay in the shadows of political life, exercising influence behind the scenes on matters of central concern to them through a variety of methods, licit and illicit. As a result, the political party arena has something of the quality of a vacuous game, noisy and emotional, but often only mildly relevant to the real power plays going on.

Mozambique

The United Nations, various European governments (especially the Italian government), and European party foundations working alongside or through the UN played a significant role in helping Mozambique end its civil war in the early 1990s and make a transition to democracy. Helping the two opposing political forces, Frelimo and Renamo, make the transition to being political parties and competing in a multiparty system was a crucial part of this effort. The very substantial international financial transfers to the Mozambican parties, especially to Renamo, were instrumental to this task, and the intensive advice, arm-twisting, and diplomatic engagement also helped.

The subsequent Western effort, which started in the late 1990s, to go from that initial phase of construction of the multiparty system to stimulating reforms in the overall shape and functioning of the parties, has been less successful. External aid has helped Frelimo bolster its own internal training efforts and increase the sophistication of its campaigns but it has not steered Frelimo away from the typical maladies of dominant parties, such as deep involvement in state corruption, the increasing use of co-optative methods to undercut independent actors, and a dangerous blurring of the line between party and state. Nor has externally sponsored party assistance been able to change Renamo's long-standing lack of internal democracy and continued leader-centric ways.

It is hardly surprising that the Western party programs in Mozambique of the past ten years have not had any decisive or catalytic effects on the organization or functioning of Frelimo. Originally forged in armed struggle for national liberation, and enjoying power for thirty years, Frelimo is a strongly institutionalized party with a clear sense of identity and a firmly established internal organizational culture. Frelimo's well-developed organizational capacities have allowed it to make good use of the external assistance. Frelimo has its own internal training program, for example, and has been able to fit the offers of external training support into that program, ensuring that the training matches Frelimo's own agenda and that a system existed helping those who received training to integrate it into the work within the party. Frelimo's stable place at the center of Mozambican politics and developed internal structures ensured that some modest externally sponsored training, strategic advice, and other support were unlikely to move it in any new directions, particularly to avoid the negative temptations inherent in its dominant party position.

Never having been in power and struggling as a semipermanent opposition party, Renamo is less organizationally developed than Frelimo, and presumably, less politically self-satisfied. Thus at least to some Western party aid organizations, Renamo appeared potentially more open to change than Frelimo. Yet Western training and advice has run again and again into the wall of Renamo's stubbornly leader-centric, command-style, loyalty-based organizational mode, a legacy of its origins and long period of life as an armed resistance movement. In its work with Renamo, for example, NDI tried hard and creatively to break through the blockage at the top on reform. Senior NDI representatives labored to push Afonso Dhlakama, Renamo's leader, on the need for internal reforms, to set up meetings with outside political figures who would add their weight to the same cause, and to facilitate (with the help of other Western party aid groups) Renamo's entry into Christian Democrat International, with the idea that exposure to the international party circuit would increase the leader's incentives for party modernization. Some encouraging signs of change occurred, including the holding of a party congress in 2001 (by a party not in the habit of holding such events), the formation of a political commission in the party to give advice to the leader, and the creation of a women's league for the party. The core power structure and top-down patterns of party governance did not significantly change—Dhlakama has maintained his tight grip.

Morocco

The first concentrated spurt of Western party aid in Morocco, a series of training events sponsored by IRI in the late 1990s, bounced off with little effect, as acknowledged both by persons who worked on those programs and persons who participated in them. The main parties were simply not interested in or open to the sorts of organizational reforms that the aid providers were suggesting. They were stuck in the debilitating halfway house of partial autonomy and partial dependency vis-à-vis the monarchy.

In the first half of this decade, party aid started up again and expanded in a more sustained way. As in Indonesia, the assistance is still fairly new and modest in scale relative to the size of the country and so expectations of decisive efforts would be unrealistic. Also as in Indonesia, the main Moroccan parties have existed for several decades and are stuck in deeply entrenched patterns of dysfunctionality, especially in their high degree of personalism, their ideological exhaustion, and lack of connection to the citizenry. The leadership of most of the main parties is dominated by a set of aging politicians who enjoyed their heyday in the 1960s and 1970s and are widely perceived as having become over the years a self-referential circle of political elites immersed in their own intrigues and out-of-touch with the day-to-day realities of the country.

Yet there is also now some sense of possible change in the political party scene, although less strongly so than in Indonesia. There is not a distinctly new postauthoritarian context or a process of significant, prodemocratic constitutional and electoral reforms, as in Indonesia. A gradual expansion of political space has occurred from the late 1990s to the present (although constrained in part by the monarchy's reactions to the 2003 Casablanca bombings) and the king has been calling for the parties to play a greater role in political life. In this evolutionary context, Western party aid is playing a very minor, but positive role. So far it appears that most of the main parties are unable or unwilling to move forward and carry out any significant organizational reforms. A few are trying to respond positively and the party programs are useful to them as they do.

The Socialist Party for example, one of Morocco's classic "dinosaur" parties, is at least struggling with the reform imperative. A middle generation of party activists in their 40s and 50s is pushing on senior figures for a whole series of organizational reforms, from opening up the process of becoming a party member to revitalizing the party's socialist ideology. The Western-sponsored training workshops, seminars, and informal consultations are useful to those activists, both in providing them with relevant ideas and information, and giving them moral support in their struggle. Nevertheless, such aid is at most a minor helping hand. It is not yet clear whether the Socialist Party or any of the other traditional Moroccan parties will be able to overcome their accumulated inertia and problems and genuinely renovate themselves.

The rise of a strong, capable Islamist party, the Justice and Development Party, underlines the limits of party aid as a force for deep-reaching party reform. The PJD is the one party in Morocco that is doing many of the things that Western party aid providers have been pushing parties to do, such as building a well-articulated national party organization, tying its overall political message to specific bread-and-butter issues that ordinary citizens can relate to, and taking seriously its role in Parliament both to question proposed legislation and suggest alternatives. Party aid representatives, and many other political observers in Morocco, comment frequently that the PJD is the only party in the country that seems to know how to act as a party. Yet although some PJD activists have participated in Western-sponsored training events, it is evident that the PJD's strengths as a party come from its own internal initiative and discipline. More strongly stated, the one party that has the greatest ambivalence about taking part in Western aid activities is the one party that actually embodies many of the characteristics that Western aid providers are trying to promote.

Indonesia

Indonesia's political parties have been in a state of change since the return to democracy there in the late 1990s. They are adapting to the open political space and regular, genuine elections that have marked the post-Suharto period, both by learning rapidly about campaign methods and building up their party organizations. The introduction in the past several years of direct presidential elections and direct elections for provincial legislatures has also encouraged certain changes in the parties—including a greater emphasis on candidate-centric campaigning and altered power relations within the parties between individual candidates and the party leadership.

Western assistance for Indonesian parties has facilitated this process of change. The many training workshops have helped local level party activists (at whom most of the training has been directed) learn the nuts and bolts of electoral campaigning and party strengthening. More intensive training of some mid-level party cadres has encouraged them at least to try introducing some organizational reforms in their parties. The aid has not yet demonstrated a potential to help produce deeper changes in the parties, ones that would get at their core shortcomings. Despite their new campaign methods and expanded organizations, Indonesia's main political parties remain almost archetypal embodiments of the standard lament about parties—they are intensely leader-centric organizations dominated by a small circle of elite politicians who hold onto their positions atop parties seemingly indefinitely, are immersed in patronage politics, and who are far more devoted to political intrigues in the capital than the prosaic work of trying to listen to and represent a base of constituents. Indonesia's constitutional and electoral laws have been through an impressive series of prodemocratic reforms since the late 1990s but the political parties have not changed their fundamental problematic characteristics.

The only mild effects of the Western party aid to date are not surprising. The aid is new and modest in scale compared with Indonesia's huge population and territory. Moreover, Indonesia's main parties are highly resistant to basic organizational changes. Their personalistic nature is a core feature of Indonesian party life dating back to the formative period of party development in the mid-twentieth century. Their involvement in patronage is deep and fundamental to how they operate.

None of these characteristics is liable to change anytime soon, and certainly not because of scattered advice and training offered by some visitors from very distant countries. Unlike in many developing or postcommunist countries, several of the main parties in Indonesia are well-rooted in fairly clearly identifiable constituencies, reflecting their origins as socioreligious or nationalist movements. This attribute is good from the point of view of party stability—it is striking for example how similar the party line up was in the early years of this decade to that which existed in the mid-1950s when the country first held multiparty elections. It renders even more difficult the already hard task of trying to stimulate basic changes in their parties. U.S. party aid providers, which are the most active Western party aid groups working in the country, have recognized the high level of resistance to change at the top of the main parties. Accordingly, they have focused on work at the local level or among the younger generation of party cadres within the central party structures. Although such an approach makes sense, it also makes clear that the effects of such work will only be very gradual and incremental, at best.

Explaining Limited Effects

The six case studies not only bolster the basic conclusion that external party aid very rarely, if ever, has transformative effects, they help clarify the main reasons why this is true. First, they underline the fact that parties are hard organizations to help, above all because party leaders often resist reforms, but for other reasons as well. Second, they demonstrate that party aid is often limited in effect because party development is greatly determined by various broader or deeper structural conditions, upon which the party aid has little effect. Third, as the feedback from persons on the receiving end of party aid programs indicates, shortcomings in the aid itself also sometimes limit its impact. Let us consider each of these reasons in greater detail.

Resistance from the Top

As aid providers in all areas of political and economic assistance constantly discover, attempting to use externally sponsored technical assistance to change institutions in other societies is inevitably complex and difficult. Governmental and nongovernmental institutions alike, be they judiciaries, parliaments, local governments, electoral commissions, central banks, or media organizations, live in their own universe of interests, incentives, pressures, traditions, and norms, all of which shape them. Seeking to change these factors, or the way the institutions respond to these factors, is an uncertain and often tenuous endeavor. Political parties are no exception. In fact it appears that various common features of parties make them especially challenging institutions to try to assist.

To start with, most political party leaders in new or struggling democracies—who command so much authority and control over their parties' institutional direction—often resist the reforms that outside aid providers advocate. Without overstating the case, it can be said that laments about top-down resistance to change are the most common complaint that party aid providers express about their work. It would be easy, and not entirely incorrect, to attribute such resistance to a habitual stubbornness on the part of party leaders. A certain kind of personality type usually ends up at the top of parties, a type not generally characterized by humility, flexibility, or a willingness to listen to and incorporate the ideas of others. Leaders of parties in these countries are masters of asserting their own power and jealously guarding it. As such, they are not natural counterparts for external aid providers looking to inject their own ideas or otherwise guide the parties in new directions.

The frequent resistance by party leaders to reforms pushed from the outside is not primarily about bullheadedness on their part. It arises rather from the fact that many of the organizational reforms that Western party foundations or institutes advocate threaten the party leaders' hold on power. Take for example internal democratization, probably the most common, and in a sense the central organizational reform that Western party aid providers push for. What sounds to Western ears as a sensible and necessary step to advance democracy appears to most party leaders as a potentially fundamental threat to their own place atop the party. Even if internal democracy is pursued in more limited ways, such as creating a democratically elected executive committee in the party or opening up candidate selection to internal elections, party leaders will likely still feel threatened. Such measures may weaken the leader's ability to control internal developments in the party, to reward his or her closest associates and cronies, and to limit his or her ability to neutralize the aspirations of rivals within the party.

The recent example of PAN in Guatemala represents the sort of scenario that party leaders fear. At least partly in response to the urgings of Western aid providers, PAN's leadership decided in 2001 to hold a party congress, including an internal leadership election, which was not the usual practice in the party. This process ended up unleashing strong tensions and divisions among top figures in the party, resulting in the departure of Oscar Berger from the party, the loss of the 2003 presidential election, and a significant weakening of the party.

Although the clash between internal democratization and the personal interests of party leaders is especially marked, almost all of the items on the typical organizational reform agenda of party aid providers appear to most party leaders as potentially detrimental to their hold on power. Strengthening local party branches and decentralizing party management may weaken the leader's levers of control. Incorporating women more fully into the party may bolster the positions of people not loyal to the existing leadership. Rationalizing the management of party finances and diversifying sources of financial support will take away important cards from the party leader's hand. Even developing a well-established technocratic party platform may seem contrary to a party leader's interests. In Kosovo, for example, a party leader told me that he was willing formally to go along with an NDI-sponsored effort to help his party develop a conventional party platform. In his view, however, he himself, as the party founder, was the party platform, a platform based on Kosovar national unity and self-determination. A platform with policy positions on everyday issues like tax policy or heath policy would, in his thinking, only be divisive and limit the party's appeal. Thus, he said, he would allow the externally sponsored consultation on platform-writing to take place, but he did not plan to give it any real support.[4]

The frequent resistance that party leaders show in the face of reform ideas coming from the outside is not just the result of habitual stubbornness or concern about loss of power. In some cases, party leaders have a very different vision than do Western party foundations about what their party is or aims to be. As discussed in chapter 4, aid providers operate from a standard conception of what a party should be. Many party leaders in new or struggling democracies have their own conceptions, some of which are quite different. Obviously, for example, many party leaders view their parties as vehicles for the pursuit of their own personal political ambitions, especially in presidential systems where the concentration of power in the office of the presidency focuses much political competition on a single office. In such cases, party leaders are often not interested in building a long-term party constituency base or learning how to represent citizens' interests. They may not care much about how the party does in legislative elections. Their overriding concern is winning the next presidential race, by whatever means possible. Thus, many of the organizational messages that party aid providers deliver fall on deaf ears.

If parties are operating in a parliamentary rather than a presidential system, their leaders may still maintain a conception of party function at odds with that of party aid groups. For example, they may view the party first and foremost as an instrument for getting themselves and their close followers into parliament in order to enjoy the perquisites of parliamentary membership. Beyond that goal they may not be very concerned with whether the party manages to increase its vote and thus not very motivated to work on strengthening the party's constituency among its existent base.

More broadly, the term "party" covers many types of organizations in developing or postcommunist countries, some that actually conform to the conventional meaning of that term and some that do not. Those that do not might be more accurately described by other terms, such as lobby tools for powerful business interests, ethnic associations, administrative vehicles for an incumbent power apparatus, nationalist movements, defeated (or victorious) guerrilla organizations, or religious movements. If aid providers simply assume that organizations formally labeled as parties necessarily share most of the organizational aspirations and political assumptions of idealized Western parties they will likely end up lamenting their lack of interest in or resistance to reform. Yet what they are encountering is not resistance to reform per se so much as a different conception (healthy or unhealthy as it may be for democracy's sake) of the organization's nature and purpose.

Each of these reasons why party leaders often block the reforms urged on them—intrinsic stubbornness, fear of loss of power within the party, and a different conception of party interests—can be quite strong on its own, enough to derail most aid efforts. Moreover, these factors often go together, presenting party aid groups with a truly daunting challenge. To cite just one of many possible examples, Mozambique's Renamo Party has in recent years presented external aid providers with a triple-rooted resistance to reform, despite what party aid representatives accurately diagnose as a strong need for Renamo to carry out a whole series of reforms if it wishes to compete more successfully. Renamo's leader, Dhlakama, is suspicious of many suggested reforms because they might loosen his near-total grip on the party. He operates from a particular vision of the party—as a heroic, moral source of resist-

ance to what he believes is a party that resorts to illegal or otherwise illegitimate means to hold onto power. Despite other personal values, such as
courage and persistence, he is an extremely stubborn, egocentric person dis-
inclined to listen carefully to or follow the advice of outsiders.

Hard to Help

Parties are hard organizations to help, not just because party leaders often
resist reforms. Some of the changes that party aid providers typically recommend, even if they are not necessarily threatening to the personal interests of
the party leaders, are not of great interest to many people within the parties
generally. As discussed in chapter 4, built into the standard menu of party aid
is a conception of virtuous politics: Parties should care about their constituents and not treat them merely as voters; negative personalistic campaigning should be avoided because it is destructive of democratic culture;
practical, issue-based campaigning is good because it helps clarify and articulate interests, and so forth. Yet many parties are focused on short-term vote-
maximization—especially given the heavy, even fatal price that parties pay if
they fail to get into power in any one election. Therefore they are usually
uninterested in those ideas about campaigning and party building that reflect
either a notion of political virtue for democracy's sake or a longer-term conception of bottom-up party building. In short, some training and advice to
parties will have less uptake than aid providers hope for because they want to
learn different things than what the outsiders are offering.

Many parties in new or struggling democracies are also hard to help
because of the very sorts of organizational weaknesses that aid providers identify as problems to be remedied. Many parties struggle to attract educated, talented young cadres because they cannot compete with the salaries offered by
businesses, NGOs, and even government ministries. Moreover, many young
people are unattracted to party work out of the pervasive aversion to partisan
politics in developing and postcommunist countries. Training programs and
other types of aid for organizational reform sometimes fall on poor human
soil and prove frustrating as a result. More generally, the weak institutionalization common in parties in new or struggling democracies—the shortage of
permanent staff, incoherent, disorganized management structures, and lack of
financial resources—makes it hard for them to articulate what kinds of assistance they most need, to take advantage of what they are offered, and to build
over time on whatever progress they do make. As with other types of
institution-building assistance, party aid providers face the dilemma that

those institutions that most need basic organizational strengthening are least well-positioned to take advantage of aid dedicated to that end.

Finally, parties are difficult to assist because although they exist formally as discrete institutions, many are integral parts of broader, often rather amorphous patronage networks that are very hard to influence or modify, whether from the outside or the inside. When patronage systems are well-established, which is the case in many developing and postcommunist countries, parties are one of a set of mechanisms by which powerful elites assert their influence and ensure their continued hold on power. Money flows into parties from the top—whether bled off from the state coffers, or brought in from wealthy persons buying influence through party contributors. It then flows down out the bottom to ensure the parties' control over voters—through payments to local bosses and notables who have influence over local communities or to citizens through various forms of largesse. Such systems operate according to a logic far removed from the representational ideals of Western party aid providers and are remarkably good at absorbing attempted reforms in any one part without changing overall.

For example, teaching parties door-to-door campaigning, a popular emphasis of party aid, runs into the fact that citizens expect parties to be distributors of money, jobs, and other benefits, not organizations that actually expect citizens to join and work on behalf of merely for the promise of interest representation. Parties may be wary of giving up their reliance on local bosses or notables to deliver votes. Urging parties not to sell places on their party lists to wealthy bidders runs up against the fact that parties depend on the funds from such sales. Adopting transparency of party financing might cripple some parties financially.

All this does not mean that patronage systems are unchangeable and that parties existing within such systems cannot adopt democratizing reforms. It underlines the fact that what may appear to be rational reforms that should on paper help parties compete more effectively (like door-to-door campaigning) may be resisted by many parties as being contrary to their interests. Often the norms and practices of political patronage systems are murky or purposely hidden. As a result, aid providers attempting to insert themselves inside the system as agents of change have a very hard time developing clear knowledge about the actual reality of how parties are operating and what relationship parties have to the overall system of political power.

Underlying Conditions and Structures

Party aid has only limited effects not only because parties are hard organizations to try to help, but also because parties are shaped by a whole set of underlying conditions and structures upon which party aid usually has no bearing. This is a problem with most types of foreign aid that seek to change a particular institution or set of institutions. The aid almost inevitably focuses on the institution itself, not on all the surrounding forces and factors that play a major role in determining its shape and functioning. Because parties in many countries are part of the central nervous system of a country's political corpus, the range of broader conditions and structures that are relevant to their development is unusually wide. Therefore, party aid is especially challenged to make a difference.

To start with, basic features of the overall political system will have significant effects on party development. If, for example, political space in the country is highly restricted, political parties (other than the governing party) will usually be crippled. No matter what their level of determination or skills, party aid providers will have a hard time building up their organizational capacity. This has increasingly become the case, for example, in Russia during the first half of this decade. Or if nonelected figures or forces, such as a monarch, a religious hierarchy, or a military elite, control the main levers of political power, party development will be undermined or at least stunted. Morocco's weak party development of the last several decades embodies this problem.

As discussed in chapter 3, any number of underlying social, economic, or other structural features also greatly influence the course and shape of political party development in a society. Widespread poverty and socioeconomic marginalization create fertile ground for clientelism and patronage politics. Weak rule of law encourages corruption, low levels of accountability, and other deformations of party politics. Enduring authoritarian legacies, both psychological and institutional, make it hard for parties to build real ties to citizens. A constricted range of economic policy choices due to pressures of globalization undercuts ideological differentiation of parties, at least on standard right-left lines.

As it is presently conceived and carried out in most cases, party aid does not address these sorts of broader conditions and structural factors that weigh so heavily on party development. This fact reflects a basic reality of party aid—given the modest amounts of money that aid donors are willing to devote to the issue, party foundations and institutes naturally focus on the more manageable-sized target of the parties themselves rather than on the many larger issues bearing on party development, such as poverty and weak rule of law. It also reflects a broader tendency that occurs in some other areas of democracy-related institution building aid (such as with programs to reform judiciaries or strengthen parliaments). This is the impulse of specialists in a particular kind of institution (whether it is judiciaries, legislatures, parties, or something else) to try to strengthen counterpart institutions in other countries using a standard set of institutional-strengthening tools with little regard for the context in which the institution is embedded.

Of course when party aid groups work in a country, usually other areas of foreign aid are focusing on many of the larger conditions and structural issues, such as poverty reduction, rule-of-law strengthening, or democratic civic education. One could argue, in a kind of reassertion of the basic modernization thesis (that still, after all these years, underlies much development aid), that party development in most new or struggling democracies is being supported indirectly by the overall set of political and economic assistance programs carried out in them. There may well be some truth to this idea but it is too general to be of much use.

In some cases, economic or political aid programs that might seem to address crucial structural factors relating to party development may have little real link to the process of political party strengthening. For example, a crucial element for the development of a varied, active set of political parties in a new or struggling democracy is access to television and radio. If opposition parties are kept off national television and radio, they will have a very hard time no matter what they learn about message development and grassroots organizing. One might assume therefore that aid programs in the media domain will be helpful in this regard, given that media aid usually strives to bolster independent media. Yet the media aid to a particular country may end up being focused, for perfectly legitimate reasons when viewed in a strictly media development perspective, on support for independent newspapers and not seek to do anything about the political restrictiveness of national television and radio. Thus a key structural issue hurting party development will not necessarily be ameliorated, or even addressed, by an aid program in the media sector. Even if a media assistance program aims to foster independent electronic media, it may not succeed. Such programs do not have much leverage in situations where a government is determined to maintain a monopoly over the main media outlets.

In some cases there even arise contradictions or tensions between certain types of economic or political assistance programs and political party development. A large-scale privatization campaign, for example, may contribute to economic growth but allow powerholders to use it to steer substantial assets into the hands of cronies and political allies. That outcome may have dramatic, and possibly very deleterious, effects on the shape of political party development, by producing a further concentration of power in the ruling party.

Weakness of the Standard Method

It might well be tempting, especially for party aid providers, to go no further than the aforementioned two explanations of the lack of transformative effects of party aid. In other words, it would be comfortable for them to say that because parties are hard organizations to help and because party aid only gets at a small part of the overall set of factors shaping politics, decisive, catalytic effects rarely flow from such assistance. In talking with people in parties that are on the receiving end of such aid, it becomes obvious that the common shortcomings of party assistance outlined in chapter 5 also contribute to its modest effects. The sorts of parallel provider-recipient narratives about the frustrations of party aid that are described above in connection with Romania and Russia are very common.

Many of the flexible party resource relationships that aid providers establish seem to be missed opportunities to stimulate, support, and help sustain internal reform in counterpart parties. Far too much party training has a tired, rote quality and involves much too little follow-up to produce significant effects. The pervasive cultivation of party-to-party cooperative ties through study tours and other exchanges often amounts to little in terms of actual party reform. As noted in chapter 5, some party aid groups are trying to reduce the deficiencies in the standard method and try some new approaches, but it is only a slow process of change, the results of which will appear only gradually over time.

Modest Positive Effects

Although transformative effects of party aid are scarce, modest positive effects are often apparent. If one examines parties that have participated in some party aid programs, small signs of change can frequently be identified, changes that can be linked with the aid activities.

Better Campaigning

In new or struggling democracies, one frequently can observe an increasing sophistication over time in the campaign methods that parties use. In general, a professionalization of election campaigning has taken place all around the world (where multiparty elections are held) in the past several decades. In established democracies this trend was initially part of the shift from mass-based parties to catch-all parties and it then intensified over the past several decades as the influence of mass media on campaigns increased. New or struggling democracies are subjected to the same pressures and incentives for the professionalization of election campaigning. The rapid spread of for-hire political consultants working in election campaigns around the world is one element (both a reflection and a contributing factor) of it.

In countries where authoritarianism has just in the past decade or two given way to competitive elections, parties have been scrambling to learn the ropes of electioneering. Western party aid has clearly contributed to that learning process. Visiting or observing parties that have taken part in campaign training activities, one can see that some of them have learned to sharpen their messages, develop better publicity materials, incorporate information gained from polling, be more strategic in the deployment of resources, become more effective at recruiting and using campaign volunteers, and so forth. Although some of this is self-learning (and the Darwinian effect of parties that fail to improve their campaigning losing elections and sometimes disappearing), some of it also is the result of externally sponsored assistance. To take just a few examples from the case study countries, in Romania some of the opposition parties that received extensive U.S. and British training on campaign methods in the 1990s carried out more sophisticated campaigns in the 1996 national elections as compared with the 1992 elections, and clearly made use of some of the techniques they were taught. In Indonesia, several parties made use in the 2004 parliamentary elections of some of the grassroots campaign methods that they had received training about from external actors. In Russia, in the 2003 Duma elections SPS showed some elements of learning about campaign methods that reflected the influence of the U.S.- and German-sponsored campaign training that it received.[5]

The fact that party aid often has fairly definite effects in this domain is not surprising. Many of the elements of effective campaigning are discrete, widely transferable techniques that are not difficult to teach, and which parties can adopt without having to make major changes in their underlying structures. As discussed just above, most parties perceive a tangible interest in learning these things. They may not be very interested in the full range of methods and ideas that party aid providers offer—they may ignore what they perceive as the nonessential virtue-oriented campaign methodologies—but they are motivated to get the core techniques.

Although positive effects of campaign-related assistance are common, drawing a larger judgment about the value of this type of party aid is complicated by a hard question: does helping parties in a new or struggling democracy to professionalize their campaign methods advance democracy in that country? One can argue for the affirmative by asserting that better-organized, better-executed campaigns will cause parties to engage more citizens in the democratic process and perhaps build the representative function of the party or parties.

Yet a contrary argument is also possible. The professionalization of election campaigning in established democracies is often blamed as a factor in the loss of citizens' interest in party politics and the hollowing out of modern democracies. Citizens become politically alienated as parties learn to test messages in focus groups until the messages and candidates seem to say only what the research indicates is most effective for hitting key "hot buttons," not what the parties or candidates actually believe. Many elements of mounting an effective campaign have little to do with creating genuine bonds between parties and constituents but rather treating voters as opportunistic targets for the most superficial and temporary loyalty. It often seems in established democracies that the more artfully parties learn to persuade people to vote for them, the less represented citizens feel by their parties.

The debate over the prodemocratic value of campaign-related aid can be taken further. On the one hand, one can argue that it is intrinsically prodemocratic to help parties in a multiparty system campaign more vigorously and effectively because voters will have more choices and the possibility of democratic alternation will likely be enhanced. Against that view, however, one can pose the following question. If the main parties in a country are a set of elite-oriented, corrupt entities seeking power primarily to advance their own fortunes, what is the value of helping those parties learn to campaign more skillfully, thereby strengthening their ability to maintain a hold on the political system?

Small Steps on Organizational Development

In addition to advancements in campaign methods one can also observe some parties in new or struggling democracies taking positive steps on organizational development. In some cases it appears fairly clear (from analyzing the timing of the changes and interviewing key people within the parties about the process of internal party change) that these steps were prompted by externally funded assistance activities.

Some of the case study countries provide various examples in this regard. In Russia, the Yabloko party in the early years of this decade undertook some internal reforms along the lines of what external aid providers had long been urging, such as reorganizing the senior management level to clarify responsibilities and professionalize party administration, and liberalizing the membership process. In Guatemala, PAN took some steps toward internal democratization in between the last two national elections, including holding a party congress and primary elections for some candidate posts. In Mozambique, as noted previously, Renamo followed Western advice on a few fronts such as forming a senior executive commission in the party, holding a party congress, and establishing a women's league. In Indonesia, Western training efforts appear to have prompted a few parties to adopt more open candidate selection procedures.

The changes are almost always small and incremental. In most cases they are piecemeal; sometimes they are part of a larger, although still gradual, set of internal reforms. As discussed earlier in this chapter, it is hard to identify cases of parties that as a result of externally funded assistance have made fundamental organizational changes that have solved the core characterisitics that drew party aid providers in to work with them, such as establishing top-down, leader-centric organizational structures or reducing significant corruption. The hard question is whether the small positive steps will deepen over time and cumulate in major organizational changes.

Party aid providers take the optimistic view. They often describe what they are doing as "planting seeds of change" and argue that over time these seeds will take root and grow into large reforms. Their confidence often seems based in a rather vague sense of naturalness about political party development, as though once parties get exposed to the right ideas and have more time to try out new practices they will naturally evolve in the direction of "good parties." This sense of naturalness about party development is remarkably untouched in many cases by any apparent awareness of the deeply entrenched reasons, internal to the parties themselves and related to the underlying structural conditions, why the parties have the organizational characteristics that they do.

To the extent that party aid providers elaborate any theory of how to stimulate organizational change it could be summarized as having three core ideas:

- Exposing top party officials to the need for change and the ways of accomplishing it will lead them to believe in the need for and possibility of reforms and put them into practice.
- Training up-and-coming young and mid-level party cadres will turn them into agents of change within the parties who over time will find ways to make reforms come about in their parties.

- Identifying and training reform-oriented local leaders and cadres within a party will help them make use of their distance from the party's central hierarchy to try out important reforms and then over time to push these reforms "upstream" into the party's main organization.

These are intuitively attractive ideas that have a commonsense appeal and serve as a convenient base for programming. They, however, are not based on well-researched longitudinal case studies that examine organizational changes in parties over time. Because most party aid representatives work in any one country only for several years at most before moving on to another assignment, they rarely actually see whether these theories prove true, that is, whether seeds of change take root and grow. They are often surprisingly unaware, and uninterested, in all the previous aid that may have been directed at the parties, no matter how similar it may have been to what they are attempting to do now. As a result, the hard but crucial question about aid for organizational development—what happens when the various sorts of externally sponsored stimuli for change run up against the underlying forces and structures that primarily shape parties—remains surprisingly unexplored.

Emergent Norms of Party Organization

Many of the different elements of international assistance aimed at parties—such as the countless party-by-party training events, the multiparty dialogues, the regional fora for parties, and the standard setting exercises by the party internationals—emphasize the same issues and values about party organization and behavior, from internal democracy and the inclusion of women to financial transparency and anticorruption. As a result, the cumulation of these varied activities over time is contributing to the growing idea in some new or struggling democracies that there are international norms or standards for how parties in a democracy are supposed to be and to act. To take just one example, in Latin America, where the regional exercises to discuss the state of political parties have been most extensive and formalized, it is common within political circles to talk about an agenda for party reform as though its core elements, such as internal democracy and anticorruption, are not just appealing ideas but actual norms. This effect is similar to the emergence and diffusion in the developing and postcommunist worlds over the past twenty years of some basic international norms or standards for elections in a democracy. In both cases there is no initial formalized process of norm setting. Instead, diverse international aid actors with similar points of view on the core issues all work to spread the core values and over time the values start to gain some traction as norms.

As in any realm where soft international norms (lacking any enforcement mechanism) are developing, the effect of them on the actual behavior of the relevant actors is far from clear. They create or add to a certain kind of pressure on the parties, both by helping crystallize and channel public dissatisfaction with the parties around some specific ideas for change and by creating some sense of a united international expectation about parties as well. Yet at the same time they are quite toothless and easy to ignore. This double perspective is evident when one interviews party officials in the regions where there has been a large amount of party work, such as Central and Eastern Europe or Latin America. Party representatives, many of whom having taken part in more than one international party assistance activity, talk knowingly and seriously about the need for greater internal democracy, constituency outreach, financial transparency, inclusion of women, better-defined platforms, and the like. Listening to them it is hard not to believe that party aid is contributing to an important socialization of party elites into a common set of normative expectations about party organization and behavior. Yet then when one observes the stubbornness with which their parties continue about their set ways in practice, all the nice talk about the imperatives for reform seems less impressive. The role of party aid in helping establish and spread international norms about parties is real, yet the effects of these norms in practice are still only very tentative.

CHAPTER EIGHT

Party System Aid

During this decade, a new type of party aid has expanded rapidly: programs to support the development of party systems overall. Unlike the other forms of party aid, such efforts do not proceed party by party, giving training, advice, and other support to help strengthen or reform individual parties. Instead they seek to foster changes in all of the parties in a country at once, via modifications of the underlying legal and financial frameworks in which parties are anchored, or changes in how the parties relate to and work with each other.

Party system programs that address the legal framework for parties often concentrate on political party law, to help a country clarify the legal basis of its parties and stimulate changes in how the parties operate, such as by creating requirements for internal party democracy. Electoral systems have significant effects on the shape of political party development, but for reasons discussed below are not usually the target of party system aid initiatives. Programs targeting the financial basis of parties are a rapidly expanding area, one that seeks to reduce the endemic corruption in party systems by establishing or fortifying systems to regulate campaign finance and party finance generally.

Initiatives to facilitate less conflictive, more productive interparty relations in different countries are also multiplying. Their most common tools are formal or informal multiparty dialogue processes designed to improve communication among parties, reduce the time and energy parties spend fighting over petty issues, and encourage parties to work together on prodemocratic systemic reforms, such as constitutional or electoral reform. The myriad efforts by a wide range of party aid providers to increase the role of women in parties can be considered a further type of party system aid. Some of these undertakings are training programs for individual parties and are part of the general domain of party aid aimed at the organizational development of parties. Some are designed to change legal and regulatory provisions bearing on the participation of women in politics or find other routes toward systemic change.

Party system work is the preferred approach of multilateral organizations, such as UNDP, the OAS, and International IDEA, as well as of some other recent entrants, such as NIMD. Multilateral organizations gravitate to a system-oriented approach because it accords with their comparative advantages or inclinations—their political neutrality and long-term developmental outlook—and it deemphasizes what they lack compared with the party foundations and institutes, that is, expertise on the nuts and bolts of political campaigning and party building. Some of the larger party foundations or institutes are also trying out programs that focus on systemic issues as part of their search for new ways of operating and their desire to respond to areas of heightened international concern, like party finance and the inclusion of women. Much of this growing domain of party system work is new and still in the experimentation and testing stage; specific methods are only starting to be defined and little is yet known about effects over time.

Electoral System

One might assume that aid providers seeking to support reform in the legal framework for parties in a country would focus on the electoral system. After all, as Western political scientists have extensively debated, the kind of electoral system a country coming out of nondemocratic rule chooses has major implications for the evolution of its political party system.[1] Very generally speaking, majoritarian (and single member plurality) systems usually produce a few large parties, whereas proportional representation systems have a greater tendency to produce multiple smaller parties. Assisting a country in its process of writing or revising its electoral law can therefore potentially have significant effects on the basic contours of its party system.

In fact, however, electoral system reform is not a major focus of party system initiatives, for several reasons. First, aid providers are getting interested in party system work now, but most new or struggling democracies have already established their electoral system, having done so during or soon after their break in the 1980s or 1990s from dictatorial rule. Once an electoral system is put in place in the period of early transitional flux, it is often difficult to persuade political elites to reopen the issue (at least the macro-level question of what sort of representational system to use; often many small modifications relating to the electoral process are pursued after the overall law is in place) because the vested interests in the system are usually significant. Second, although the effects that electoral system choices can have on political party development are fundamental along certain dimensions—such as on the number and size of parties a country will develop—they are less likely to have direct effects on the issues that most concern party aid providers, such as parties' lack of internal democracy or the spread of political corruption.

Third, the implications of different electoral system choices for party development are only one of many factors that a government (or an aid organization working with a government) will consider as it engages in electoral law reform. The International IDEA handbook on electoral systems design, for example, lists "encouraging political parties" as just one of ten criteria for designing an electoral law, along with other major considerations, such as "making elections accessible and meaningful" and "facilitating stable and efficient government."[2] Most of the international assistance that has gone into electoral reform has been part of the electoral assistance domain and focused much more on building free and fair elections than on party development per se.

Political Party Law

Aid groups involved in political party assistance are giving increasing attention to political party law in new or struggling democracies. By party law it is meant the state laws that concern "what constitutes a political party, the form of activity in which parties may engage, and what forms of party organization and behavior are appropriate."[3] In a minority of cases, party law is embodied in a special political party law. In most countries, party law is embodied in a variety of laws (often including the general electoral law, a law on political finance, and a law on political campaigning), administrative regulations, court decisions, and, often (at least in the developing world), in the national constitution itself.

Governments in new or struggling democracies have been establishing or reworking their political party laws during the last twenty to thirty years as the Third Wave of democracy has spread. It is only recently that party aid providers have started focusing on this area and getting involved in trying to facilitate or influence the process. The appeal to aid providers of work on party law is strong, especially in situations where they have provided training or other technical assistance to problematic parties and have failed to have much effect. Working directly on party law holds out the possibility of getting at some of the governing structures that determine the shape of parties, and having some effect on all the parties at once.

In countries that have very little party law, aid providers push for the establishment of such laws, frequently in the form of a single overarching party law. Where countries already have a substantial body of party law, aid providers seek to support whatever impulse exists in the society for additions or reforms to the law. Of course party aid providers do not want just any party law, they aim to support party law that will, in their view, underpin or actively generate a vibrant, prodemocratic party system. For example, regarding party establishment and registration requirements, they usually push for a law that is fair, clear, and not burdensome. If the country is one in which power is monopolized by one group and challengers are blocked even from forming a party, party aid providers will try to ensure that the party law is not a source of obstacles to party formation. If the country is one in which political power is highly dispersed or fragmented among dozens of parties, party aid providers may encourage provisions that set a higher threshold of requirements to start or register a party.

Regarding parties' internal operations, party aid providers often urge establishing specific legal requirements relating to internal democracy in parties. These may include rules about holding party congresses, electing party officers, maintaining a gender balance within the party's management, and other similar stipulations. Party aid work also now deals extensively with the issue of regulating party finance. This area of party law work has become very large and is therefore considered separately in the next section of this chapter.

The prodemocratic interest of party aid providers in party law reforms is not necessarily shared by the governments or major parties in the countries where they work. As Kenneth Janda points out, party law serves a variety of functions in different countries, many of which are not necessarily prodemocratic at all, from shielding power holders against robust challengers to limiting the role of parties altogether.[4] The recent experience of Russia with political party "reform" is a good example in this regard. Since 2001, Russian President Vladimir Putin has pushed through a series of shrewdly designed party law modifications that have seriously undercut opposition parties. A new party law of 2001 significantly raised the registration requirements (signatures needed and regional presence) for parties, pushing out the smaller regional parties that had been making some gains. A new election law enacted in 2005 further hit small parties by prohibiting independent candidates in legislative elections (small parties having previously used independent candidates as a way to compete in elections for which they otherwise could not qualify), increasing the amount of funds parties need to have on hand to compete in elections, and raising the threshold for entry into parliament from 5 percent to 7 percent. A new political party law enacted in 2005 tightened yet again the requirements for forming new parties, making it very difficult for any new parties to enter the already atrophied Russian party scene. Some 2005 amendments to the electoral law created still further obstacles to opposition party development by, among other things, prohibiting parties not represented in the Duma from forming blocs to try to get past the heightened vote threshold for parliamentary representation.

Even when changes in party law are the cooperative project of all the main parties in a country, both those in the government and the opposition, some part of the underlying motivation may not be democracy strengthening, no matter how the project is billed. The main parties may, for example, decide to raise the requirements for party formation with the justification that they are trying to reduce party fragmentation, while their real interest is building a higher fence around the political ground they have staked out for themselves. The recent party law reform in Peru, for example, which is discussed in more detail below, was an effort by the main political forces to encourage a consolidation of Peru's notoriously unstable party system. Yet at the same time it also represented a desire of the main parties of the time to fortify their collective place in the system.

Aid providers can play two different roles in assisting political party law reform. Their most basic and common role is as a background supporter of a law reform process—providing comparative information to the relevant political actors about party laws in other countries, sponsoring workshops or other events at which the law-writing process can be debated and discussed, and quietly urging the main actors to stay on course. In Morocco for example, NDI played a very modest supporting role of this type in the process leading up to the enactment of a new political party law in 2005. NDI helped provide information about party laws to some of the main parties and convened seminars with parties to discuss the key choices and issues in the process of law-drafting.

Aid groups sometimes, although much less frequently, take on a more active role in political party law reform. They can try to stimulate interest in it where the issue is not actively on the agenda and back or even help organize a coalition of actors that will push for such reforms. International IDEA played such a role in Peru in the late 1990s and early years of this decade, working in close partnership with Transparencia. As Peru moved away from the authoritarian Fujimori years, the weakness of the country's political parties was one of the most noticeable of its democratic shortcomings. With the idea of strengthening parties, Transparencia and IDEA forged a campaign to stimulate the passage of a political party law (there was no overarching party law on the books), creating and supporting an interparty working group that produced a draft law that, after various modifications, was enacted in 2003.

The Peruvian law contains a number of provisions designed to consolidate the party scene (by reducing the number of very small or "briefcase" parties), through high signature requirements for party registration and public funding for some training activities and to stimulate prodemocratic internal party reforms, including greater financial transparency, internal election requirements, and a 30 percent gender quota for party leadership posts. Getting these provisions into the law was a struggle. The parties resisted some (such as strict financial transparency requirements) while fearing the public's disapproval of others (such as public funding for the parties). The effect of the law on Peru's fragmented, unstable party scene is as yet unclear. The law has not, as some hoped, reduced the number of parties (the number of parties has climbed from twenty-three to more than thirty) or led to any decisive steps toward internal democratization. It at least provides a legal basis to work from in the process of political party strengthening and some procedural and substantive goals for parties that are the product of a consensual, democratic process.

The Peruvian experience points to the general fact that the effects of political party law reform as a tool for strengthening political party development are not yet really known. Even in the minority of cases in which the writing or rewriting of a party law is significantly motivated by prodemocratic intentions, there are obvious limits to what outsiders can achieve through supporting such processes. To start with, law reform projects in every domain, from commercial law to criminal law, struggle to have effects on what are almost always stubborn sociopolitical or socioeconomic patterns and conditions. Changes in laws will produce changes on the ground only if they are internalized by the relevant actors, which occurs only through some combination of effective education, implementation, and enforcement.

More specifically regarding political party laws, clarifying the rules about establishing and registering parties may help smooth one initial part of the process of political party development. If a regime is determined to put obstacles in the way of opposition forces, it will find ways to do so no matter what the political party law says. Similarly, it may be useful to have some requirements in a party law regarding internal democratic procedures of parties but it is unlikely that such requirements, on their own, are going to have major effects on the core organizational patterns of parties, such as their highly hier-archical nature and lack of rootedness. One does not overturn centuries of patrimonial or neopatrimonial structures and habits with a few procedural measures relating to internal party democracy. Nevertheless such provisions may be useful at least as a way of articulating an ideal and setting out some guideposts to work toward.

Moreover, there is no set answer to the question of what sort of political party law will most help support democratic party development. Established democracies vary extremely widely in how they regulate parties, from sys-tems with very few legal requirements and provisions, such as Australia, to ones with detailed regulation of party organization and activity, such as Ger-many. Even those established democracies that do have well-elaborated sys-tems of party regulation usually developed such systems long after parties were active and well-established. The legal provisions came into place more to codify party realities than to guide party development or sharply reshape it. This fact should also cause party aid providers to be cautious about assum-ing that work on party law reform is a likely path to healing the ills of parties in new or struggling democracies.

Party Financing

The financing of political parties (including both financing for election cam-paigns and the regular, ongoing costs of running a party) has surged in this decade as an area of donor attention. Programs to assist new or struggling democracies develop their systems of regulation concerning party financing multiply rapidly year by year. Aid organizations are flocking to this area out of their broader interest in trying to reduce corruption in developing and postcommunist countries. Money in politics is at the core of corruption; party financing is a core part of money in politics. Hence, the relentless search for effective anticorruption methods has led a wide range of donor organizations—bilateral aid agencies, multilateral development banks, inter-national NGOs, and private foundations—to the party finance domain. Some of these aid organizations working on the problem of party finance, such as the multilateral development banks, are motivated primarily by the desire to help reduce corruption for the beneficial effects lowered corruption will have on the overall socioeconomic development of the countries in question. Whatever effects their party finance programs have on political party development in the target countries is a greatly secondary concern. Other aid groups involved in party finance work, however, like IFES, are motivated in significant part by an interest in bolstering political party development. The actual content of party finance programs designed from these two different perspectives (anticorruption and party development) is often quite similar. Party finance programs rooted in a party development perspective, however, may give greater attention to issues such as the inequality and scarcity of resources for parties rather than focusing just on the issues of transparency and legality. In short, all aid work on party finance affects political parties; some of it is primarily designed to do so and such work can be considered a form of direct rather than just indirect party assistance.

Problematic party financing creates or contributes to many political ills. With regard to political party development, analysts usually highlight three dimensions of party financing that can create distortions.[5] First, corruption in party financing—such as candidates or parties taking contributions in return for favors or the illegal steering of state resources to party coffers or campaigns—has many harmful effects on parties. It distorts and weakens the representational function of parties, renders parties poor vehicles for mobilizing citizens to value and participate in the democratic process, and contributes to the centralization of party structures (by concentrating resources at the top and discouraging party leaders from sharing their power).

Second, the scarcity of resources that is characteristic of party financing in many poor countries also hurts party development. Underresourced parties are unable to build coherent party organizations, invest in training for their workers, or carry out the sorts of large-scale outreach that will allow them to build a constituency. Scarcity of resources also often increases party fragmentation (as small, poor parties are unable to gain a broad base) and makes parties vulnerable to influence or takeover by criminal groups with ready cash.

Third, inequality of resources, another problematic dimension of party financing in many new or struggling democracies, also leads to unequal or otherwise distorted representation, and widespread political alienation. The rich are able to control certain parties and use them to protect their interests; the average citizen loses belief in the value of democratic participation. Gross inequalities of resources of parties reinforce dominant party systems in many countries, systems that usually wind up with serious antidemocratic characteristics.

New or struggling democracies vary widely in their legal and regulatory systems for governing party finance. Some have almost no systems at all, leaving party financing essentially unregulated. Others have extensive laws and regulations as well as institutions for enforcing them. The basic response to the challenge of doing more on party financing is to strengthen whatever system is in place or create one if none exists. Although these systems vary greatly in their specific features, there is a common menu of measures from which systems are assembled. Various specialized publications, such as International IDEA's *Handbook on Funding of Political Parties and Election Campaigns*, describe the array of elements that go into party financing systems.[6] These elements are only summarized very briefly here:[7]

- *Disclosure of income or expenditures.* Candidates and parties may be required to report either income (donations or in-kind contributions from individuals, businesses, or other organizations) or expenditures, usually campaign related.
- *Limitations or restrictions on income or expenditures.* Contributions to candidates or parties may be limited in size and frequency. Contributions from certain sources may be prohibited, such as from professional associations, unions, foreign-owned corporations, or foreign entities. Campaign expenditures may be restricted to a set amount. Certain types of expenditures, such as vote-buying or purchasing of advertising time on television and radio, may be prohibited.
- *Providing media access.* Candidates or parties may be granted free, equal time on television and radio.
- *Public funding.* Candidates and parties may be reimbursed by the state for part or all of their campaign expenses, receive regular state funding for core party costs, or receive state funding on a matching basis with private funding.

The administration and enforcement of the system for regulating party financing will usually be the responsibility of the country's national electoral management body or some other governmental body such as the national audit agency or ministry of justice. In recent years, NGOs in some countries— including think tanks, anticorruption groups, or civic education organizations—have taken an active role in monitoring the party finance system and publicizing its shortcomings.

Although this menu of party financing regulatory approaches is widely agreed upon, there is tremendous variation in the ways individual national systems of party finance regulation are designed and implemented, and the specific elements they contain. Every item on this standard menu is the subject of wide-ranging debates about its utility and appropriateness in different contexts. Public funding, for example, is extremely controversial, with well-rehearsed arguments lined up on both sides. Proponents argue that it strengthens party development, promotes fairness, and reduces corruption. Opponents contend that it can isolate parties from society, block the entry of new political actors into a system, and aggravate public cynicism about parties. Not only is there little consensus about what is the best approach to reducing or solving problems of party finance in any particular country, this is an area in which as Michael Pinto-Duschinsky writes, "purity in political financing is not a topic on which the West is entitled to preach virtue to developing democracies."[8] Party financing problems are widespread and serious in established democracies. The problems of money in politics are not problems open to solution but rather to a long-term process of alleviation and management.

Aid organizations are trying many things in their effort to help countries improve the inevitably stubborn set of problems surrounding their party finance systems. As with other areas of aid that go through an early boom phase, hurriedly organized seminars and training workshops on the subject have proliferated as have many superficial efforts to export laws and regulations from Western democracies. At the same time, more serious efforts are also starting to take place. Looking closely into this swarm of activities, one can discern a number of distinct approaches:

- *Encouragement and technical assistance to governments.* Aid providers can encourage a government to give attention to and do something about party financing and then provide the relevant officials and lawmakers with comparative information about practices in other countries, opportunities to discuss and learn about comparative experiences, and advice about how to proceed.
- *Building impetus for reform.* An aid provider interested in taking a more activist approach than merely encouraging a top-down reform process can attempt to help nurture a broader societal interest in and push for reform. One way to do this is by partnering with policy institutes or public interest NGOs of the country in question and supporting those organizations in researching the problems of party finance, studying possible reforms, developing activities to stimulate public awareness and interest, and launching some type of citizen (or combined civil society–political party) campaign for reform.[9]
- *Strengthening party capacity.* Aid providers often work directly with the parties on party finance issues—strengthening the capacity of parties to raise money, helping them learn how to abide by existing or new laws

and regulations on party finance, or providing them information and training on possible ways to reform the existing party finance system.

- *Strengthening enforcement capacity.* Assistance is sometimes provided to help bolster the governmental organizations that are responsible for enforcing the party finance system through training, material assistance, or other forms of capacity-building.
- *NGO monitoring.* Some aid providers fund local NGO monitoring efforts in which think tanks, anticorruption NGOs, or other civic groups carry out research, documentation, and publicity on the compliance of candidates and parties with party finance laws and regulations, usually in connection with an election campaign. In some cases there are major monitoring campaigns around an election involving multiple organizations and extensive investigation and publicity. International NGOs have helped develop and disseminate the methodologies for such monitoring work, as for example the Open Society Justice Initiative's *Handbook on Monitoring Election Campaign Finance.*[10]

Several features of this burgeoning donor concern with party financing are worth noting. It represents the area of party aid with the widest range of aid organizations involved because it connects to the crowded field of anticorruption assistance. The heterogeneity of assistance produces a large number of different approaches and a certain amount of positive experimentation in a domain that needs new ideas and insights. The potential danger is that the multiplicity of underlying interests and philosophies of the many different aid actors will produce confused and sometimes contradictory efforts in any one country.

As is often the case with a new donor enthusiasm, much of the first wave of programming on party finance work has consisted of high-profile conferences, agenda-setting exercises, awareness raising, and the production of hortatory declarations and action plans long on good intentions but short of actual backing within the countries concerned. Such activities may be a necessary or at least inevitable part of getting a new area of assistance under way but it is essential to move quickly beyond this phase in order to avoid simply producing cynicism in the relevant publics and miss the chance to refine methods and approaches before the main donors lose interest and move on to some new enthusiasm.

As with other areas of foreign aid in which legal and regulatory systems are at issue, aid providers working on party finance are often swayed by the temptation of formalistic solutions—pushing other governments to quickly enact new laws and regulations and providing them with off-the-shelf models. Such formalistic approaches rarely have much positive effect because the new laws and regulations are not rooted in any real buy-in from the affected groups, capacity for implementation and enforcement is lacking, and there is usually insufficient knowledge about the law within the society. They are likely to be especially ineffective in the party finance domain given that this is an area where the laws and regulations often have little controlling effect, even in established democracies with relatively solid rule-of-law systems. As Pinto-Duschinsky says about party finance laws generally, "scholars of political funding have almost exhausted the vocabulary of contempt in describing the ineffectiveness of these rules." [11]

Furthermore, despite the fact that glaring problems with party finance confront most aid-providing countries, aid organizations still habitually recommend to others their own country's approaches and methods. This is evident, for example, regarding public funding of parties. Public funding is the norm in much of Europe but much less used in the United States. Accordingly, aid groups from Europe prescribe public funding to officials in new or struggling democracies much more readily than do U.S. aid groups.

With respect to effects, much of the aid work relating to party finance is new and perhaps not yet ripe for assessments. Modest expectations are even more in order here than in other areas of democracy aid. This is true because efforts to strengthen party finance systems in new or struggling democracies are inevitably limited by the overall weak state of the rule of law in these countries. Moreover, as the continued travails of established democracies on this issue make clear, the problem of money in politics is one of the most vexing challenges that all democracies face.

The rush of donor activity in this domain has undoubtedly helped raise the awareness of many people in new or struggling democracies about the importance and possibility of trying to tackle the problems of party finance. Whether over time this burst of activity will translate into deep-reaching, effective ameliorative measures remains to be seen. As is the case in other areas in which external aid providers take on very large-scale, entrenched sociopolitical or socioeconomic problems, lasting progress will only be made when a whole set of factors comes together, including political will for change on the part of key elites, the necessary underlying institutional base to support change, and a lack of powerful spoilers.

Aid providers can try to help such factors come about, but their ability to do so is usually limited. They can expose key political elites to information about the shortcomings of the existing political finance regime in their country and ideas for possible remedial measures. Exposure alone does not create real political will to undertake hard changes. Through training and other technical assistance, aid providers can help bolster the necessary institutional underpinnings for a strengthened party finance regime but such institutional reform is almost always painfully slow and partial. They can usually do little to thwart persons determined to circumvent the new regime.

Where such factors emerge largely on their own, due to a fortuitous political transition process or other type of favorable juncture, well-targeted assistance can help a party finance reform process move ahead. Indonesia for example, has managed to move away from the Suharto years with an impressive and still growing set of core political structural reforms, including fundamental changes in their electoral system. A balanced distribution of power among the principal political actors has helped to ensure that no one dominant group is able to stymie finance and other systemic reforms. Party finance reform has advanced as part of the electoral changes with modest but substantive technical assistance provided from the outside (primarily by IFES)—including cooperative information to help frame the available policy choices and strategic advice at some key moments to relevant lawmakers—proving helpful.

Where a broader constellation of positive factors is not present, similarly well-crafted and even vigorous external assistance almost always bounces off. The entrenched interests in new or struggling democracies, especially those where one political party or group has a dominant position, simply override any finance reform impetus coming from other parts of the society or from the outside. For example, various U.S. and European aid providers supported some well-designed party finance monitoring and other reforms by Russian civil society groups in the late 1990s and early years of this decade. The powerfully centralized, entrenched political apparatus dominating Russian politics largely negated the effort.

Interparty Dialogues

Another form of party system aid is support for interparty dialogues. These are dialogue processes in which representatives of the political parties of a country get together regularly over several months, or sometimes even years, to discuss and work on matters of mutual interest. Such dialogues can take various forms. They may be high-level, formal processes in which party leaders, or secretary-generals of parties, meet in a structured setting. They may also involve mid-level party cadres and less formal meetings. They may be directed at a prespecified goal or they may be open-ended; they may be highly public and accessible or closed-door and quiet. They are not the same as inter-party negotiations held to try to end a civil war. Rather they take place in peacetime, as one element of a larger democratization process.

The aims of such dialogues are generally twofold. Dialogue processes are created to be a protected space separate from the conventional political arena, in which the parties can communicate with each other, get to know each other better on a personal basis, overcome conflicts, and build a base for cooperation. Sponsors of interparty dialogue also often hope that parties will use the dialogue process to work together on political reform measures such as electoral law reform, party finance issues, or other elements of the political rules of the game. Most or many of the parties in the dialogue are usually represented in the country's national legislature and thus could in theory pursue the same political reform projects there. The hope, however, is that being somewhat separate from the accumulated pressures and blockages of the legislature, a dialogue will be a more flexible, productive process. Also, in the dialogues, unlike in legislatures, parties can focus exclusively on party-specific issues. Dialogues are also sometimes organized in the lead-up to elections to provide the parties with a mechanism for talking as a group with the electoral commission to clarify procedures or head off electoral disputes before they solidify.

The role of external organizations as supporters of such dialogues varies. Sometimes an outside group will actually plant the idea and build a dialogue process from scratch. In other cases it will respond to an initiative coming from the parties. Outside groups can serve as a neutral broker or umpire among the parties to keep the dialogue on track, as well as a provider of comparative technical expertise, underwriter of workshops and seminars, and source of strategic and tactical advice. Supporting an interparty dialogue best suits an external organization with a clear reputation for political neutrality. UNDP is the most active organization involved in such work, with NIMD and the OAS also active players, although the German *Stiftungen* and the U.S. party institutes have successfully sponsored multiparty dialogues relating to national agenda-setting, electoral processes, and other political issues in some countries. Aiding dialogues is relatively low-cost but labor-intensive, requiring a subtle hand to help a process move ahead without getting in the way of what has to be a process forged by the parties themselves.

Latin America has had the most interparty dialogues, reflecting the particular interest of UNDP's Latin America bureau in such work and also the fact that Latin American political systems are on the whole well-suited to such efforts, not having many dominant party systems (dominant parties not being usually productive dialogue partners) and having a long, albeit troubled history of multipartyism. Probably the most extensive, elaborate interparty dialogue, at least this decade, has been in Guatemala. It consisted of two parallel, externally sponsored dialogue processes. In 2000, the OAS established the Forum of Political Parties at the request of the main Guatemalan parties. The parties sought a formal dialogue process to help advance on electoral and other political reforms that were called for in the 1994 peace accords but on which little progress had yet been made. The forum brought together the secretary-general of each party every month or two, up to and through the 2003 elections.

In the forum the parties developed a draft bill on electoral and party reform that was eventually enacted into law. Although it did not end up incorporating the provisions for internal democracy that some people hoped it would, the bill raised the threshold for entry into Congress to 5 percent, to reduce party fragmentation. The forum also served as a place for the parties to discuss various issues in the lead-up to the 2003 elections, one result of which was the parties agreeing on a code of electoral ethics. When the ruling party violated the code by using violence against some demonstrators several months before the elections, the forum suspended it from the group.

During the same years, UNDP, with support from NIMD, established the Multiparty Dialogue. Each Guatemalan party chose two representatives—mid-level to senior party cadres—to serve on the dialogue. They met many times together over the course of several years, carrying on discussions, participating in numerous training seminars, and working together on a common agenda, called the Shared National Agenda, that was launched before the 2003 elections to serve as a suggested basis of action for the next government. The representatives in the dialogue also carried out numerous meetings within their parties at the national and regional levels to discuss the Shared National Agenda. The idea of the agenda was to reverse the pattern of fractious, unproductive governments by encouraging the next government to focus on a widely agreed set of core policy goals. The hope was that if the new government would do so it would accomplish useful policy objectives and build credit in the public for all the participating parties, thereby starting to reverse the parties' extremely low public credibility. The forum and the dialogue operated separately from each other but in a generally reinforcing manner, despite some confusion at times about the differences between the two and occasional patches of rivalry and friction.

From the experience of these dialogue efforts in Guatemala and elsewhere, some basic lessons about their utility as an approach to strengthening party systems can be drawn. Dialogues are an inherently appealing idea—after all, who can be against dialogue? Yet to avoid wasting effort and to help design them to be as useful as possible in particular contexts, it is necessary to look hard at their intended functions. In considering supporting the establishment of an interparty dialogue in a country, one can start by asking whether there appears to be a real need for a new space in which parties can meet to get to know one another better and work together. Are the political elites in fact unfamiliar with each other across party lines? Are there unproductive tensions and conflicts between the parties, beyond the normal interparty competition, that might be reduced through dialogue? Is there a reason why the parties should not just try to use the national and local legislative bodies as places to learn to work together?

In Guatemala conditions were favorable along these lines. After decades of civil war and centuries of gross socioeconomic inequality, Guatemalan political society was deeply divided. The parties lacked basic lines of communication among themselves and gummed up the governance process with constant skirmishes over matters of minor import. Due both to structural weakness of the institution and the fact that many parties failed to gain representation in it, the Guatemalan Congress was a poor forum for the parties to try to learn to work together better.

In other countries, the need for an interparty dialogue to foster communication among the parties might not be present, even though the parties are very troubled. In many weak democracies, the political elites from the main parties know each other very well and do not lack formal or informal opportunities to discuss and debate political matters. An external aid group coming in and setting up a special closed door forum for the parties risks aggravating the public's belief that the main parties are a collusive elite that spends more time making deals with each other than serving their constituents. A country with a political situation like Nicaragua's for example, where the two main political parties have a recent history of mutually self-interested pacts, has little room or need for an interparty dialogue, unless the exercise were somehow directed at reducing collusive interparty behavior.

A second line of questions that can be asked about a possible interparty dialogue is whether the parties will be able to learn to work together productively on some reform items of substance, so that the dialogue is not just a talk shop. Do there appear to be some common interests among the main parties on reforming the rules of the game? In Guatemala the peace accords constituted a preexisting base of consensus on which the parties could build. Even despite that however they were unable to agree on many elements of a party law (such as the introduction of gender quotas) beyond the raised threshold for entry into Congress. The Shared National Agenda was also built on that base. Useful and important though it was, it represented only a consensus on a broad list of *what* needed to be done, not a consensus on *how* those goals should be pursued. Thus the parties came to agreement that poverty reduction was a key national objective, but did not reach or even seek consensus on what type of policy, such as a probusiness, low-tax growth plan versus a redistributive, high-tax social protection approach, should be adopted to achieve it.

In many other new or struggling democracies there is little basis of common interest for pursuing electoral or other political reforms due to well-drawn lines in the sand. Where dominant parties hold sway for example, important reforms that might help level the playing field, such as on party finance or media access, are usually blocked from the start. In Tanzania, for example, a country with a long-standing dominant party (the Revolutionary Party of Tanzania [CCM]) that has been in power for decades, NIMD has in the past several years sponsored an interparty dialogue. The dialogue has provided the main parties with a forum to discuss various issues and increased communication among them. It has not yet, however, contributed to any movement on significant political reforms, a process largely blocked by the overweening position of the CCM. In short, dialogue processes may help clarify the lines or expose the real issues at stake but they cannot alter the underlying imbalances of power and entrenched interests that often thwart reforms.

Women in Parties

Another area of party aid that has grown rapidly in recent years and seeks to produce not only changes in individual parties but often also in party systems overall is assistance to foster greater inclusion of women. Almost all party aid providers are active in this area. The widespread embrace of work in this domain reflects a general consensus on the part of aid organizations that women in new or struggling democracies are significantly underrepresented in political parties (and political life generally), with adverse effects on women, on parties (due to their being inadequately representative), and society generally. The growing ubiquity of work on inclusion of women in parties also reflects the fact that such efforts can fairly easily find a place in almost any type of political context, from successful democratic transitions to semiauthoritarian and even authoritarian regimes. In the largely autocratic Middle East for example, an important element of the U.S. government's new push for democratization is a greater role for women in political life.

Women-focused political party aid seeks to get more women into parties and to bolster their power, influence, and effectiveness once in. It also tries to get women's policy concerns included in party platforms, and taken seriously by parties. Aid organizations also try to encourage changes in the political party structures and internal organizational cultures of parties to make them more supportive of women. Another major objective of such work is increasing the number of viable women candidates for whatever elected offices, local, regional, and national, are up for election.

Much women-focused work is, like all party aid, rooted in training—for women party cadres on how to be effective within parties, for all party cadres on the importance of including women fully in party life, for women candidates on campaigning, and for newly elected women on governance. Aid providers also push for key institutional reforms in parties, including creating women's leagues within parties, opening management structures to women, establishing internal party quotas for women managers and candidates, and provisions in party laws requiring more representation of women in party management structures.

Party aid providers sometimes also foster collaboration among women from diverse parties and political groups within a country or a region, through networking events or associations. These efforts aim to allow women political activists to share experiences and learning across party lines and to create informal networks of support for politically active women. NDI and IRI are following this approach at a broader level, setting up a joint project to create a global electronic network of women in politics to serve various support and information functions.

Aid to promote the greater inclusion of women in parties is one part of the much larger domain of external assistance to promote a greater role for women in politics generally.[12] If there are many actors involved in women-in-party work, there are countless ones involved in women-in-politics work, including bilateral aid agencies, international NGOs, development banks, private foundations, national NGOs, and many more. They seek to bolster the role of women in politics at all different levels and from many angles: getting more women into national and local governments, encouraging greater responsiveness of political institutions to women's policy concerns, and fostering grassroots political participation by women. This broad women-in-politics agenda can be seen in turn as just one element of a still larger agenda of women's empowerment that has been spreading around the world in recent decades, an agenda that spans and interconnects the social, political, economic, and cultural domains.

Despite the burgeoning number of programs to strengthen the role of women in parties, there has been very little systematic work to assess its effects. I have not attempted such an assessment as part of this study, and confine the discussion of its effects to a few impressionistic remarks.

It is clear even from quite unsystematic observation that the role of women in political parties in most new or struggling democracies is growing. More women are active within parties in most countries. Women in senior positions, including leadership positions, although still few, are gradually increasing in number. Women's leagues within parties are multiplying, and women's issues are more frequently incorporated into party platforms. Many parties are making more serious efforts to reach out to women voters. The causes of these changes are multiple, and they relate to the broader trend toward women's empowerment generally. It is very difficult to sort out the importance of the specific domain of women-related party aid. Nevertheless it seems clear that the push party aid providers are giving to greater inclusion of women in political parties is contributing to the positive trend. One cannot help but be struck in visiting party aid programs that there is often a high level of interest and energy in activities that involve women activists. This is especially true at training events for women candidates, cadres, or organizers at the provincial level, where the sense of possibility of change is often greater than it is closer to the centers of power in the parties.

Yet although changes in the place of women in parties are noticeable in most new or struggling democracies, it remains only a very limited evolution. As discussed in the previous chapter, political parties are hard organizations to change through external assistance. Strengthening the role of women in a party inevitably touches on the same issues of power and control that make other types of internal reforms difficult and slow, not to mention the often deeply rooted social beliefs and attitudes that underlie the male-dominated state of most parties. Looking at the parties in the case study countries, for example, one sees dismayingly little change in the very weak presence of women in the top levels of party leadership structures, whether in Guatemala, Indonesia, Mozambique, Morocco, Romania, or Russia. The inclusion of women generally in the parties in these countries, and in most other countries in the developing and postcommunist worlds, remains poor. Of course the limited progress should hardly be surprising. Even in the political parties of most countries on the aid-providing side, such as Germany, Great Britain, and the United States, many decades of grappling with the challenge of bolstering the place of women in politics has resulted in only slow progress. In the United States, for example, the percentage of women in Congress is 14.9 percent, which is lower than the average percentage of women in legislatures in Africa and Asia. The Nordic countries are exceptional in the progress they have made on women's inclusion, but even there progress came only after decades of work.

Moreover, when examining the effects of party aid on the role of women in parties, it is also important to note that women run a real danger of being co-opted by political parties.[13] Parties will often use women to gain votes or establish connections with the grassroots, but resist incorporating them into decision-making structures, supporting their candidacies, allowing them to fill positions of influence or responsibility, or taking their opinions into account. In many African political parties, for example, women feature prominently in large party rallies as entertainers, recruiters, and party workers but are virtually absent within the central party hierarchy. Women in Indonesia report that parties will encourage them to run for office in order to gain votes, but refuse to support their campaigns once they do so.

More broadly, regarding the role of women in legislative or other political bodies, change can be measured more easily at least in the simple numerical sense, and a positive trend can be observed. The number of women in local and national legislative bodies in the developing and postcommunist worlds is slowly increasing. In sub-Saharan Africa, for example, the percentage of women in national parliaments rose from 1997 to 2006 from 10.4 percent to 16.6 percent. In Asia the increase was from 13.1 percent to 15.9 percent. A mix of causal factors is at work here too, but the various aid programs to train female candidates, remove legal and other structural obstacles to women's political participation, and bolster civic education for women are undoubtedly a positive contributing factor in that mix, one that is not decisive but not trivial either.

A vigorous debate exists over the effects of the increased number of women in legislatures and other political offices. Many Western groups supporting efforts to fuel this trend assume that a higher proportion of women in positions of power will lead to substantive improvements in the responsiveness of political systems to women's interests. Yet some analysts question this assumption or argue that it is at best only partially valid. The presence of moderately greater numbers of women in positions of power may not be sufficient to reverse well-entrenched political patterns rooted in socioeconomic structures and sociocultural value systems that work against women's interests. The women who come to power as a result of quotas or other structured methods of increasing the formal representation of women may be kept on the sidelines of power through informal means, or they may be part of the same elite social networks that dominate political life and not really represent any widening perspective or representational reach. Nevertheless the growing numbers of women in legislatures around the world is a positive trend, very slow though it may be, one that promises to make political systems more representative over time.

A Start

It is a natural evolution of political party assistance to expand from trying to help individual parties to strengthen party systems overall. Even though aid efforts directed at party systems are still fairly new, one can observe at least some signs of an emergent consensus—at least among party aid providers—on some of the important elements of such work. For example a consensus about key features of prodemocratic political party law are spreading and starting to affect internal debates in different countries about political party law reform. Although aid providers often pursue different specific approaches to party finance reform, they mostly share various general ideas about the nature of the problem and the range of useful ways of tackling it. Similarly, initiatives aimed at promoting greater inclusion of women have become very widespread and are provoking societies that traditionally gave little attention to the issue to consider it. Thus party system aid appears to be starting to influence at least debates and thinking in some new or struggling democracies about basic choices concerning the framework for political party development.

At the same time, however, aid programs aimed at party systems face important challenges. Above all, as has been encountered in other areas of reforms to basic laws, such as the domains of criminal law or commercial law, helping produce changes in the laws themselves is often relatively easy. Ensuring that new or reformed laws actually produce the desired changes in the behavior of organizations and individuals is a much harder task. Underneath the new laws are entrenched structures and interests, resistant to change. Thus focusing on party system reform rather than parties themselves is a way of going underneath parties to get at the underlying legal or normative frameworks that shape them. Yet underneath those frameworks is a much larger set of political, economic, social, and cultural factors that determine why parties and other political institutions are the way they are. Party system aid represents an effort to go deeper into political party development, but it is only a very partial step in that direction.

PART FOUR

Conclusions

CHAPTER NINE

Going Deeper

The troubled state of political parties in new or struggling democracies is a central challenge to democratization. Parties that are highly leader-centric, organizationally weak, corrupt and captive of wealthy financial backers, ideologically incoherent, poorly rooted in society, and narrowly focused on electioneering fail to fulfill core democratic functions. They do not represent citizens' interests well, effectively incorporate citizens into the political process, present voters with clearly defined alternatives, or govern skillfully once in power. Not only is the pervasiveness of parties' shortcomings striking, so too is their similarity across the highly varied economic, political, social, and cultural contexts of these countries. This similarity is the result of the commonality of certain key conjunctural and structural factors, including the pattern of democratic compression characteristic of the Third Wave of democracy, as well as the weak rule of law, the persistence of poverty and inequality in many places, the shrinkage of the state resulting from market reforms, the narrowed range of policy choices in the context of globalization, the prevalence of presidential systems, and the continuing power of post authoritarian antipolitical legacies.

Yet problematic, aggravating, and disappointing though they are, political parties are necessary, even inevitable. No workable form of democratic pluralism as been invented that operates without political parties. Some civil society enthusiasts may dream that a superempowered civil society might obviate the need for political parties but no society is close to that vision. It is hard to envisage how civil society organizations could take on the principal responsibility for representing citizens' interests (and by necessity then competing among themselves for influence and power) without taking on something like the form of political parties. Although they are often hollowed out, unstable, grasping, and profoundly unpopular, political parties are not going to disappear from new or struggling democracies anytime soon. As long as Western and multilateral organizations seek to support democratic transitions around the world, they will continue to have to confront political parties and find ways to help them better fulfill at least some of their core prodemocratic functions.

As the troubled state of political parties in new or struggling democracies makes clear, the efforts over the past twenty-five years by Western party aid organizations to bolster and advance political party development in many of these countries has had at best very limited effects. Party aid has strengthened the capacity of numerous parties to carry out electoral campaigns, stimulated some of them to introduce modest internal reforms, and helped widely disseminate within political party circles ideas about the roles parties should play in a democracy and the organizational characteristics that match best with these roles. Yet party aid has only very rarely had transformative impact on the basic organizational make-up and operational features of recipient parties.

The limited effect of party aid has several causes. Parties turn out to be very difficult organizations to assist. Party leaders, who usually have most of the power within parties, often feel threatened by the reforms that party aid providers advocate, such as increasing financial transparency or decentralizing managerial authority, and they resist them accordingly. The very organizational weaknesses that draw party aid providers in to try to help parties, such as shallow human resources and dysfunctional managerial methods, render parties poorly equipped to take advantage of and build on externally sponsored assistance efforts. Moreover, unlike in other areas of democracy assistance, such as elections administration or rule-of-law reform, Western aid groups seeking to support political party development in other countries are not able to draw upon a secure, widely accepted domestic model of success. Instead, given the troubled state of parties in many of the established democracies themselves, party aid providers face constant questions at home and abroad about how they can do what they do with any confidence or coherence. The party model from which they operate has the palpable character of an idealized or mythic model.

The effects of party aid also tend to be quite limited because the main determinants of the make-up and methods of parties in the recipient countries are an array of underlying economic, political, social, and cultural conditions that are largely beyond its ambit. This gap between the reach of tightly focused institution-building programs and the underlying causes of the deficiencies of the institutions in question is a fundamental problem almost all types of democracy aid face. It is especially wide regarding political parties because the domain of electoral politics and parties is especially personalistic and informal rather than technocratic and rationalistic.

Chronic methodological weaknesses in party aid itself have also undercut its effects. Organizations carrying out party assistance have relied all too often on stale, cookie-cutter methods, such as supply driven, repetitive, short-term trainings, seminars, conferences, and consultancies in which fly-in Western experts with little knowledge of the local scene lecture or advise political party activists on how to reform their parties. Party aid has often overemphasized campaign-related skills at the expense of long-term organizational development. Those party aid groups that have focused more on long-term party building have often fallen into the trap of cozy party-to-party relationships that produce little real impetus for change. Moreover, many party aid groups have clung to the fraternal method even as the relevance of the traditional European ideological party families has declined, especially in regions where party aid is now spreading, such as Africa, Asia, and the Middle East.

Much party aid has been rooted in only cursory assessments of the local party and political scenes. It is rarely tied to any in-depth strategic analysis of the patterns of political change in the recipient country in question and the role of the parties in the overall process of attempted democratization. Instead much of the aid proceeds from the view that because parties everywhere in new or struggling democracies appear to suffer from similar shortcomings, party aid can pursue essentially the same approach all over. Few party aid groups have sponsored any serious independent evaluations of their work to take a hard look at their methods and approaches and to assess the actual effects of their work over time.

A Second Generation

Party assistance is now in a state of change. Some of the party aid organizations that have been operating for decades have started facing the fact that the standard method of helping parties often seems to produce little effect. They are responding by attempting to improve the method and trying some new approaches. The various organizations that have entered the party aid domain in this decade—which unlike the older organizations that do party aid are mostly not party foundations or institutes—have been looking for new ways of acting, ones that reflect their own distinctive organizational strengths and inclinations.

Better training methods are becoming somewhat more common, including more sustained training, more follow-up activities for participants, fewer fly-in trainers, more use of third country trainers and expertise, more training of trainers, and greater use of new educational technologies, such as distance learning. Some party aid groups are experimenting with more extensive prior analyses of the party scene in a country before establishing a program there. There is some growth in post-hoc evaluations to extract lessons learned.

Party aid is marked by movement away from single-party efforts toward multiparty programs. The multiparty focus often involves more systematic attempts to affect the overall party system in a country. These take the form of initiatives to foster horizontal learning among parties, to spread norms about good party behavior within the political elite, to bridge the gap between parties and civil society, and to increase the role of women in politics. The growing field of programs aimed at party systems also includes support for reforms in the basic rules and regulations that govern party life, such as political party law and laws relating to party finance.

These many attempted improvements of the standard method and the new lines of system-oriented assistance are still only tentative. They represent only one part of a party aid domain still significantly rooted in its traditional approaches. Nevertheless it is clear that international party assistance is in transition. The first generation of party aid, which was coterminous with the Third Wave of democracy (the last quarter of the twentieth century), and primarily based in party-to-party relationships of solidarity and support within the major European ideological families, is giving way. A new generation of party aid is emerging, one potentially defined both by more incisive and diverse methods of stimulating and supporting change in individual parties and a broader set of initiatives in and around parties to bolster party systems as a whole and to integrate such work into democracy building and development work generally.

The Limits of Moderate Reform

Although a new generation of party aid is starting to be identifiable, much more needs to be done to advance it and make it cohere. An agenda for strengthening party aid and helping bring this second generation of assistance to fruition is fairly clear. The various lines of improvement and innovation that party aid providers have begun experimenting with need to be embraced and taken forward by a wider range of party aid actors. This means many things:

- Abandoning cozy party-to-party cooperative relationships that lack any real focus on how party reform can be stimulated, supported, and sustained.
- Avoiding the tendency to devote substantial amounts of program resources to party exchanges, especially poorly planned study tours, dignitary-rich conferences, and short-term parliamentary delegations in either direction.
- Incorporating and expanding the many possible improvements in training methods, with a focus on creating sustained learning experiences and the opportunity for genuine follow-up and practical application.
- Devoting more resources to serious going-in assessments of the political parties and overall political life in a country before setting up party aid programs there.
- Ceasing to send to complex foreign political contexts Western campaign experts who know little about the local scene and reflexively prescribe a stock set of ideas about high-octane campaigning as a recipe for party strengthening and reform.
- Going deeper and further with programs to bolster the representational character of parties, by broadening efforts to bridge the gap between parties and civil society (beyond just NGOs), taking more steps to understand the rise of new social movements and their potential ties to the party domain, continuing to support the inclusion of women in parties, and supporting new forms of citizen representation at the local level.
- Taking forward the new efforts to strengthen party systems, by learning more about how to make multiparty dialogues effective, help new legal frameworks on party finance gain teeth, and stimulate useful progress on party law reform.
- Carrying out many more independent, searching evaluations of party aid programs that question basic assumptions about methods, assess long-term effects on parties, and relate the effects to the recipient country's overall political development.

If the community of party aid providers follows this path of moderate reform, what will likely be achieved? To put it differently, what is reasonable to expect of party aid? The question of reasonable expectations is relevant to every area of democracy aid, yet is rarely asked or properly answered. As discussed in chapter 7, the international policy community lurches between investing democracy assistance with unrealistic expectations or dismissing it as insignificant. Establishing a realistic middle ground regarding expected results and effects remains a necessary task both for democracy aid generally and party aid specifically.

Even if party aid providers do make significant progress on the path of moderate reform, expectations about impact must be kept modest. Parties will remain difficult organizations to assist both because of their organizational weaknesses and the marked tendency of party leaders to feel threatened by and resistant to many of the reforms that aid providers prescribe. Even when aid is strengthened and improved along the lines discussed above, it generally does not touch the various conjunctural and structural conditions that primarily shape parties.

We can expect party aid to help bring about some positive changes in parties and party systems, especially where the broader political environment is moving in a somewhat positive direction and party assistance is brought to bear in a concentrated, sustained fashion. Party assistance programs can stimulate some parties to try grassroots outreach methods, introduce some measures of internal democracy, spend more time elaborating party platforms, give greater place to women in the party hierarchy, pursue dialogues and other bridge-building activities with civil society organizations, establish internal training programs for party personnel and experiment with merit-based promotion practices, reach out more vigorously to youth, recognize and take seriously citizens' dissatisfaction with parties, give local branches more autonomy, and at least acknowledge the need for greater financial transparency and probity.

Regarding party systems, external assistance can sometimes help create real opportunities for parties to engage in serious dialogue, introduce in the political arena comparative knowledge about party law reform choices, stimulate interest in strengthening legal frameworks to regulate party finance, and reduce structural obstacles to the participation of women in electoral politics.

In short, party aid can sometimes help stimulate and support a host of gradualistic, incremental reforms in parties and party systems. These reforms may help parties do a better job over time of aggregating and articulating citizens' interests, engaging citizens in the democratic process, and governing more effectively once in power. The aid is unlikely, however, to produce decisive changes in the basic organization and operation of parties. That is to say, we are unlikely to see in most new or struggling democracies party aid changing the relentlessly electoralist character of most parties, reversing the leader-centric, personalist nature of most party organizations; eliminating or even substantially reducing party corruption; introducing ideological coherence into party politics; overcoming deep patterns of patriarchy; infusing citizens with discerning, engaged attitudes about democratic politics; and making parties principled actors that eschew petty infighting, partisan squabbles, and unseemly self-interest.

As with other areas of democracy aid, arriving at realistic expectations about the effects of party assistance is a somewhat deflating process. The serious problems that draw outside groups in to take on the challenge of working with political parties are unlikely to be substantially overcome, although some modest lines of improvement are possible. Again, as with other areas of democracy aid, it would in fact be surprising if it were possible for a few outside groups to arrive in a society, spend a few million dollars (or often less) per year for several years on various training programs and other technical assistance activities and in so doing produce or facilitate a transformation of some of the central political institutions in the country. An essential challenge for party aid providers, as for democracy promoters generally, is to find the motivation and energy to persevere with and keep striving to improve what is often vexing work in highly problematic local contexts while accepting that the effects of their work will be modest at best and unlikely in and of themselves to lead to any fundamental changes in the troubled state of the particular institutions with which they work.

Going Deeper

Is it possible for party aid to go deeper, to go beyond the path of moderate reforms and develop more assertive or incisive methods that would produce more fundamental effects? The answer is uncertain but the question is worth exploring. One approach to going deeper would be for aid providers to try to directly address the underlying structural factors that primarily shape parties in new or struggling democracies. For example, aid providers could in theory try to design a party development program that attempted to alleviate or otherwise change some of the key determinants of problematic parties in a country, such as the weak rule of law, high levels of poverty or inequality, an economic policy context that constrains basic policy choices, a presidential system that constrains party development, and the antipolitical attitudinal legacies of earlier authoritarian rule. In practice, however, this is unlikely to happen. Although Western aid agencies and foreign ministries often make political party development one of their areas of attention in their democracy-building portfolio in a country, it is not such a high priority for them that they would be prone to build large-scale efforts on sweeping issues such as the rule of law and poverty for the sake of that goal. Even if they did, it is hardly clear they could produce decisive results in these areas that would actually make a transformative difference in the shape and operation of political parties. Trying to change the basic conditions in a country, for example, of socio-economic marginalization and vulnerability conditions that underlie the patterns of political patronage and thus have major consequences for political party life, is not something donor actors have been very successful at in many places. Similarly, numerous rule-of-law programs have been established but it is hard to point to many new or struggling democracies where basic institutional shortcomings of the rule of law have been substantially cured.

A different way that party aid might try to go deeper is by focusing on the relationship of the parties in a country to the overall distribution of power in that political system and trying to affect that distribution in ways that might contribute to democratization. A framework for thinking about party systems in this way—in terms of the relationship of parties to the distribution and exercise of power in the society—was presented in chapter 3. This was the taxonomy of party system types divided between party systems in largely nondemocratic countries (single-party systems, emasculated multiparty systems, and malign dominant party systems) and in relatively democratic countries (benign dominant party systems, unstable pluralistic party systems, and stable pluralistic party systems). Each of these types of systems presents a different challenge for aid providers interested in trying to think about party development from the perspective of the power relations and their relationship to democratization.

For example, in countries with emasculated multiparty systems, aid providers interested in working on political party development might view their central task not as helping parties become more internally democratic, less corrupt, more inclusive of women, and so forth. Instead they could focus on finding ways to help parties gain a more important position in the political system, to challenge those political actors that hold most of the power and keep parties down.

In Morocco, for example, which is a prime example of an emasculated multiparty system (due to the dominant political position of the monarchy), standard party aid confronts sharp structural limits. Training parties in campaign methods and in the basics of party organization may help prepare parties for the day when they gain a more important role in Morocco's political life. Such efforts struggle for traction in a context where the parties do not have much real power and are not taken very seriously by the public or the entrenched power sector of the society. The conventional training and other party reform efforts do not have much effect on the parties' overall political power, which depends greatly on the king and whether he decides to circumscribe his role and devolve significant power to the elected government.

If outside democracy promotion actors want to go deeper in supporting political party development in Morocco, doing so means pushing at the core political power arrangements of the country, and in particular, finding ways to encourage or pressure the king to move further on the path of democratic reform to which he has committed himself publicly. Outside party aid organizations are themselves not much in a position to engage in political suasion with the king or use diplomatic or economic carrots and sticks to encourage him to move ahead with political reforms. Such tasks fall more naturally to foreign ministries or other governmental bodies. If conceived in this broader way, therefore, support for party development ends up on their plate. Of course there is no guarantee of success. Various Western governments have for some time been gently urging the king to move ahead with democratization. There is little indication that such efforts have done much to speed up his naturally cautious, very slow approach. Even those Western governments, such as the U.S. government, that have encouraged Moroccan democratization are divided in themselves over how hard to push. Although they would like Morocco to lead the way to become a model of a successful path of gradualist reform leading to real democratization, they are as wary as the king of any rapid process of change, concerned that it might unleash sociopolitical forces that would take advantage of the opening to pursue extremist agendas.

Party aid groups inevitably have a limited role to play in the larger issue of the overall evolution of the political system. They can at least try, however, as for example NDI has done, to help Moroccan parties and other political actors focus on the core power conundrum that undercuts Moroccan parties. They can do this through work on constitutional reform, which represents the institutional heart of the deeper question of political change. Programs can be carried out that help the parties learn about comparative experiences with constitutional reform and meet as a group to formulate strategies for addressing the issue. Such efforts are in and of themselves unlikely to play any major role in changing Morocco's political life but at least they draw attention, and may make some modest contribution, to the central issue that will shape Morocco's political party development in the next five to ten years.

Russia also represents an emasculated party system (possibly en route to becoming a dominant party system if the Kremlin ends up vesting significant power in Unity, the party it has created to serve its interests). The weak, manipulated position of the parties is partially a product of the presidential system that discourages party development in various formal and informal ways. It is also the result of the authoritarian behavior of the Kremlin since 2000 and the strong antiparty legacy that the failed Soviet system left behind. Outside political assistance is very unlikely to be able to do anything to help produce or facilitate a structural change in Russia's presidential system. At the same time, doing whatever possible to limit President Putin's authoritarian drive is probably the most relevant form of support for party development.

As one Russian opposition party activist emphasized in an interview—the near-elimination of independent radio and television in Russia has been devastating to political party development. If Western governments wish to support Russian party development, he emphasized, they would do better to concentrate on exerting pressure for independent media than continuing with conventional training programs that do nothing to increase the limited political space available to parties. As with Morocco, if more broadly conceived, promoting party development in Russia would become the task of a wider range of outside actors than just political party groups, including Western leaders themselves. Again as with Morocco, this fact raises the question of how interested Western leaders actually are in Russian democratization. For most of Putin's time in office, U.S. and European leaders have made little objection to his soft authoritarian march, valuing Russian cooperation on economic and security matters.

In malign dominant power systems, like Belarus or Zimbabwe, where a ruling party has a stranglehold on power and is bent on frustrating the efforts of other parties to gain any significant power, party development hinges greatly on whether that stranglehold can be broken or loosened. Therefore, attempting to support party development might include various activities outside the immediate party domain such as exerting diplomatic pressure on the government's poor human rights performance and trying to bolster any existing independent sources of authority as power, such as judiciaries, independent media, or civil society activist groups. Or they might take the form of the multifaceted assertive electoral assistance campaigns that some U.S. and European democracy promotion organizations have mounted in recent years, such as in Belarus, Georgia, Serbia, and Ukraine. These campaigns support a broad set of civic groups and opposition political parties struggling to challenge a democratically dubious regime that is trying to legitimate its rule through elections. As discussed in chapter 6, the partisan nature of these campaigns causes controversy and pushback in the recipient countries. They face serious questions of legitimacy to the extent they appear to be regime change ventures rooted in the near-term foreign policy interests of the United States or other sponsoring countries rather than broader prodemocracy campaigns to support a free and fair election regardless of the outcome.

Even in democratic systems, the distribution and exercise of political power is also deeply interlinked with political party development and could more explicitly be the focus of party-related programs. Consider, for example, countries with benign dominant party systems, like Botswana, Mozambique, and South Africa. It is certainly possible in such contexts (in the sense of there being sufficient political space) to carry out conventional party training programs. Doing so is unlikely, however, to be very effective in terms of facilitating party development. Given the sharply unbalanced nature of the parties, the ruling party will usually be able to better take advantage of the assistance (having more party cadres, and often the funds necessary to build on the training activities with follow-up measures) and only grow in relative strength as a result of external assistance offered across the board to parties. The weaknesses of the opposition parties are often structurally rooted (such as an inability to generate sufficient funds to compete effectively due to the ruling party's controlling grip on the economic elite) with the result that training and other conventional types of aid will do little to change them. A key issue for party development in such situations is how much the dominant party entrenches its position and moves the country in the direction of a malign rather than benign dominant party system. The principal symptom of such an entrenchment is when the ruling party begins to blur the line between itself and the state. If it effectively fuses itself with the state—such as by channeling state resources to the party and completely populating the state with party-based personnel—other parties will have an extremely hard time gaining any ground.

Therefore a different way to support party development in such contexts, beyond conventional party reform programs, would be to focus on trying to help fortify the endangered line between the ruling party and the state. This might entail various types of initiatives—supporting studies by independent research institutes to identify and publicize the process of politicization of the state, supporting advocacy NGOs that carry out work to limit political uses of state resources, strengthening whatever safeguards exist within state agencies against party-state abuse, such as audit committees or governmental ombudsmen, and sponsoring multiparty dialogue processes to help create more opportunities for opposition parties to push systemic reforms, like party finance reforms. All such efforts would effectively be trying to affect the power balance in the country—that is, to check the power of the dominant party—and thus would likely not be easy. Nevertheless they would at least be focused on one of the key issues determining the overall course of party development.

Unstable distributed party systems are especially hard cases for party aid. This is true both in countries where parties have long failed to develop stable roots or forms, as in Brazil, Peru, and the Philippines, and countries where stable systems have recently collapsed, such as Venezuela. Party aid providers acknowledge in private that conventional assistance programs for parties gain little traction in such settings. Parties are exposed to ideas and knowledge about party reform and party building but continue to come and go from the political scene or, in the case of collapsed parties, to remain marginal. It is not a lack of knowledge about the methods of party building that is causing the chronic party instability. Deeper factors are at work, although it is not always clear what they are. Political scientists debate the causes of party instability, such as why Poland has failed to develop stable parties whereas Hungary has, or why Brazil lacks stable parties while Chile has them. They offer varying explanations, from differing social structures to the contrasting roles of particular leaders, without necessarily finding any definitive answers. It is not clear that party aid providers are going to be able to find ways of going beyond the conventional aid menu in such countries, futile though that menu usually proves to be.

The case of Guatemala highlights one possible explanation for party instability but also the difficulties aid providers would encounter if they attempted to address it directly. Insight into the cause of the persistent party instability in Guatemala can be understood by drawing a contrast with one of its neighbors, El Salvador. Both countries suffered through more than two decades of bloody civil war in which leftist insurgents based in remote provinces battled against a harshly repressive rightist military government representing the interests of the country's traditional socioeconomic elite. Both countries returned to elected civilian rule in the mid-1980s and ended their civil conflicts in the early 1990s. Yet whereas Guatemala has experienced highly unstable political party life since the return to civilian rule, Salvadoran politics have been characterized by a high degree of party stability with two large parties dominating the scene, the National Republican Alliance (ARENA) on the right and the former guerrilla movement turned party, the Farabundo Martí Liberation Front (FMLN) on the left.

Boiling a very complex comparative picture down to essentials, the main reason for this striking difference in party life appears to be the following: In El Salvador the civil war was a struggle between two strong sides that fought to a stalemate, with both being forced to accept that it could not destroy the other and would have to live with it in some way. As they began to move from war to peace, both sides decided to commit themselves to developing and backing a strong party that would represent their interests in electoral politics. The two main parties that emerged were rooted in the underlying power structures of the society, the popularistic leftist movement on the one side, and the business elite on the other.

A different process occurred in Guatemala. The civil war did not end in stalemate. The Guatemalan guerrillas were much weaker than their Salvadoran counterparts and were basically defeated by the Guatemalan security forces. When peace came, what remained of the rebel movement dedicated some effort to becoming a political party (the rebels splintered into several parties). They had neither the extensive popular base, strong organization, or political leadership skills that the Salvadoran guerrillas had. Their parties failed to gain much ground and quickly ended up on the political margins. The military-backed business elite did not invest significant energy or resources in building up one main political party. They chose to back different parties and candidates in successive elections, acting opportunistically from behind the political curtain rather than in a sustained, focused way through one party. In addition, some of the hardcore elements in the Guatemalan security forces continued to interfere in politics after the end of the civil war, undercutting democratic political life through intimidation, shady dealings and other behind-the-scenes maneuvering.

Thus in Guatemala, unlike El Salvador, the main power structures and forces that shaped the civil conflict did not translate into a few coherent, well-grounded parties. Despite many successive elections, the connection between the country's parties and the real holders of power remains weak. Not surprisingly, therefore, the many trainings and other institution-building programs by outside aid providers have not had much effect on Guatemala's party instability.

Whether it would be possible to go deeper to get at the roots of the instability is unclear. One approach might be to try to facilitate a more sustained, concentrated engagement by the business elite in party building, using the Salvadoran case as an example. Trying to change the Guatemalan business elite's traditional preference for acting behind the scenes to protect its interests and the contempt some parts of that elite maintain for democracy is not something mild external aid efforts can do. Similarly, trying to help some Guatemalan parties become genuinely rooted in the country's traditionally marginalized indigenous population sounds like a good idea, but faces profound obstacles that go to the very roots of Guatemalan society. It is certainly worth trying to go beyond the conventional approaches to party building in Guatemala to understand the underlying causes of the country's chronic party instability. The closer one gets to understanding the core causes, the more daunting the task of trying to help overcome them appears. This same reality likely prevails with each of the cases of countries that have relatively free political competition but a long record of party instability.

Finally there is the category of stable distributed party systems, such as those found in some parts of Central and Eastern Europe and Latin America (and of course in many long-established democracies). This is the one category of party system in the developing and postcommunist worlds that does not present any special challenges for democratization in terms of an unbalanced distribution of power or a disconnect between power structures and parties. Instead these are systems in which the normal organizational and operational shortcomings of parties often constitute the main challenges for aid providers looking to support political party development. Nevertheless, looking closely at these systems as a group, one can identify various special problems or issues that sometimes turn up. In some countries, such as Bangladesh, the two main parties, though somewhat stable and balanced in terms of overall power, are caught up in a dangerous pattern of increasing conflict, which results in destructive governmental dysfunctionality and threatens to degenerate into violence. Other countries appear to be in danger of sliding from a distributed power configuration into a dominant party system, due to the increasing grip of the ruling party and debilitation on the opposition's side. Argentina—where the Peronist Party is taking on some of the troubling characteristics of a malign dominant party—is one such case. Other distributed party systems face the challenge of incorporating rapidly rising social movements or other social groups that have traditionally been shut out, and to do so without the whole system breaking apart. The Bolivian political system, for example, is struggling to peacefully incorporate a newly powerful political actor—the indigenous movement led by President Evo Morales.

Each of these special problems or challenges constitutes a potential special focus for party aid providers seeking to go beyond the conventional menu of party strengthening activity toward a more politically strategic approach. Party aid in such places for example could concentrate on reducing conflict among parties in cases of aggravated standoffs in the party system, attempting to head off the slide toward a dominant party situation where a pluralist system is becoming unbalanced, or facilitating the adjustment of a party system to the incorporation of surging movements or other actors.

Challenges

All of these possible broader approaches to aiding party development are set forth only as very preliminary ideas to stimulate thinking about the challenge of going beyond standard approaches rooted in institutional modeling. Going deeper clearly entails some major challenges. First, it will require party aid organizations to develop a greater capacity for political analysis of recipient countries. Such analysis needs to go fully into the local political realities of each country while also applying some sort of comparative framework for assessing the role of parties in political development. Party aid providers have to begin to connect their programs more seriously to such analysis, to avoid falling back on the assumption that predesigned programs can basically be quickly tailored to fit any context. The funders behind party aid groups have to be willing to support more serious analytic preparation and redesign institutional incentives, not to reward the low-cost nature of cookie-cutter approaches.

Second, the institutional boundaries of party aid will have to expand. Going beyond conventional approaches means understanding and working with a variety of sectors in recipient societies around political parties, such as media organizations, advocacy groups, and legal institutions. It means applying levers other than just aid, such as diplomatic pressure. This implies that a wider range of organizations on the aid providers' side will need to be involved than just the usual set of traditional party aid organizations, from civil society aid groups to foreign ministries. Broadening the institutional basis of party work is both practically and conceptually difficult. It requires mobilizing new actors to get involved in a field that many are wary of (due to the unpromising nature of many political parties). It requires organizing and engaging them around a persuasive conception of the wider set of factors bearing on party development and an integrated vision of how different types of aid and other external interventions can be effectively brought to bear.

A third challenge of going deeper is dealing with the inevitably greater political sensitivity of efforts that confront the core power structures and arrangements in another society. Such efforts are necessarily more politically pointed or assertive than conventional approaches. In many countries, especially for example those with emasculated party systems or malign dominant party systems, an overconcentration of power is a primary obstacle to party development. Supporting efforts by people within the society to challenge that overconcentration will usually run into resistance. This has been evident in the cases where aid providers have stood behind opposition coalitions in semiauthoritarian countries. Greater resistance is likely to occur in all cases where aid providers go beyond the normally unassertive standard approaches to get closer to the political bone, even when it is not a question of support for political opposition groups per se. It is one thing, for example, for an external aid group to go to the African National Congress in South Africa and propose some typical multiparty training programs. It would be quite different and more controversial to go to them and propose a series of activities specifically designed to clarify and sharpen the boundary between the ANC and the South African state.

Political assertiveness is especially fraught with problems in the current global context of heightened suspicion about the whole enterprise of Western democracy promotion. It is an unfortunate fact that party aid providers are starting to evolve toward more politically incisive understandings of and approaches to party development at the very time when the overall climate for democracy promotion is extremely touchy, due to larger factors such as the Iraq War and the U.S. war on terrorism that have put off many people around the world from the very idea of democracy promotion. In this context it becomes especially incumbent upon party aid providers to show that it is possible to be more political in the design and implementation of their work in a principled way. That is to say they must become more political in service of prodemocratic principles, not in service of the near-term strategic interests of their funding government.

Notes

Chapter One

1. Samuel P. Huntington, *The Third Wave: Democratization in the Late Twentieth Century* (Norman, OK: University of Oklahoma Press, 1991). On the ebbing of the Third Wave see Larry Diamond, "Is the Third Wave Over?" *Journal of Democracy* 7, no. 3 (July 1996): 20–37; and Thomas Carothers, "The End of the Transition Paradigm," *Journal of Democracy* 13, no. 1 (January 2002): 5–21.

2. Cross-regional analysis is difficult due to lack of conformity of public opinion polls across different regions. Nevertheless the pattern of party unpopularity is clear. Richard Rose and Neil Munro find that on average only 11 percent of citizens in Central and Eastern Europe trust political parties, in *Elections and Parties in New European Democracies* (Washington, D.C.: Congressional Quarterly Press, 2003). Richard Rose's *New Baltic Barometer VI: A Post-Enlargement Survey* (Glasgow: University of Strathclyde, 2005) found that an average of only 10 percent of citizens in the Baltic states trusted political parties. Regarding the former Soviet Union, in 2001, only 7 percent of Russians trusted political parties, that number since 1994 having never risen above 14 percent. See Richard Rose, *A Decade of New Russia Barometer Surveys* (Glasgow: University of Strathclyde, 2002). An IFES survey, *Citizens' Awareness and Participation in Armenia Survey 2004* (Washington, D.C.: IFES, 2004), found that only 17 percent of Armenians somewhat trusted governing parties whereas only 19 percent somewhat trusted opposition parties. One year after the Orange Revolution in Ukraine, only 9 percent of Ukrainians said that parties serve the interests of the Ukrainian people and only 5 percent were members of a political party, according to another IFES survey, *Public Opinion in Ukraine, November 2005* (Washington, D.C.: IFES, 2005).

Concerning Latin America, an *Economist* report on the Latinobarometro, "The Latinobarometro Poll: Democracy's Low-Level Equilibrium," *Economist*, August 12, 2004, states that confidence in political parties hovered just below 20 percent and has been significantly lower during the past decade. Fernando Esteves, et al., *Democracy and Latin America: Towards Citizen's Democracy, Statistical Compendium* (New York: UNDP, 2005) highlights that in almost every country in the region, political parties consistently enjoy the least confidence of all public institutions. Mitchell A. Seligson's analysis of Mexico, Central America, and Colombia in *The Political Culture of Democracy in Mexico, Central America and Colombia, 2004* (Nashville, TN: Vanderbilt University Press, Latin American Public Opinion Project, 2004) shows that political parties are rated lowest of all public institutions. The Afrobarometer Network, in *Afrobarometer Round 2: Compendium of Comparative Results from a 15-Country Survey*, Working Paper 34 (March 2004), finds that only 55 percent of Africans consider multiparty government necessary, whereas 40 percent state that "political parties cause division and confusion ... it is therefore unnecessary to have many [of them] in this country." About half of Africans trust their ruling party, whereas only 23 percent trust the opposition party, as reported in Afrobarometer Network, *Key Findings about Public Opinion in Africa*, Briefing Paper 1 (April 2002). Relevant public opinion polls are scarce in the Middle East, but a 2005 poll by Al Arabiya found that 61 percent of respondents reported that lack of confidence in political parties actually prevented them from political participation (Al Arabiya Opinion Survey of the Arab Street 2005, World Economic Forum 2005, available at www.weforum.org/ site/homepublic.nsf/Content/Surveys%5CAl+Arabiya+Opinion+Survey+of+the+Arab+Street +2005. In Jordan, only 6 percent of people surveyed in 2004 felt that existing political parties represent the political, social, and economic aspirations of the population; in 2005 this number rose to 9.8 percent. See Public Opinion Poll Unit, *Democracy in Jordan 2005* (Amman: Center for Strategic Studies, University of Jordan, 2005).

The East Asia Barometer 2001–2002 revealed a low trust in parties in most parts of Asia. China's party trust rating was exceptionally high at 94 percent. Without China, the regional level of trust is 26.4 percent (*East Asia Barometer 2001–2002*). South Asians have a higher degree of trust in their parties, but still see them as profoundly corrupt and self-interested. Sixty-two percent of Pakistanis, for example, think that parties only serve their own interests and a mere 13 percent believe they represent the public interest, as elaborated in Gulmina Bilal, "Restoring Public Confidence in Political Parties," *News International*, September 26, 2005. In East and Southeast Asia, only 9.1 percent of the population considers political parties an important social group, as discussed in Takashi Inoguchi, *Values and Lifestyles in Urban Asia: A Cross-Cultural Analysis* (Tokyo: University of Tokyo, 2005). Even in Korea, a more established democracy, trust in political parties was only 15 percent in 2001, down from 20 percent in 1997 (*East Asia Barometer 2001–2002*), and Yun-han Chu, Larry Diamond, and Doh Chull Shin, "Halting Progress in Korea and Taiwan," *Journal of Democracy* 12, no. 1 (January 2001): 122–36.

3. Ivan Doherty, "Democracy Out of Balance: Civil Society Can't Replace Political Parties," *Policy Review* (April & May 2001): 25–35.

4. Two early articles provided some overview of the field of political party assistance: Joshua Muravchik, "U.S. Political Parties Abroad," *Washington Quarterly* 12, no. 3 (Summer 1989): 91–100, and Michael Pinto-Duschinsky, "Foreign Political Aid: The German Political Foundations and Their U.S. Counterparts," *International Affairs* 67, no. 1 (1991): 33–63. The small set of more recent writings on the subject includes Peter Burnell, ed., *Globalising Democracy: Party Politics in Emerging Democracies* (London: Routledge, 2006); Gero Erdmann, *Hesitant Bedfellows: The German Stiftungen and Party Aid in Africa. An Attempt at an Assessment*, Working Paper no. 184/50 (Warwick, UK: Centre for the Study of Globalisation and Regionalisation, December 2005); Krishna Kumar, "Reflections on International Party Assistance," *Democratization* 12, no. 4 (August 2005): 506–28; Stefan Mair, "Germany's Stiftungen and Democracy Assistance: Comparative Advantages, New Challenges," in *Democracy Assistance: International Co-operation for Democratization*, ed. Peter Burnell (London: Frank Cass, 2000);

USAID Political Party Development Assistance (Washington, D.C.: USAID Center for Democracy and Governance, April 1999); and Jos van Wersch and Jereon de Zeeuw, *Mapping European Democracy Assistance*, Working Paper no. 36 (The Hague: Netherlands Institute of International Relations, November 2005).

5. Two examples of USAID-commissioned evaluations of party work are ARD, Inc., *An Assessment of Political Party Building in Ukraine* (Arlington, VA: ARD, May 2000); and Management Systems International, *Evaluation of the Activities of the International Republican Institute and the National Democratic Institute in Albania, Bulgaria, Ukraine, and Lithuania* (Washington, D.C.: MSI, April 1996).

Chapter Two

1. There is a burgeoning literature on party development in Central and Eastern Europe. Some important works include Jane Leftwich Curry and Joan Barth Urban, eds., *The Left Transformed in Post-Communist Societies: The Cases of East-Central Europe, Russia and Ukraine* (Oxford: Rowman and Littlefield, 2003); Abby Innes, "Party Competition in Postcommunist Europe: The Great Electoral Lottery," *Comparative Politics* 35, no. 1 (2002): 85–104; John Ishiyama, ed., *Communist Successor Parties in Post-Communist Politics* (Commack, NY: Nova Science Publishers, 1999); John Ishiyama and András Bozóki, "Adaptation and Change: Characterizing the Survival Strategies of the Communist Successor Parties," *Journal of Communist Studies and Transition Politics* 17, no. 3 (September 2001): 32–51; Anna Maria Grzymala-Busse, *Redeeming the Communist Past: The Regeneration of Communist Parties in East Central Europe* (New York: Cambridge University Press, 2002); Herbert Kitschelt, Zdenka Mansfeldova, Radoslaw Markowski, and Gábor Tóka, *Post-Communist Party Systems: Competition, Representation, and Inter-Party Cooperation* (Cambridge: Cambridge University Press, 1999); Tomáš Kostelecký, *Political Parties after Communism* (Baltimore: Johns Hopkins University Press, 2003); Anatoly Kulick and Susanna Pshizova, *Party Politics in Post-Soviet Europe and the Baltics* (Westport, CT: Harcourt Education, 2005); Paul Lewis, *Political Parties in Post-Communist Eastern Europe* (London: Routledge, 2000); Paul Lewis, ed., *Party Development and Democratic Change in Post-Communist Europe: The First Decade* (London: Frank Cass, 2001); Frances Millard, *Elections, Parties and Representation in Post-Communist Europe* (Hampshire, UK: Palgrave, 2004); Geoffrey Pridham, "Complying with the European Union's Democratic Conditionality: Transnational Party Linkages and Regime Change in Slovakia, 1993–1998," *Europe-Asia Studies* 51, no. 7 (November 1999): 1221–44; Geoffrey Pridham and Attila Ágh, eds., *Prospects for Democratic Consolidation in East-Central Europe* (New York: Manchester University Press, 2001); Richard Rose and Neil Munro, *Elections and Parties in New European Democracies* (Washington, D.C.: Congressional Quarterly Press, 2003); Aleks Szczerbiak and Séan Hanley, *Centre-Right Parties in Post-Communist East-Central Europe* (Abingdon: Taylor and Francis, 2004); James Toole, "Straddling the East-West Divide: Party and Communist Legacies in East Central Europe," *Europe-Asia Studies* 55, no. 1 (January 2003): 101–18; Hubert Tworzecki, *Learning to Choose: Electoral Politics in East-Central Europe* (Stanford: Stanford University Press, 2003); and Ingrid Van Biezen, *Political Parties in New Democracies: Party Organization in Southern and East-Central Europe* (Basingstoke, UK: Palgrave Macmillan, 2003).

2. Ishiyama, *Communist Successor Parties*; and Grzymala-Busse, *Redeeming the Communist Past*.

3. Lewis, ed., *Party Development and Democratic Change*, 202.

4. Kostelecký, *Political Parties after Communism*.

5. Political parties in the former Soviet Union have attracted less scholarly attention than parties in Central and Eastern Europe. Some of the important studies include Vladimir Babak, Demian Vaisman, and Aryeh Wasserman, *Political Organization in Central Asia and Azerbaijan* (London: Frank Cass, 2004); Jack Bielasiak, "The Institutionalization of Electoral and Party Systems in Postcommunist States," *Comparative Politics* 34, no. 2 (January 2002): 189–210; Paul Chaisty, "Party Cohesion and Policy-Making in Russia," *Party Politics* 11, no. 3 (May 2005): 299–318; Kathleen Collins, "Clans, Pacts and Politics in Central Asia," *Journal of Democracy* 13, no. 3 (July 2002): 137–52; Nadia Diuk, "The Next Generation," *Journal of Democracy* 15, no. 3 (July 2004): 59–66; Grigorii V. Golosov, "Electoral Systems and Party Formation in Russia: A Cross-Regional Analysis," *Comparative Political Studies* 36, no. 8 (October 2003): 912–35; Grigorii V. Golosov, *Political Parties in the Regions of Russia* (Boulder, CO: Lynne Rienner, 2004); Henry E. Hale, "Why Not Parties? Electoral Markets, Party Substitutes, and Stalled Democratization in Russia," *Comparative Politics* 37, no. 2 (January 2005): 147–66; Henry E. Hale, "Yabloko and the Challenge of Building a Liberal Party in Russia," *Europe-Asia Studies* 56, no. 7 (November 2004): 993–1020; Henry E. Hale, "The Origins of United Russia and the Putin Presidency: The Role of Contingency in Party-System Development," *Demokratizatsiya* 12, no. 2 (Spring 2004): 169–94; John Ishiyama and Ryan Kennedy, "Superpresidentialism and Political Party Development in Russia, Ukraine, Armenia and Kyrgyzstan," *Europe-Asia Studies* 53, no. 8 (December 2001): 1177–91; Anatoly Kulik and Susanna Pshizova, eds., *Political Parties in Post-Soviet Space* (Westport, CT: Praeger, 2005); John Löwenhardt, *Party Politics in Post-Communist Russia* (London: Frank Cass, 1998); Michael McFaul, "Political Parties," in *Between Dictatorship and Democracy: Russian Post-Communist Political Reform*, eds. Michael McFaul, Nikolai Petrov, and Andrei Ryabov (Washington, D.C.: Carnegie Endowment, 2004); Michael McFaul, *Party Formation and Non-Formation in Russia*, Working Paper no. 12 (Washington, D.C.: Carnegie Endowment, May 2000); Arthur H. Miller and Thomas F. Klobucar, "The Development of Party Identification in Post-Soviet Societies," *American Journal of Political Science* 44, no. 4 (October 2000): 667–85; Regina Smyth, "Strong Partisans, Weak Parties? Party Organizations and the Development of Mass Partisanship in Russia," *Comparative Politics* 38, no. 2 (January 2006): 209–28; Lucan Way, "Pluralism by Default in Moldova," *Journal of Democracy* 13, no. 4 (October 2002): 127–41; and David White, *The Russian Democratic Party Yabloko: Opposition in a Managed Democracy* (Burlington, VT: Ashgate Publishing, 2006).

6. Way, "Pluralism by Default," 136–37.

7. Collins, "Clans, Pacts and Politics in Central Asia."

8. Diego Achard and Luiz E. González, *A Challenge to Democracy: Political Parties in Central America, Panama and Dominican Republic* (San Jose, Costa Rica: Inter-American Development Bank, International IDEA, Organization of American States and United Nations Development Programme, 2005); Katrina Burgess and Steven Levitsky, "Explaining Populist Party Adaptation in Latin America: Environmental and Organizational Determinants of Party Change in Argentina, Mexico, Peru and Venezuela," *Comparative Political Studies* 36, no. 8 (October 2003): 881–911; Michael Coppedge, "The Evolution of Latin American Party Systems," in *Politics, Society and Democracy: Latin America*, eds. Scott Mainwaring and Arturo Valenzuela (Boulder, CO: Westview Press, 1998); Michael Coppedge, "Political Darwinism in Latin America's Lost Decade," in *Political Parties and Democracy*, eds. Larry Diamond and Richard Gunther (Baltimore: Johns Hopkins University Press, 2001); Torcuato S. Di Tella,

History of Political Parties in Twentieth-Century Latin America (New Brunswick, NJ: Transaction Publishers, 2004); Roberto Espíndola, "Political Parties and Democratization in the Southern Cone of Latin America," *Democratization* 9, no. 3 (Autumn 2002): 109–30; Steven Griner and Daniel Zovatto, *From Grassroots to the Airwaves—Paying for Political Parties and Campaigns in the Caribbean* (Washington, D.C.: Organization of American States and International IDEA, 2005); Steven Levitsky, *Transforming Labor-Based Parties in Latin America: Argentine Peronism in Comparative Perspective* (Cambridge: Cambridge University Press, 2003); Raul L. Madrid, "Indigenous Parties and Democracy in Latin America," *Latin American Politics and Society* 47, no. 4 (Winter 2005): 161–79; Scott Mainwaring and Timothy R. Scully, eds., *Christian Democracy in Latin America: Electoral Competition and Regime Conflicts* (Stanford: Stanford University Press, 2003); Scott Mainwaring, "Party Systems in the Third Wave," in *The Global Divergence of Democracies*, eds. Larry Diamond and Marc F. Plattner (Baltimore: Johns Hopkins University Press, 2001); Scott Mainwaring and Matthew Soberg Shugart, *Presidentialism and Democracy in Latin America* (Cambridge: Cambridge University Press, 1997); Alejandro Moreno, *Political Cleavages: Issues, Parties and Consolidation of Democracy* (Boulder, CO: Westview Press, 1999); Kenneth Roberts and Erik Wibbels, "Party Systems and Electoral Volatility in Latin America: A Test of Economic, Institutional, and Structural Explanations," *American Political Science Review* 93, no. 3 (September 1999): 575–90; Christopher Sabatini, "The Decline of Ideology and the Rise of 'Quality of Politics' Parties in Latin America," *World Affairs* (Fall 2002): 106–10; Christopher Sabatini, "Latin America's Lost Illusions: Decentralization and Political Parties," *Journal of Democracy* 14, no. 2 (April 2003): 138–50; Hans Stockton, "Political Parties, Party Systems, and Democracy in East Asia: Lessons from Latin America," *Comparative Political Studies* 34, no. 1 (Summer 2003): 1–39; and Donna Lee Van Cott, *From Movements to Parties in Latin America: The Evolution of Ethnic Politics* (Cambridge: Cambridge University Press, 2005).

9. Coppedge, "Political Darwinism," 174–79; and Di Tella, *History of Political Parties.*

10. Di Tella, *History of Political Parties,* 187–89.

11. Roberts and Wibbels, "Party Systems and Electoral Volatility in Latin America."

12. Sabatini, "The Decline of Ideology."

13. Sabatini, "Decentralization and Political Parties."

14. Matthijs Bogaards, "Crafting Competitive Party Systems: Electoral Laws and the Opposition in Africa," *Democratization* 7, no. 4 (Winter 2000): 163–90; Michael Bratton and Nicolas van de Walle, *Democratic Experiments in Africa: Regime Transitions in Comparative Perspective* (Cambridge: Cambridge University Press, 1997); Peter Burnell, "The Party System and Party Politics in Zambia: Continuities Past, Present and Future," *African Affairs* 100 (2001): 239–63; Patrick Chabal and Jean-Pascal Daloz, *Africa Works: Disorder as Political Instrument* (London: The International African Institute, 1999); Larry Diamond and Marc F. Plattner, eds., *Democratization in Africa* (Baltimore: Johns Hopkins University Press, 1999); Gero Erdmann, "Party Research: Western European Bias and the 'African Labyrinth,'" *Democratization* 11, no. 3 (June 2004): 63–87; Hermann Giliomee and Charles Simkins, eds., *The Awkward Embrace: One-Party Domination and Democracy* (Cape Town: Tafelberg Publishers Ltd., 1999); Michelle Kuenzi and Gina Lambright, "Party Systems Institutionalization in 30 African Countries," *Party Politics* 7, no. 4 (2001): 437–68; Carrie Manning, "Assessing African Party Systems after the Third Wave," *Party Politics* 11, no. 6 (November 2005): 77–127; Edward R. McMahon, "Catching the 'Third Wave' of Democratization? Debating Political Party Effectiveness in Africa since 1980," *African and Asian Studies* 3, no. 3/4 (2004): 295–320; Minion K. C. Morrison, "Political Parties in Ghana through Four Republics: A Path to Democratic Consolidation,"

Comparative Politics (July 2004): 421–41; John Mukum Mbaku and Julius O. Ihonvbere, *Multiparty Democracy and Political Change: Constraints to Democratization in Africa* (Burlington, VT: Ashgate Publishing, 1998); Shaheen Mozaffar and James R. Scarritt, "The Puzzle of African Party Systems," *Party Politics* 11, no. 4 (July 2005): 399–421; Magnus Öhman, *The Heart and Soul of the Party: Candidate Selection in Ghana and Africa* (Uppsala, Sweden: Uppsala University, 2004); Vicky Randall and Lars Svåsand, "Political Parties and Democratic Consolidation in Africa," *Democratization* 9, no. 3 (Autumn 2002): 30–52; M. A. Mohamed Salih, ed., *African Political Parties: Evolution, Institutionalism and Governance* (London: Pluto Press, 2003); Raymond Suttner, "Democratic Transition and Consolidation in South Africa: The Advice of 'the Experts,'" *Current Sociology* 52, no. 5 (September 2004): 755–73; Raymond Suttner, "Transformation of Political Parties in Africa Today," *Transformation: Critical Perspectives on South Africa* 55 (2004): 1–27; Roger Southall, *Democracy in Africa: Moving Beyond a Difficult Legacy* (Pretoria, South Africa: HSRC Publishers, 2003); Oda van Cranenburgh and Petr Kopecký, "Political Institutions in New Democracies: (Not so) Hidden Majoritarianism in Post-Apartheid South Africa," *Acta Politica* 39 (2004): 279–96; and Nicolas van de Walle, "Presidentialism and Clientelism in Africa's Emerging Party Systems," *Journal of Modern African Studies* 42, no. 2 (2003): 297–321.

15. Van de Walle, "Presidentialism and Clientelism," 299.

16. M. A. Mohamed Salih, "Conclusions," in *African Political Parties*, ed. M. A. Mohamed Salih (London: Pluto Press, 2003).

17. Randall and Svåsand, "Political Parties and Democratic Consolidation in Africa."

18. Southall, *Democracy in Africa*, 30; Suttner, "Transformation of Political Parties in Africa," 2–9.

19. Van de Walle, "Presidentialism and Clientelism," 305.

20. Bratton and van de Walle, *Democratic Experiments in Africa*.

21. Abdo Baaklini, Guilain Denoeux, and Robert Springborg, *Legislative Politics in the Arab World: The Resurgence of Democratic Institutions* (Boulder, CO: Lynne Rienner, 1999); Ellen Lust-Okar, "Divided They Rule: The Management and Manipulation of Political Opposition," *Comparative Politics* 36, no. 2 (January 2004): 159–79; Ellen Lust-Okar and Amaney Ahmad Jamal, "Rulers and Rules: Reassessing the Influence of Regime Type on Electoral Law Formation," *Comparative Political Studies* 35, no. 3 (April 2002): 337–66; Roger Owen, *State, Power, and Politics in the Making of the Middle East*, 2nd ed. (New York: Routledge, 2000); Oliver Schlumberger, "The Arab Middle East and the Question of Democratization: Some Critical Remarks," *Democratization* 5, no. 4 (Winter 2000): 104–32; Frank Tachau, ed., *Political Parties of the Middle East and North Africa* (Westport, CT: Greenwood Press, 1994); Carrie Rosefsky Wickham, *Mobilizing Islam: Religion, Activism, and Political Change in Egypt* (New York: Columbia University Press, 2002); and Michael J. Willis, "Political Parties in the Maghrib: The Illusion of Significance?" *The Journal of North African Studies* 7, no. 2 (Summer 2002): 1–22.

22. Lust-Okar and Ahmad Jamal, "Rulers and Rules."

23. *Political Attitudes of the Moroccan Public* (Casablanca: Association Maroc 20/20, December 2001), 8.

24. Daniel Brumberg, "Liberalization versus Democracy," in *Uncharted Journey: Promoting Democracy in the Middle East*, eds. Thomas Carothers and Marina Ottaway (Washington, D.C.: Carnegie Endowment, 2005), 15–36.

25. Nathan J. Brown, Amr Hamzawy, and Marina Ottaway, *Islamist Movements and the Democratic Process in the Arab World: Exploring the Gray Zones*, Carnegie Paper no. 67 (Washington, D.C.: Carnegie Endowment, March 2006).

26. The grassroots success of the Muslim Brotherhood in Egypt is a primary case in point. See Wickham, *Mobilizing Islam.*

27. Craig Baxter et al., *Government and Politics in South Asia*, 5th ed. (Boulder, CO: Westview Press, 2002); Amrita Basu, *Women, Political Parties and Social Movements in South Asia* (Geneva: United Nations Research Institute for Social Development, 2005); Manali Desai, "Party Formation, Political Power and the Capacity for Reform: Comparing Left Parties in Kerala and West Bengal, India," *Social Forces* 80, no. 1 (September 2001): 37–60; Neil DeVotta, "Illiberalism and Ethnic Conflict in Sri Lanka," *Journal of Democracy* 13, no. 1 (January 2002): 84–98; John Hickman, "Explaining the Two-Party System in the Sri Lankan National Assembly," *Contemporary South Asia* 8, no. 1 (March 1999): 29–40; Subrata K. Mitra, Mike Enskat, and Clemens Spiess, eds., *Political Parties in South Asia* (Westport, CT: Praeger, 2004); Rounaq Jahan, "Bangladesh in 2002: Imperiled Democracy," *Asian Survey* 43, no. 1 (January/February 2003): 222–29; Susanne Hoeber Rudolph and Lloyd I. Rudolph, "New Dimensions of Indian Democracy," *Journal of Democracy* 13, no. 1 (January 2002): 52–66; Aqil Shah, "Democracy on Hold in Pakistan," *Journal of Democracy* 13, no. 1 (January 2002): 67–75; and E. Sridharan and Ashutosh Varshney, "Toward Moderate Pluralism: Political Parties in India," in *Political Parties and Democracy*, eds. Larry Diamond and Richard Gunther (Baltimore: Johns Hopkins University Press, 2001).

28. Baxter et al., *Government and Politics in South Asia.*

29. Sridharan and Varshney, "Toward Moderate Pluralism."

30. Jahan, "Bangladesh in 2002."

31. Jean Blondel, "The Role of Parties and Party Systems in the Democratization Process," in *Democracy, Governance and Economic Performance: East and Southeast Asia*, eds. Ian Marsh, Jean Blondel, and Takashi Inoguchi (New York: United Nations University Press, 1999); Yunhan Chu, "The Legacy of One-Party Hegemony in Taiwan," in *Political Parties and Democracy*, eds. Larry Diamond and Richard Gunther; Aurel Croissant, *Electoral Politics in Southeast and East Asia* (Singapore: Friedrich Ebert Stiftung, 2002); Larry Diamond and Marc F. Plattner, eds., *Democracy in East Asia* (Baltimore: Johns Hopkins University Press, 1998); Larry Diamond and Doh Chull Shin, eds., *Institutional Reform and Democratic Consolidation in Korea* (Stanford: Hoover Institution Press, 2000); Lowell Dittmer, Haruhiro Fukui, and Peter N. S. Lee, eds., *Informal Politics in East Asia* (Cambridge: Cambridge University Press, 2001); Amy L. Freedman, *Political Change and Consolidation: Democracy's Rocky Road in Thailand, Indonesia, South Korea and Malaysia* (New York: Palgrave Macmillan, 2006); James Gomez, *Between Freedom and Censorship: Asian Political Parties in Cyberspace* (Potsdam, Germany: Liberal Institute, Friedrich Naumann Stiftung, 2005); Eva-Lotta Hedman and John T. Sidel, *Philippine Politics and Society in the Twentieth Century: Colonial Legacies, Post-Colonial Trajectories* (New York: Routledge, 2000); Shuxian Jian and Lijun Sheng, *The Communist Party of China and Political Parties in Southeast Asia: A Comparative Study of India, Indonesia, the Philippines, South Korea and Thailand* (Singapore: Eastern University Press, 2003); Dwight Y. King, *Half-Hearted Reform: Electoral Institutions and the Struggle for Democracy in Indonesia* (Westport, CT: Praeger Publishers, 2003); Surin Maisrikrod, "Political Reform and the New Thai Electoral System: Old Habits Die Hard?" in *How Asia Votes*, eds. John Fuh-sheng Hsieh and David Newman (New York: Seven Bridges Press, 2002); Peter M. Manikas and Laura L. Thornton, *Political Parties in Asia* (Washington, D.C.: National Democratic Institute for International Affairs, 2003); Ian Marsh, Jean Blondel, and Takashi Inoguchi eds., *Democracy, Governance, and Economic Performance: East and Southeast Asia* (New York: United Nations University Press, 1999); Duncan McCargo, "Thailand's Political Parties: Re ¹, Authentic, and Actual," in *Political Change*

in Thailand: Democracy and Participation, ed. Kevin Hewison (London: Routledge, 1997); Paige Johnson Tan, "Anti-Party Reaction in Indonesia: Causes and Implications," *Contemporary Southeast Asia* 24, no. 3 (December 2002): 484–508; Benjamin Reilly, *Political Parties and Political Engineering in the Asia Pacific Region* (Honolulu: East-West Center, 2003); and Wolfgang Sachsenröder and Ulrike E. Frings, eds., *Political Party Systems and Democratic Developments in East and Southeast Asia: Vol. II, East Asia* (Aldershot, UK and Burlington, VT: Ashgate Publishing, 1998).

32. Diamond and Plattner, *Democracy in East Asia*.

33. Manikas and Thornton, *Political Parties in Asia*, 3.

34. Hedman and Sidel, *Philippine Politics and Society in the Twentieth Century*.

35. McCargo, "Thailand's Political Parties."

Chapter Three

1. Some of the key writings on the historical evolution of political parties include Maurice Duverger, *Political Parties* (New York: Wiley, 1951); Joseph LaPalombara and Myron Weiner, eds., *Political Parties and Party Development* (Princeton, NJ: Princeton University Press, 1966); Seymour Martin Lipset and Stein Rokkan, *Party Systems and Voter Alignments* (New York: Free Press, 1967); Robert Michels, *Political Parties: A Sociological Study of the Oligarchical Tendencies of Modern Democracy* (New York: Hearst's International Library, 1915); Angelo Panebianco, *Political Parties: Organization and Power* (New York: Cambridge University Press, 1988); and Giovanni Sartori, *Parties and Party Systems: A Framework for Analysis*, vol. 1 (Cambridge: Cambridge University Press, 1976). Some more recent general works on the historical evolution of parties in established democracies include Hans Daalder, "The Rise of Parties in Western Democracies," in *Political Parties and Democracy*, eds. Larry Diamond and Richard Gunther (Baltimore: Johns Hopkins University Press, 2001); David Broughton and Mark Donovan, eds., *Changing Party Systems in Western Europe* (London: Pinter Publishers, 1998); and Alan Ware, *Political Parties and Party Systems* (New York: Oxford University Press, 1995).

2. The literature on the contemporary condition of political parties in established democracies is vast. Kenneth Janda provides a useful literature review and bibliography in "Comparative Political Parties: Research and Theory," in *Political Science: The State of the Discipline II*, ed. Ada W. Finifter (Washington, D.C.: American Political Science Association, 1993), 163–92. Some important works on post–catch-all party change in the established democracies include Russell Dalton, *Democratic Challenges, Democratic Choices* (New York: Oxford University Press, 2004); Russell Dalton and Martin Wattenberg, eds., *Parties without Partisans: Political Change in Advanced Industrial Democracies* (New York: Oxford University Press, 2004); Richard Gunther, José Ramón Montero, and Juan J. Linz, eds., *Political Parties: Old Concepts and New Challenges* (Oxford: Oxford University Press, 2002); Peter Mair, *Party System Change: Approaches and Interpretations* (New York: Oxford University Press, 1999); Peter Mair, "Myths of Electoral Change and the Survival of Traditional Parties," *European Journal of Political Research* 24 (1993): 121–33; Thomas Poguntke, "Anti-Party Sentiment: Conceptual Thoughts and Empirical Evidence: Explorations in a Minefield," *European Journal of Political Research* 29 (1996): 319–44; Philippe C. Schmitter, "Parties Are Not What They Once Were," in *Political Parties and Democracy*, eds. Larry Diamond and Richard Gunther; and Steven Wolinetz, *Party Systems* (Hampshire, UK: Ashgate Publishing, 1998).

3. Richard Katz and Peter Mair, "Changing Models of Party Organization and Party Development: The Emergence of the Cartel Party," *Party Politics* 1, no. 1 (1995): 5–28; and Thomas Poguntke, "New Politics and Party Systems," *West European Politics* 10 (1987): 76–88. An illuminating analysis of different ideas about post–catch-all parties is provided in Steven B. Wolinetz, "Beyond the Catch-All Party: Approaches to the Study of Parties and Party Organization in Contemporary Democracies," in *Political Parties: Old Concepts and New Challenges*, eds. Richard Gunther, José Ramón Montero, and Juan J. Linz (Oxford: Oxford University Press, 2002).

4. Van Biezen makes a similar argument with specific reference to post-1989 party development in Central and Eastern Europe although she casts the difference as that between traditional European party development consisting of a process of "movement from society towards the state" whereas in postcommunist party development "parties can be seen to originate as parties of the state." See Ingrid van Biezen, "On the Theory and Practice of Party Formation and Adaptation in New Democracies," *European Journal of Political Research* 44 (2005): 147–74, 169.

5. Richard Gunther and Larry Diamond, "Types and Functions of Parties," in *Political Parties and Democracy*, eds. Diamond and Gunther.

6. David Kovick, "Political Parties, Reform and Corruption in Asia: An Examination of Eight Asian Countries," in *Political Parties in Asia*, eds. Peter M. Manikas and Laura L. Thornton (Washington, D.C.: National Democratic Institute, 2003).

7. Ann L. Craig and Wayne A. Cornelius, "House Divided: Parties and Political Reform in Mexico," in *Building Democratic Institutions: Party Systems in Latin America*, eds. Scott Mainwaring and Timothy R. Scully (Stanford: Stanford University Press, 1995); and Soledad Loaeza, "The National Action Party (PAN): From the Fringes of the Political System to the Heart of Change," in *Christian Democracy in Latin America: Electoral Competition and Regime Conflicts*, eds. Scott Mainwaring and Timothy R. Scully (Stanford: Stanford University Press, 2003).

8. Vicky Randall has explored many of these same issues, both with respect to the common features of parties in developing countries and the causes of these features. See for example, Vicky Randall, "Political Parties and Social Structure in the Developing World," in *Handbook of Party Politics*, eds. Richard Katz and William Crotty (Thousand Oaks, CA: Sage Publishing, 2005); Vicky Randall, "Party Systems and Voter Alignments in the New Democracies of the Third World," in *Party Systems and Voter Alignments Revisited*, eds. Lauri Karvonen and Stein Kuhnle (London: Routledge, 2000); and Vicky Randall and Lars Svåsand, "Party Institutionalization in New Democracies," *Party Politics* 8, no. 1 (2002): 5–29. Scott Mainwaring's work on Latin American political parties, in particular his analysis of party institutionalization, has been influential in analyses of parties throughout the developing world. See Scott Mainwaring and Timothy R. Scully, "Party Systems in Latin America," in *Building Democratic Institutions: Party Systems in Latin America*, eds. Scott Mainwaring and Timothy R. Scully (Stanford: Stanford University Press, 1995). He has recently applied his framework cross-regionally in *Party System Institutionalization and Party System Theory after the Third Wave of Democratization*, Working Paper no. 319 (Notre Dame, IN: Kellogg Institute, April 2005).

9. On the results of rule-of-law assistance see, generally, Thomas Carothers, ed., *Promoting the Rule of Law Abroad: In Search of Knowledge* (Washington, D.C.: Carnegie Endowment, 2006).

10. Some of the most important writings include Andre Blais and Louis Massicotte, "Electoral Systems," in *Comparing Democracies 2*, eds. Lawrence LeDuc, Richard G. Niemi, and Pippa Norris (London: Sage Publications, 2002); David M. Farrell, *Electoral Systems: A Com-*

parative Introduction (New York: Palgrave, 2001); Donald L. Horowitz, "Electoral Systems: A Primer for Decision Makers," *Journal of Democracy* 14 (October 2003): 115–27; Richard Katz, *Democracy and Elections* (New York: Oxford University Press, 1997); Arend Lijphart, *Electoral Systems and Party Systems: A Study of 27 Democracies 1945–1990* (Oxford: Oxford University Press, 1994); Douglas W. Rae, *The Political Consequences of Electoral Laws*, rev. ed. (New Haven, CT: Yale University Press, 1972); Andrew Reeve and Alan Ware, *Electoral Systems: A Comparative and Theoretical Introduction* (London: Routledge, 1992); Giovanni Sartori, *Comparative Constitutional Engineering: An Inquiry into Structures, Incentives and Outcomes*, 2nd ed. (New York: New York University Press, 1997); and Giovanni Sartori, "The Party Effects of Electoral Systems," in *Political Parties and Democracy*, eds. Larry Diamond and Richard Gunther (Baltimore: Johns Hopkins University Press, 2001).

11. Juan Linz, "The Perils of Presidentialism," *Journal of Democracy* 1, no. 1 (1990): 51–69; and Alfred Stepan and Cindy Skach, "Constitutional Frameworks and Democratic Consolidation: Parliamentarism versus Presidentialism," *World Politics* 46 (1993): 1–22. Mainwaring and Shugart take issue with some of Linz's arguments about presidentialism in Scott Mainwaring and Matthew Soberg Shugart, "Conclusions: Presidentialism and the Party System," in *Presidentialism and Democracy in Latin America*, eds. Scott Mainwaring and Matthew Soberg Shugart (Cambridge: Cambridge University Press, 1997).

12. On the issue of party decline in the United States, see Amy D. Burke, "Party Decline: A Primer," *The American Prospect* 38 (May/June 1998): 44–45; John J. Coleman, *Party Decline in America: Policy, Politics, and the Fiscal State* (Princeton, NJ: Princeton University Press, 1996); Bruce Keith, et al., *The Myth of the Independent Voter* (Berkeley: University of California Press, 1992); and Martin P. Wattenberg, *The Decline of American Political Parties, 1952–1996* (Cambridge, MA: Harvard University Press, 1998). On party decline more generally in the established democracies, see Russell Dalton and Martin Wattenberg, eds., *Parties without Partisans: Political Change in Advanced Industrial Democracies* (Oxford: Oxford University Press, 2000); Russell Dalton, *Democratic Choices, Democratic Challenges* (Oxford: Oxford University Press, 2004); Peter Mair, "Myths of Electoral Change and the Survival of Traditional Parties," *European Journal of Political Research* 24 (1993): 121–33; Thomas Poguntke, "Anti-Party Sentiment: Conceptual Thoughts and Empirical Evidence: Explorations into a Minefield," *European Journal of Political Research* 29 (1996): 319–44; Anders Widfeldt, "Party Membership and Party Representativeness," in *Citizens and the State*, eds. Hans-Dieter Klingemann and Dieter Fuchs (Oxford: Oxford University Press, 1995).

Chapter Four

1. The information in this section about party aid actors is drawn from (1) interviews and conversations with representatives of the party aid organizations concerned, (2) their websites, annual reports, and other organizational documents, and (3) the small body of independent writings on party aid, which are cited at specific points in the text, as relevant.

2. Jos van Wersch and Jereon de Zeeuw, *Mapping European Democracy Assistance*, Working Paper no. 36 (The Hague: Netherlands Institute of International Relations, November 2005), 7.

3. Cited in Stefan Mair, "Germany's Stiftungen and Democracy Assistance: Comparative Advantages, New Challenges," in *Democracy Assistance: International Co-operation for Democratization*, ed. Peter Burnell (London: Frank Cass, 2000), 131.

4. Van Wersch and de Zeeuw, *Mapping European Democracy Assistance*, 7–24.

5. Ibid., 3.

6. *A Handbook on Working with Political Parties* (New York: United Nations Development Programme, 2006).

7. Mair, "Germany's Stiftungen," 129–31.

8. Van Wersch and de Zeeuw, *Mapping European Democracy Assistance*, 13–16.

9. These percentage estimates were supplied directly to the author by IRI and NDI.

10. Paul E. Sigmund, "The Transformation of Christian Democratic Ideology: Transcending Left and Right, or Whatever Happened to the Third Way?" in *Christian Democracy in Latin America: Electoral Competition and Regime Conflicts*, eds. Scott Mainwaring and Timothy R. Scully (Stanford: Stanford University Press, 2003), 70.

11. Fritz Plasser and Gunda Plasser, *Global Political Campaigning: A Worldwide Analysis of Campaign Professionals and Their Practices* (Westport, CT: Praeger, 2002).

12. The factual material and analysis in this section was primarily derived from interviews with representatives of the party aid organizations concerned and with representatives of parties that participated in the aid programs.

13. See Carrie L. Manning, *The Politics of Peace in Mozambique: Post-Conflict Democratization, 1992–2000* (Westport, CT: Praeger, 2002), 105–11.

14. Interview in Maputo, with a representative of an international organization that worked on the 1994 and 1999 elections in Mozambique, May 2004.

15. Interview in Maputo, with USAID representative who worked on the party fund for the 1999 elections, May 2004.

Chapter Five

1. See Thomas Carothers, *Aiding Democracy Abroad: The Learning Curve* (Washington, D.C.: Carnegie Endowment, 1999), ch. 5.

2. Some of the *Stiftungen* used to give money to counterpart parties but stopped doing so in the 1980s after a scandal about such a payment led to a lawsuit and a ruling by the German constitutional court disallowing the *Stiftungen* from making such payments. See Stefan Mair, "Germany's Stiftungen," 131.

3. Author interview with member of Guatemalan Congress, April 2004.

4. Gero Erdmann, *Hesitant Bedfellows: The German* Stiftungen *and Party Aid in Africa. An Attempt at an Assessment*, Working Paper no. 184/50 (Warwick, UK: Centre for the Study of Globalisation and Regionalisation, December 2005).

5. National Democratic Institute for International Affairs, *Peru's Political Party System and the Promotion of Pro-Poor Reform* (Washington, D.C.: NDI, 2005), and National Democratic Institute for International Affairs, *Bolivia's Political Party System and the Incentives for Pro-Poor Reform* (Washington, D.C.: NDI, 2005).

6. Netherlands Institute for Multiparty Democracy, *Political Institutions Interactive Assessment* (The Hague: NIMD, 2005).

7. National Democratic Institute for International Affairs, *Political Party Accountability: Principles and Realities* (Final Report) (Washington, D.C.: NDI, 2003).

8. Christopher Sabatini, "Whom Do International Donors Support in the Name of Civil Society?" *Development in Practice* 12, no.1 (February 2002): 7–19.

9. The Nordic researchers are only at the exploratory stage but are at least pushing hard on a problem that merits attention.

Chapter Six

1. Fred Weir and Howard LaFranchi, "The East-West Stakes over Ukraine," *Christian Science Monitor* (November 26, 2004). The Kremlin used a wider range of tools than just money to try to influence the Ukrainian elections, including personal political influences, economic pressure, and the invocation of cultural ties. See Iris Kempe and Iyrna Solonenko, "International Orientation and Foreign Support," in *Presidential Election and Orange Revolution: Implications for Ukraine's Transition*, eds. Helmut Kurth and Iris Kempe (Kyiv: Friedrich Ebert Stiftung, 2005).

2. Author interview with director of the Bucharest office of one of the German *Stiftungen*, in Bucharest, September 2003.

3. U.S. State Department Briefing, June 27, 1995.

4. International Republican Institute, "Haiti Election Alert," June 27, 1995.

5. Walt Bogdanich and Jenny Nordbert, "Mixed U.S. Signals Helped Tilt Haiti toward Chaos," *New York Times*, January 29, 2006, 1, 8–10.

6. Lorne Craner, "A False Picture of Aristide," *Washington Times*, February 13, 2006, A19.

7. United States Agency for International Development, *USAID Political Party Assistance Policy*, September 2003, 1.

8. Author interview with representative of a European conservative party foundation, June 2003.

9. Thomas Carothers, "Ousting Foreign Strongmen: Lessons from Serbia," in *Critical Mission: Essays on Democracy Promotion*, ed. Thomas Carothers (Washington, D.C.: Carnegie Endowment, 2004).

10. See Dennis Krivosheev, "Belarus's External Relations," and Teresa Dumasy, "Belarus's Relations with the European Union: A Western Perspective," in *Contemporary Belarus: Between Dictatorship and Democracy*, eds. Elena A. Korosteleva, Colin W. Lawson, and Rosalind J. Marsh (London: Routledge, 2003); and John L. Löwenhardt, "Belarus and the West," in *Post-Communist Belarus*, eds. Stephen White, Elena Korosteleva, and John L. Löwenhardt (Oxford: Rowman and Littlefield, 2005). For discussions of the regime's reactions to real and perceived Western intervention, see Graeme P. Herd, "Colorful Revolutions and the CIS: 'Manufactured' versus 'Managed' Democracy?" *Problems of Post-Communism* 52, no. 2 (March–April 2005): 3–18; and David R. Marples and Lyubov Pervushina, "Belarus: Lukashenko's Red October," *Problems of Post-Communism* 52, no. 2 (March–April 2005): 19–28.

11. For a discussion of Western support of attempted and accomplished color revolutions, and regime reactions to them throughout the former Soviet Union, see Herd, "Colorful Revolutions and the CIS." For an assessment of the overall role that Western democracy assistance played in the revolutions of Serbia, Georgia, and Ukraine, see Michael McFaul, "Transitions from Post-Communism," *Journal of Democracy* 16, no. 3 (July 2005): 5–20. For detailed documentation of Western involvement in Ukraine's Orange Revolution, see Oleksandr Sushko and Olena Prystayko, "Western Influence," in *Revolution in Orange: The Origins of Ukraine's Democratic Breakthrough*, eds. Anders Åslund and Michael McFaul (Washington D.C.: Carnegie Endowment, 2006); and Iris Kempe and Iyrna Solonenko, "International Orientation and Foreign Support," in *Presidential Election and Orange Revolution: Implications for Ukraine's Transition*, eds. Helmut Kurth and Iris Kempe (Kyiv: Friedrich Ebert Stiftung, 2005). An account of Western political involvement in Georgia prior to the Rose Revolution is found in Charles H. Fairbanks Jr., "Georgia's Rose Revolution," *Journal of Democracy* 15, no. 2 (April 2004): 110–25.

12. Steven Lee Myers, "Bringing Down Europe's Last Ex-Soviet Dictator," *New York Times Sunday Magazine*, February 26, 2006, 48.

13. See for example Ian Traynor, "Tick, Tick: Regime Change in Europe, Made in America," *The Guardian*, November 27, 2004.

Chapter Seven

1. Author interview with Ebert Stiftung representative, Rabat, Morocco, May 2005.

2. Attila Ágh, *The Europeanization of Social Democracy in East Central Europe* (Bonn: Friedrich Ebert Stiftung, May 2004), 4–7.

3. Author interview with representative of Konrad Adenauer Stiftung, Moscow, October 2003.

4. Author interview with leader of Kosovar political party, Pristina, Kosovo, February 2003.

5. Sarah Mendelson analyzes the effects of U.S. party aid on the campaign practices of Russian recipient parties in "Democracy Assistance and Political Transition in Russia," *International Security* 25, no. 4 (Spring 2001): 68–106.

Chapter Eight

1. The literature on the effects of electoral systems on parties and party systems is very large. Some of the major works include David Farrell, *Electoral Systems: A Comparative Introduction* (New York: Palgrave, 2001); David L. Horowitz, "Electoral Systems: A Primer for Decision Makers," *Journal of Democracy* 14, no. 4 (October 2003): 115–27; Douglas W. Rae, *The Political Consequences of Electoral Laws*, rev. ed. (New Haven, CT: Yale University Press, 1972); and Giovanni Sartori, "The Party Effects of Electoral Systems," in *Political Parties and Democracy*, eds. Larry Diamond and Richard Gunther (Baltimore: Johns Hopkins University Press, 2001).

2. Andrews Reynolds, Ben Reilly, and Andrew Ellis, *Electoral System Design: The New International IDEA Handbook* (Stockholm: International IDEA, 2005).

3. Kenneth Janda, *Political Parties and Democracy in Theoretical and Practical Perspectives: Adopting Party Law* (Washington, D.C.: National Democratic Institute, 2005), 3.

4. Ibid., 8–18.

5. Reginald Austin and Maja Tjernström, eds., *Funding of Political Parties and Election Campaigns* (Stockholm: International IDEA, 2003); Shari Bryan and Denise Baer, eds., *Money in Politics: A Study of Party Financing in 22 Countries* (Washington, D.C.: National Democratic Institute, 2005); Peter Burnell and Alan Ware, eds., *Funding Democratisation* (Manchester, UK: Manchester University Press, 1998); Jānis Ikstens, et al., *Campaign Finance in Central and Eastern Europe* (Washington, D.C.: International Foundation for Election Systems, 2002); Michael Johnston, *Political Parties and Democracy in Theoretical and Practical Perspectives: Political Finance Policy, Parties and Democratic Development* (Washington, D.C.: National Democratic Institute, 2005); National Democratic Institute for International Affairs, *Funding of Political Parties: An International Comparative Study* (Washington D.C.: National Democratic Institute, 1998); United States Agency for International Development, *Money in Politics Handbook: A Guide to Increasing Transparency in Emerging Democracies* (Washington, D.C.: USAID, 2003); and Marcin Walecki, *Political Money and Corruption*, IFES Political Finance White Paper Series (Washington, D.C.: IFES, 2004).

6. Austin and Tjernström, eds., *Funding of Political Parties and Election Campaigns*.

7. Alan Ware, "Conclusion," in *Funding Democratisation*, eds. Peter Burnell and Alan Ware (Manchester, UK: Manchester University Press, 1998).

8. Michael Pinto-Duschinsky, "Financing Politics: A Global View," *Journal of Democracy* 13, no. 4 (October 2002): 69–85, 72.

9. Sefakor Ashiagbor, *Party Finance Reform in Africa* (Washington, D.C.: National Democratic Institute, 2005).

10. Open Society Justice Initiative, *Monitoring Election Campaign Finance: A Handbook for NGOs* (New York: Open Society Institute, 2005).

11. Pinto-Duschinsky, "Financing Politics," 80.

12. Patricia Ahern, Paul Nuti, and Julia M. Masterson, *Promoting Gender Equity in the Democratic Process: Women's Paths to Political Participation and Decisionmaking* (Washington, D.C.: International Center for Research on Women and the Centre for Development and Population Activities, 2000); Julie Ballington and Azza Karam, eds., *Women in Parliament: Beyond Numbers. A New Edition* (Stockholm: International Institute for Democracy and Electoral Assistance, 2005); Lane Kenworthy and Melissa Malami, "Gender Inequality in Political Representation: A Worldwide Comparative Analysis," *Social Forces* 78, no. 1 (September 1999): 235–68; Arend Lijphart, *Electoral Systems and Party Systems: A Study of 27 Democracies 1945–1990* (Oxford: Oxford University Press, 1994); Fiona J. Macaulay, "Cross-Party Alliances around Gender Agendas: Critical Mass, Critical Actors, Critical Structures, or Critical Junctures," UN document no. EGM/EPWD/2005/EP.12 (December 12, 2005); Management Systems International and International Foundation for Elections Systems, *Women in Politics: An Analysis of Donor Strategies* (Washington, D.C.: U.S. Agency for International Development Global Bureau Center for Democracy and Governance, 1998); Amy Mazur, "The Impact of Women's Participation and Leadership on Policy Outcomes: A Focus on Women's Policy Machineries," UN doc. no. EGM/EPWD/2005/EP.5 (December 12, 2005); National Democratic Institute for International Affairs, *Nominating for Change: Strengthening Women's Position in Political Parties* (Jakarta and Washington, D.C.: National Democratic Institute for International Affairs, 2003); Barbara Nelson and Najma Chowdhury, eds., *Women and Politics Worldwide* (New Haven, CT: Yale University Press, 1994); and Shirin M. Rai, *International Perspectives on Gender and Democratisation* (New York: St. Martin's Press, 2000).

13. Helena Catt, "How Can Women MPs Make a Difference? Reconsidering Group Representation and the Responsible Party Model," Occasional Paper No. 6 (Belfast: Queen's University, October 2003); Joni Lovenduski, et al., "Making an Impact," in *Women in Parliament: Beyond Numbers. A New Edition*, eds. Julie Ballington and Azza Karam (Stockholm: International Institute for Democracy and Electoral Assistance, 2005); Amy Mazur, "The Impact of Women's Participation and Leadership on Policy Outcomes: A Focus on Women's Policy Machineries," UN doc. no. EGM/EPWD/2005/EP.5 (December 12, 2005); Rosa Lina T. Miranda, "Impact of Women's Participation and Leadership on Outcomes," UN doc. no. EGM/EPWD/2005/EP. 7 (December 12, 2005); and Hung-En Sung, "From Victims to Saviors? Women, Power and Corruption," *Current History* 105, no. 689 (March 2006): 139–43.

Bibliography

Achard, Diego, and Luiz E. González. *A Challenge to Democracy: Political Parties in Central America, Panama and Dominican Republic.* San Jose, Costa Rica: Inter-American Development Bank, International IDEA, Organization of American States, and United Nations Development Programme, 2005.

Ágh, Attila. *The Europeanization of Social Democracy in East Central Europe.* Bonn: Friedrich Ebert Stiftung, May 2004.

ARD, Inc. *An Assessment of Political Party Building in Ukraine.* Arlington, VA: ARD, May 2000.

Ashiagbor, Sefakor. *Party Finance Reform in Africa.* Washington, D.C.: National Democratic Institute, 2005.

Austin, Reginald, and Maja Tjernström, eds. *Funding of Political Parties and Election Campaigns.* Stockholm: International IDEA, 2003.

Baaklini, Abdo, Guilain Denoeux, and Robert Springborg. *Legislative Politics in the Arab World: The Resurgence of Democratic Institutions.* Boulder, CO: Lynne Rienner, 1999.

Babak, Vladimir, Demian Vaisman, and Aryeh Wasserman. *Political Organization in Central Asia and Azerbaijan.* London: Frank Cass, 2004.

Ballington, Julie, and Azza Karam, eds. *Women in Parliament: Beyond Numbers,* 2nd ed. Stockholm: International Institute for Democracy and Electoral Assistance, 2005.

Basu, Amrita. *Women, Political Parties and Social Movements in South Asia.* Geneva: United Nations Research Institute for Social Development, 2005.

Baxter, Craig, et al. *Government and Politics in South Asia,* 5th ed. Boulder, CO: Westview Press, 2002.

Bielasiak, Jack. "The Institutionalization of Electoral and Party Systems in Postcommunist States." *Comparative Politics* 34, no. 2 (January 2002): 189–210.

Blondel, Jean. "The Role of Parties and Party Systems in the Democratization Process." In *Democracy, Governance and Economic Performance: East and Southeast Asia.* Edited by Ian

Marsh, Jean Blondel, and Takashi Inoguchi. New York: United Nations University Press, 1999.

Bogaards, Matthijs. "Crafting Competitive Party Systems: Electoral Laws and Opposition in Africa." *Democratization* 7, no. 4 (Winter 2000): 163–90.

Blais, Andre, and Louis Massicotte. "Electoral Systems." In *Comparing Democracies 2*. Edited by Lawrence LeDuc, Richard G. Niemi, and Pippa Norris. London: Sage Publications, 2002.

Bogdanich, Walt, and Jenny Nordbert. "Mixed U.S. Signals Helped Tilt Haiti toward Chaos," *New York Times*, January 29, 2006, 1, 8–10.

Bratton, Michael, and Nicolas van de Walle. *Democratic Experiments in Africa: Regime Transitions in Comparative Perspective*. Cambridge: Cambridge University Press, 1997.

Broughton, David, and Mark Donovan, eds. *Changing Party Systems in Western Europe*. London: Pinter Publishers, 1998.

Bryan, Shari, and Denise Baer, eds. *Money in Politics: A Study of Party Financing in 22 Countries*. Washington, D.C.: National Democratic Institute, 2005.

Burgess, Katrina, and Steven Levitsky. "Explaining Populist Party Adaptation in Latin America: Environmental and Organizational Detriments of Party Change in Argentina, Mexico, Peru and Venezuela." *Comparative Political Studies* 36, no. 8 (October 2003): 881–911.

Burnell, Peter. "The Party System and Party Politics in Zambia: Continuities Past, Present and Future." *African Affairs* 100 (2001): 239–63.

———, ed. *Globalising Democracy: Party Politics in Emerging Democracies*. London: Routledge, 2006.

Burnell Peter, and Alan Ware, eds. *Funding Democratisation*. Manchester, UK: Manchester University Press, 1998.

Carothers, Thomas. *Aiding Democracy Abroad: The Learning Curve*. Washington, D.C.: Carnegie Endowment, 1999.

———. "Ousting Foreign Strongmen: Lessons from Serbia." In *Critical Mission: Essays on Democracy Promotion*. Edited by Thomas Carothers. Washington, D.C.: Carnegie Endowment, 2004.

———, ed. *Promoting the Rule of Law Abroad: In Search of Knowledge*. Washington, D.C.: Carnegie Endowment, 2006.

———. "The End of the Transition Paradigm." *Journal of Democracy* 13, no. 1 (January 2002): 5–21.

Catt, Helena. "How Can Women MPs Make a Difference? Reconsidering Group Representation and the Responsible Party Model." Occasional Paper No. 6. Belfast: Queen's University (October 2003).

Chabal, Patrick, and Jean-Pascal Daloz. *Africa Works: Disorder as Political Instrument*. London: The International African Institute, 1999.

Chaisty, Paul. "Party Cohesion and Policy-Making in Russia." *Party Politics* 11, no. 3 (May 2005): 299–318.

Chu, Yun-han, Larry Diamond, and Doh Chull Shin. "Halting Progress in Korea and Taiwan." *Journal of Democracy* 12, no. 1 (January 2001): 122–36.

Coleman, John J. *Party Decline in America: Policy, Politics, and the Fiscal State.* Princeton, NJ: Princeton University Press, 1996.

Collins, Kathleen. "Clans, Pacts and Politics in Central Asia." *Journal of Democracy* 13, no. 3 (July 2002): 137–52.

Coppedge, Michael. "The Evolution of Latin American Party Systems." In *Politics, Society and Democracy: Latin America.* Edited by Scott Mainwaring and Arturo Valenzuela. Boulder, CO: Westview Press, 1998.

———. "Political Darwinism in Latin America's Lost Decade." In *Political Parties and Democracy.* Edited by Larry Diamond and Richard Gunther. Baltimore: Johns Hopkins University Press, 2001.

Craig, Ann L., and Wayne A. Cornelius. "House Divided: Parties and Political Reform in Mexico." In *Building Democratic Institutions: Party Systems in Latin America.* Edited by Scott Mainwaring and Timothy R. Scully. Stanford: Stanford University Press, 1995.

Cranenburgh, Oda van, and Petr Kopecký. "Political Institutions in New Democracies: (Not so) Hidden Majoritarianism in Post-Apartheid South Africa." *Acta Politica* 39 (2004): 279–96.

Craner, Lorne. "A False Picture of Aristide." *Washington Times,* February 13, 2006, A19.

Croissant, Aurel, ed. *Electoral Politics in Southeast and East Asia.* Singapore: Friedrich-Ebert Stiftung, 2002.

Curry, Jane Leftwich, and Joan Barth Urban, eds. *The Left Transformed in Post-Communist Societies: The Cases of East-Central Europe, Russia and Ukraine.* Oxford: Rowman and Littlefield, 2003.

Daalder, Hans. "The Rise of Parties in Western Democracies." In *Political Parties and Democracy.* Edited by Larry Diamond and Richard Gunther. Baltimore: Johns Hopkins University Press, 2001.

Dalton, Russell. *Democratic Challenges, Democratic Choices.* New York: Oxford University Press, 2004.

Dalton, Russell, and Martin Wattenberg, eds. *Parties without Partisans: Political Change in Advanced Industrial Democracies.* New York: Oxford University Press, 2004.

DeVotta, Neil. "Illiberalism and Ethnic Conflict in Sri Lanka." *Journal of Democracy* 13, no. 1 (January 2002): 84–98.

Di Tella, Torcuato S. *History of Political Parties in Twentieth-Century Latin America.* New Brunswick, NJ: Transaction Publishers, 2004.

Diamond, Larry. "Is the Third Wave Over?" *Journal of Democracy* 7, no. 3 (July 1996): 20–37.

Diamond, Larry, and Marc F. Plattner, eds. *Democratization in Africa.* Baltimore: Johns Hopkins University Press, 1999.

———, eds. *Democracy in East Asia.* Baltimore: Johns Hopkins University Press, 1998.

Diamond, Larry, and Doh Chull Shin, eds. *Institutional Reform and Democratic Consolidation in Korea.* Stanford: Hoover Institution Press, 2000.

Diamond, Larry, and Richard Gunther, eds. *Political Parties and Democracy*. Baltimore: Johns Hopkins University Press, 2001.

Dittmer, Lowell, Haruhiro Fukui, and Peter N.S. Lee, eds. *Informal Politics in East Asia*. Cambridge: Cambridge University Press, 2001.

Diuk, Nadia. "The Next Generation." *Journal of Democracy* 15, no. 3 (July 2004): 59–66.

Doherty, Ivan. "Democracy Out of Balance: Civil Society Can't Replace Political Parties." *Policy Review* (April & May 2001): 25–35.

Dumasy, Teresa. "Belarus's Relations with the European Union: A Western Perspective." In *Contemporary Belarus: Between Dictatorship and Democracy*. Edited by Elena A. Korosteleva, Colin W. Lawson, and Rosalind J. Marsh. London: Routledge, 2003.

Duverger, Maurice. *Political Parties*. New York: Wiley, 1951.

Erdmann, Gero. *Hesitant Bedfellows: The German* Stiftungen *and Party Aid in Africa. An Attempt at an Assessment*. Working Paper no. 184/50. Warwick, UK: Centre for the Study of Globalisation and Regionalisation, December 2005.

———. "Party Research: Western European Bias and the 'African Labyrinth.'" *Democratization* 11, no. 3 (June 2004): 63–87.

Espíndola, Roberta. "Political Parties and Democratization in the South Cone of Latin America." *Democratization* 9, no. 3 (Autumn 2002): 109–30.

Fairbanks Jr., Charles H. "Georgia's Rose Revolution." *Journal of Democracy* 15, no. 2 (April 2004): 110–25.

Farrell, David M. *Electoral Systems: A Comparative Introduction*. New York: Palgrave, 2001.

Freedman, Amy L. *Political Change and Consolidation: Democracy's Rocky Road in Thailand, Indonesia, South Korea and Malaysia*. New York: Palgrave Macmillan, 2006.

Giliomee, Hermann, and Charles Simkins, eds. *The Awkward Embrace: One Party Domination and Democracy*. Cape Town: Tafelberg Publishers Ltd., 1999.

Golosov, Grigorii V. "Electoral Systems and Party Formation in Russia: A Cross-Regional Analysis." *Comparative Political Studies* 36, no. 8 (October 2003): 912–35.

———. *Political Parties in the Regions of Russia*. Boulder, CO: Lynne Rienner, 2004.

Griner, Steven, and Daniel Zovatto. *From Grassroots to the Airwaves—Paying for Political Parties and Campaigns in the Caribbean*. Washington, D.C.: Organization of American States and International IDEA, 2005.

Grzymala-Busse, Anna Maria. *Redeeming the Communist Past: The Regeneration of Communist Parties in East Central Europe*. New York: Cambridge University Press, 2002.

Gunther, Richard, José Ramón Montero, and Juan J. Linz, eds. *Political Parties: Old Concepts and New Challenges*. Oxford: Oxford University Press, 2002.

Hale, Henry E. "Why Not Parties? Electoral Markets, Party Substitutes, and Stalled Democratization in Russia." *Comparative Politics* 37, no. 2 (January 2005): 147–66.

———. "Yabloko and the Challenge of Building a Liberal Party in Russia." *Europe-Asia Studies* 56, no. 7 (November 2004): 993–1020.

———. "The Origins of United Russia and the Putin Presidency: The Role of Contingency in Party-System Development." *Demokratizatsiya* 12, no. 2 (Spring 2004): 169–94.

Herd, Graeme P. "Colorful Revolutions and the CIS: 'Manufactured' Versus 'Managed' Democracy?" *Problems of Post-Communism* 52, no. 2. (March–April 2005): 3–18.

Hickman, John. "Explaining the Two-Party System in the Sri Lankan National Assembly." *Contemporary South Asia* 8, no. 1 (March 1999): 29–40.

Horowitz, Donald L. "Electoral Systems: A Primer for Decision Makers." *Journal of Democracy* 14 (October 2003): 115–27.

Huntington, Samuel P. *The Third Wave: Democratization in the Late Twentieth Century.* Norman, OK: University of Oklahoma Press, 1991.

Ikstens, Jānis, et al. *Campaign Finance in Central and Eastern Europe.* Washington, D.C.: International Foundation for Election Systems, 2002.

Innes, Abby. "Party Competition in Postcommunist Europe: The Great Electoral Lottery." *Comparative Politics* 35, no. 1 (2002): 85–104.

International Republican Institute. "Haiti Election Alert." June 27, 1995.

Ishiyama, John, ed. *Communist Successor Parties in Post-Communist Politics.* Commack, NY: Nova Science Publishers, 1999.

Ishiyama, John, and Ryan Kennedy. "Superpresidentialism and Political Party Development in Russia, Ukraine, Armenia and Kyrgyzstan." *Europe-Asia Studies* 53, no. 8 (December 2001): 1177–91.

Ishiyama, John, and András Bozóki. "Adaptation and Change: Characterizing the Survival Strategies of the Communist Successor Parties." *Journal of Communist Studies and Transition Politics* 17, no. 3 (September 2001): 32–51.

Janda, Kenneth. "Comparative Political Parties: Research and Theory." In *Political Science: The State of the Discipline II.* Edited by Ada W. Finifter. Washington, D.C.: American Political Science Association, 1993: 163–92.

———. *Political Parties and Democracy in Theoretical and Practical Perspectives: Adopting Party Law.* Washington, D.C.: National Democratic Institute, 2005.

Jian, Shuxian, and Lijun Sheng. *The Communist Party of China and Political Parties in Southeast Asia: A Comparative Study of India, Indonesia, the Philippines, South Korea and Thailand.* Singapore: Eastern University Press, 2003.

Johnston, Michael. *Political Parties and Democracy in Theoretical and Practical Perspectives: Political Finance Policy, Parties and Democratic Development.* Washington, D.C.: National Democratic Institute, 2005.

Katz, Richard, and Peter Mair. "Changing Models of Party Organization and Party Development: The Emergence of the Cartel Party." *Party Politics* 1, no. 1 (1995): 5–28.

———. *Democracy and Elections.* New York: Oxford University Press, 1997.

Kempe, Iris, and Iyrna Solonenko. "International Orientation and Foreign Support." In *Presidential Election and Orange Revolution: Implications for Ukraine's Transition.* Edited by Helmut Kurth and Iris Kempe. Kyiv: Friedrich Ebert Stiftung, 2005.

King, Dwight Y. *Half-Hearted Reform: Electoral Institutions and the Struggle for Democracy in Indonesia.* Westport, CT: Praeger Publishers, 2003.

Kitschelt, Herbert, Zdenka Mansfeldova, Radoslaw Markowski, and Gábor Tóka. *Post-Communist Party Systems: Competition, Representation, and Inter-Party Cooperation.* New York: Cambridge University Press, 1999.

Kostelecký, Tomáš. *Political Parties after Communism.* Baltimore: Johns Hopkins University Press, 2003).

Kulick, Anatoly, and Susanna Pshizova. *Party Politics in Post-Soviet Europe and the Baltics.* Westport, CO: Harcourt Education, 2005.

———, eds. *Political Parties in Post-Soviet Space.* Westport, CT: Praeger, 2005.

Kumar, Krishna. "Reflections on International Party Assistance." *Democratization* 12, no. 4 (August 2005): 506–28.

LaPalombara, Joseph, and Myron Weiner, eds. *Political Parties and Party Development.* Princeton, NJ: Princeton University Press, 1966.

Lewis, Paul. *Political Parties in Post-Communist Eastern Europe.* London: Routledge, 2000.

———, ed. *Party Development and Democratic Change in Post-Communist Europe: The First Decade.* London: Frank Cass, 2001.

Levitsky, Steven. *Transforming Labor-Based Parties in Latin America: Argentine Peronism in Comparative Perspective.* Cambridge: Cambridge University Press, 2003.

Lijphart, Arend. *Electoral Systems and Party Systems: A Study of 27 Democracies 1945–1990.* Oxford: Oxford University Press, 1994.

Linz, Juan. "The Perils of Presidentialism." *Journal of Democracy* 1, no. 1 (1990): 51–69.

Lipset, Seymour Martin, and Stein Rokkan. *Party Systems and Voter Alignments.* New York: Free Press, 1967.

Löwenhardt, John. *Party Politics in Post-Communist Russia.* London: Frank Cass, 1998.

Lust-Okar, Ellen. "Divided They Rule: The Management and Manipulation of Political Opposition." *Comparative Politics* 36, no. 2 (January 2004): 159–79.

Lust-Okar, Ellen, and Amaney Ahmad Jamal. "Rulers and Rules: Reassessing the Influence of Regime Type on Electoral Law Formation." *Comparative Political Studies* 35, no. 3, (April 2002): 337–66.

Madrid, Raul L. "Indigenous Parties and Democracy in Latin America." *Latin American Politics and Society* 47, no. 4 (Winter 2005): 161–79.

Mainwaring, Scott. "Party Systems in the Third Wave." In *The Global Divergence of Democracies.* Edited by Larry Diamond and Marc F. Plattner. Baltimore: Johns Hopkins University Press, 2001.

Mainwaring, Scott, and Timothy R. Scully, eds. *Building Democratic Institutions: Party Systems in Latin America.* Stanford: Stanford University Press, 1995.

———, eds. *Christian Democracy in Latin America: Electoral Competition and Regime Conflicts.* Stanford: Stanford University Press, 2003.

Mainwaring, Scott, and Matthew Soberg Shugart. *Presidentialism and Democracy in Latin America*. Cambridge: Cambridge University Press, 1997.

Mainwaring, Scott, and Mariano Torcal. *Party System Institutionalization and Party System Theory after the Third Wave of Democratization*. Working Paper no. 319. Notre Dame, IN: Kellogg Institute, April 2005.

Mair, Peter. *Party System Change: Approaches and Interpretations*. New York: Oxford University Press, 1999.

———. "Myths of Electoral Change and the Survival of Traditional Parties." *European Journal of Political Research* 24 (1993): 121–33.

Mair, Stefan. "Germany's Stiftungen and Democracy Assistance: Comparative Advantages, New Challenges." In *Democracy Assistance: International Co-operation for Democratization*. Edited by Peter Burnell. London: Frank Cass, 2000.

Management Systems International. *Evaluation of the Activities of the International Republican Institute and the National Democratic Institute in Albania, Bulgaria, Ukraine, and Lithuania*. Washington, D.C.: MSI, April 1996.

Management Systems International and International Foundation for Elections Systems. *Women in Politics: An Analysis of Donor Strategies*. Washington, D.C.: U.S. Agency for International Development Global Bureau Center for Democracy and Governance, 1998.

Manikas, Peter M., and Laura L. Thornton. *Political Parties in Asia*. Washington, D.C.: National Democratic Institute for International Affairs, 2003.

Manning, Carrie L. "Assessing African Party Systems after the Third Wave." *Party Politics* 11, no. 6 (November 2005): 77–127.

———. *The Politics of Peace in Mozambique: Post-Conflict Democratization, 1992–2000*. Westport, CT: Praeger, 2002.

Marsh, Ian, Jean Blondel, and Takashi Inoguchi, eds. *Democracy, Governance, and Economic Performance: East and Southeast Asia*. New York: United Nations University Press, 1999.

Mazur, Amy. "The Impact of Women's Participation and Leadership on Policy Outcomes: A Focus on Women's Policy Machineries." UN doc no. EGM/EPWD/2005/EP.5 (December 12, 2005).

Mbaku, John Mukum, and Julius O. Ihonvbere. *Multiparty Democracy and Political Change: Constraints to Democratization in Africa*. Burlington, VT: Ashgate Publishing, 1998.

McFaul, Michael. *Party Formation and Non-Formation in Russia*. Working Paper no. 12. Washington, D.C.: Carnegie Endowment, May 2000.

———. "Political Parties." In *Between Dictatorship and Democracy: Russian Post-Communist Political Reform*. Edited by Michael McFaul, Nikolai Petrov, and Andrei Ryabov. Washington, D.C.: Carnegie Endowment, 2004.

———. "Transitions from Post-Communism." *Journal of Democracy* 16, no. 3 (July 2005): 5–20.

McMahon, Edward R. "Catching the 'Third Wave' of Democratization? Debating Political Party Effectiveness in Africa since 1980." *African and Asian Studies* 3, no. 3/4 (2004): 295–320.

Mendelson, Sarah. "Democracy Assistance and Political Transition in Russia." *International Security* 25, no. 4 (Spring 2001): 68–106.

Michels, Robert. *Political Parties: A Sociological Study of the Oligarchical Tendencies of Modern Democracy.* New York: Hearst's International Library, 1915.

Miller, Arthur H., and Thomas F. Klobucar. "The Development of Party Identification in Post-Soviet Societies." *American Journal of Political Science* 44, no. 4 (October 2000): 667–85.

Millard, Frances. *Elections, Parties and Representation in Post-Communist Europe.* Hampshire, UK: Palgrave, 2004.

Mitra, Subrata K., Mike Enskat, and Clemens Spiess, eds. *Political Parties in South Asia.* Westport, CT: Praeger, 2004.

Moreno, Alejandro. *Political Cleavages: Issues, Parties and Consolidation of Democracy.* Boulder, CO: Westview Press, 1999.

Morrison, Minion K. C. "Political Parties in Ghana through Four Republics: A Path to Democratic Consolidation." *Comparative Politics* (July 2004): 421–41.

Mozaffar, Shaheen, and James R. Scarritt. "The Puzzle of African Party Systems." *Party Politics* 11, no. 4 (July 2005): 399–421.

Muravchik, Joshua. "U.S. Political Parties Abroad." *Washington Quarterly* 12, no. 3 (Summer 1989): 91–100.

Myers, Steven Lee. "Bringing Down Europe's Last Ex-Soviet Dictator." *New York Times Sunday Magazine*, February 26, 2006, 48.

National Democratic Institute for International Affairs. *Bolivia's Political Party System and the Incentives for Pro-Poor Reform.* Washington, D.C.: National Democratic Institute, 2005.

———. *Funding of Political Parties: An International Comparative Study.* Washington, D.C.: National Democratic Institute, 1998.

———. *Nominating for Change: Strengthening Women's Position in Political Parties.* Jakarta and Washington, D.C.: National Democratic Institute, 2003.

———. *Peru's Political Party System and the Promotion of Pro-Poor Reform.* Washington, D.C.: National Democratic Institute, 2005.

———. *Political Party Accountability: Principles and Realities.* Washington, D.C.: National Democratic Institute, 2003.

Nelson, Barbara, and Najma Chowdhury, eds. *Women and Politics Worldwide.* New Haven, CT: Yale University Press, 1994.

Netherlands Institute for Multiparty Democracy. *Political Institutions Interactive Assessment.* The Hague: Netherlands Institute for Multiparty Democracy, 2005.

Öhman, Magnus. *The Heart and Soul of the Party: Candidate Selection in Ghana and Africa.* Uppsala, Sweden: Uppsala University, 2004.

Open Society Justice Initiative. *Monitoring Election Campaign Finance: A Handbook for NGOs.* New York: Open Society Institute, 2005.

Owen, Roger. *State, Power, and Politics in the Making of the Modern Middle East,* 2nd ed. New York: Routledge, 2000.

Panebianco, Angelo. *Political Parties: Organization and Power.* New York: Cambridge University Press, 1988.

Pinto-Duschinsky, Michael. "Financing Politics: A Global View." *Journal of Democracy* 13, no. 4 (October 2002): 69–85.

———. "Foreign Political Aid: The German Political Foundations and Their U.S. Counterparts." *International Affairs* 67, no. 1 (1991): 33–63.

Plasser, Fritz, and Gunda Plasser. *Global Political Campaigning: A Worldwide Analysis of Campaign Professionals and Their Practices.* Westport, CT: Praeger, 2002.

Poguntke, Thomas. "Anti-Party Sentiment: Conceptual Thoughts and Empirical Evidence: Explorations in a Minefield." *European Journal of Political Research* 29 (1996): 319–44.

———. "New Politics and Party Systems." *West European Politics* 10 (1987): 76–88.

Pridham, Geoffrey. "Complying with the European Union's Democratic Conditionality: Transnational Party Linkages and Regime Change in Slovakia, 1993–1998." *Europe-Asia Studies* 51, no. 7 (November 1999): 1221–44.

Pridham, Geoffrey, and Attila Ágh, eds. *Prospects for Democratic Consolidation in East-Central Europe.* New York: Manchester University Press, 2001.

Rae, Douglas W. *The Political Consequences of Electoral Laws,* rev. ed. New Haven, CT: Yale University Press, 1972.

Rai, Shirin M. *International Perspectives on Gender and Democratisation.* New York: St. Martin's Press, 2000.

Randall, Vicky. "Party Systems and Voter Alignments in the New Democracies of the Third World." In *Party Systems and Voter Alignments Revisited.* Edited by Lauri Karvonen and Stein Kuhnle. London: Routledge, 2000.

———. "Political Parties and Social Structure in the Developing World." In *Handbook of Party Politics.* Edited by Richard Katz and William Crotty. Thousand Oaks, CA: Sage Publishing, 2005.

Randall, Vicky, and Lars Svåsand. "Party Institutionalization in New Democracies." *Party Politics* 8, no. 1 (2002): 5–29.

———. "Political Parties and Democratic Consolidation in Africa." *Democratization* 9, no. 3 (Autumn 2002): 30–52.

Reeve, Andrew, and Alan Ware. *Electoral Systems: A Comparative and Theoretical Introduction.* London: Routledge, 1992.

Reilly, Benjamin. *Political Parties and Political Engineering in the Asia Pacific Region.* Honolulu, HI: East-West Center, 2003.

Reynolds, Andrews, Ben Reilly, and Andrew Ellis. *Electoral System Design: The New International IDEA Handbook.* Stockholm: International IDEA, 2005.

Roberts, Kenneth, and Erik Wibbels. "Party Systems and Electoral Volatility in Latin America: A Test of Economic, Institutional, and Structural Explanations." *American Political Science Review* 93, no. 3 (September 1999): 575–90.

Rose, Richard, and Neil Munro. *Elections and Parties in New European Democracies.* Washington, D.C.: Congressional Quarterly Press, 2003.

Rudolph, Susanne Hoeber, and Lloyd I. Rudolph. "New Dimensions of Indian Democracy." *Journal of Democracy* 13, no. 1 (January 2002): 52–66.

Sabatini, Christopher. "The Decline of Ideology and the Rise of 'Quality of Politics' Parties in Latin America." *World Affairs* (Fall 2002): 106–10.

———. "Latin America's Lost Illusions: Decentralization and Political Parties." *Journal of Democracy* 14, no. 2 (April 2003): 138–50.

———. "Whom Do International Donors Support in the Name of Civil Society?" *Development in Practice* 12, no.1 (February 2002): 7–19.

Sachsenröder, Wolfgang, and Ulrike E. Frings, eds. *Political Party Systems and Democratic Developments in East and Southeast Asia: Vol II, East Asia.* Aldershot, UK, and Burlington, VT: Ashgate Publishing, 1997.

Salih, M. A. Mohamed, ed. *African Political Parties: Evolution, Institutionalism and Governance.* London: Pluto Press, 2003.

Sartori, Giovanni. *Comparative Constitutional Engineering: An Inquiry into Structures, Incentives and Outcomes,* 2nd ed. New York: New York University Press, 1997.

———. *Parties and Party Systems: A Framework for Analysis,* vol. 1. Cambridge: Cambridge University Press, 1976.

Schlumberger, Oliver. "The Arab Middle East and the Question of Democratization: Some Critical Remarks." *Democratization* 5, no. 4 (Winter 2000): 104–32.

Schmitter, Philippe C. "Parties Are Not What They Once Were." In *Political Parties and Democracy.* Edited by Larry Diamond and Richard Gunther. Baltimore: Johns Hopkins University Press, 2001.

Smyth, Regina. "Strong Partisans, Weak Parties? Party Organizations and the Development of Mass Partisanship in Russia." *Comparative Politics* 38, no. 2 (January 2006): 209–28.

Southall, Roger. *Democracy in Africa: Moving Beyond a Difficult Legacy.* Pretoria, South Africa: HSRC Publishers, 2003.

Stepan, Alfred, and Cindy Skach. "Constitutional Frameworks and Democratic Consolidation: Parliamentarism versus Presidentialism." *World Politics* 46 (1993): 1–22.

Stockton, Hans. "Political Parties, Party Systems, and Democracy in East Asia: Lessons from Latin America." *Comparative Political Studies* 34, no. 1 (Summer 2003): 1–39.

Sung, Hung-En. "From Victims to Saviors? Women, Power and Corruption." *Current History* 105, no. 689 (March 2006): 139–43.

Suttner, Raymond. "Transformation of Political Parties in Africa Today." *Transformation: Critical Perspectives on South Africa* 55 (2004): 1–27.

Szczerbiak, Aleks, and Séan Hanley. *Centre-Right Parties in Post-Communist East-Central Europe.* Abingdon: Taylor and Francis, 2004.

Tachau, Frank, ed. *Political Parties of the Middle East and North Africa.* Westport, CT: Greenwood Press, 1994.

Tan, Paige Johnson. "Anti-Party Reaction in Indonesia: Causes and Implications." *Contemporary Southeast Asia* 24, no. 3 (December 2002): 484–508.

Toole, James. "Straddling the East-West Divide: Party and Communist Legacies in East Central Europe." *Europe-Asia Studies* 55, no. 1 (January 2003): 101–18.

Tworzecki, Hubert. *Learning to Choose: Electoral Politics in East Central Europe.* Stanford: Stanford University Press, 2003.

United Nations Development Programme. *A Handbook on Working with Political Parties.* New York: United Nations Development Programme, 2006.

United States Agency for International Development. *Money in Politics Handbook: A Guide to Increasing Transparency in Emerging Democracies.* Washington, D.C.: USAID, 2003.

———. *USAID Political Party Assistance Policy.* Washington, D.C.: September 2003.

———. *USAID Political Party Development Assistance.* Washington, D.C.: USAID Center for Democracy and Governance, April 1999.

Van Biezen, Ingrid. "On the Theory and Practice of Party Formation and Adaptation in New Democracies." *European Journal of Political Research* 44 (2005): 147–74.

———. *Political Parties in New Democracies: Party Organization in Southern and East-Central Europe.* Basingstoke, New York: Palgrave Macmillan, 2003.

Van Cott, Donna Lee. *From Movements to Parties in Latin America: The Evolution of Ethnic Politics.* Cambridge: Cambridge University Press, 2005.

Van de Walle, Nicolas. "Presidentialism and Clientelism in Africa's Emerging Party Systems." *Journal of Modern African Studies* 42, no. 2 (2003): 297–321.

Van Wersch, Jos, and Jereon de Zeeuw. *Mapping European Democracy Assistance.* Working Paper no. 36. The Hague: Netherlands Institute of International Relations, November 2005.

Walecki, Marcin. *Political Money and Corruption.* IFES Political Finance White Paper Series. Washington, D.C.: IFES, 2004.

Ware, Alan. *Political Parties and Party Systems.* New York: Oxford University Press, 1995.

Wattenberg, Martin P. *The Decline of American Political Parties, 1952–1996.* Cambridge, MA: Harvard University Press, 1998.

Way, Lucan. "Pluralism by Default in Moldova." *Journal of Democracy* 13, no. 4 (October 2002): 127–41.

White, David. *The Russian Democratic Party Yabloko: Opposition in a Managed Democracy.* Burlington, VT: Ashgate Publishing, 2006.

Wickham, Carrie Rosefsky. *Mobilizing Islam: Religion, Activism, and Political Change in Egypt.* New York: Columbia University Press, 2002.

Willis, Michael J. "Political Parties in the Maghrib: The Illusion of Significance?" *The Journal of North African Studies* 7, no. 2 (Summer 2002): 1–22.

Wolinetz, Steven. *Party Systems.* Hampshire, UK: Ashgate Publishing, 1998.

Wolinetz, Steven B. "Beyond the Catch-All Party: Approaches to the Study of Parties and Party Organization in Contemporary Democracies." In *Political Parties: Old Concepts and New Challenges.* Edited by Richard Gunther, José Ramón Montero, and Juan J. Linz. Oxford: Oxford University Press, 2002.

Index

About the Author

Thomas Carothers is vice president for international politics and governance at the Carnegie Endowment for International Peace and founder and director of the Democracy and Rule of Law Project. A leading authority on democratization and democracy promotion, he has worked on democracy programs for twenty years with many U.S., European, and international organizations and carried out extensive field research on democracy building around the world. He has written or edited eight books on democracy promotion, including *Promoting the Rule of Law Abroad: The Problem of Knowledge* (Carnegie Endowment, 2006), *Uncharted Journey: Promoting Democracy in the Middle East* (Carnegie Endowment, 2005), and *Critical Mission: Essays on Democracy Promotion* (Carnegie Endowment, 2004). He has also published many articles on the subject in major journals and newspapers. He is a recurrent visiting professor at the Central European University in Budapest and has lectured at universities in many countries.

Prior to joining the Carnegie Endowment, Carothers was an attorney at Arnold & Porter in Washington, D.C., and in the Office of the Legal Adviser of the U.S. Department of State. He has also been an International Affairs Fellow of the Council on Foreign Relations. He is a graduate of Harvard Law School, the London School of Economics, and Harvard College.

Carnegie Endowment
for International Peace

The Carnegie Endowment for International Peace is a private, nonprofit organization dedicated to advancing cooperation between nations and promoting active international engagement by the United States. Founded in 1910, Carnegie is nonpartisan and dedicated to achieving practical results.

Through research, publishing, convening and, on occasion, creating new institutions and international networks, Endowment associates shape fresh policy approaches. Their interests span geographic regions and the relations between governments, business, international organizations, and civil society, focusing on the economic, political, and technological forces driving global change. Through its Carnegie Moscow Center, the Endowment helps to develop a tradition of public policy analysis in the states of the former Soviet Union and to improve relations between Russia and the United States. The Endowment publishes *Foreign Policy*, one of the world's leading journals of international politics and economics, which reaches readers in more than 120 countries and in several languages.

Officers
Jessica T. Mathews, *President*
Paul Balaran, *Executive Vice President and Secretary*
Thomas Carothers, *Vice President for Studies*
Mark Medish, *Vice President for Studies*
George Perkovich, *Vice President for Studies*
Peter Reid, *Vice President for Communications*

Board of Trustees
James C. Gaither, *Chairman*
Gregory B. Craig, *Vice Chairman*
Bill Bradley
Robert Carswell
Jerome A. Cohen
Richard A. Debs
William H. Donaldson
Roger Ferguson
Donald V. Fites
William W. George
Richard Giordano
Jamie Gorelick

Stephen D. Harlan
Donald Kennedy
Robert Legvold
Stephen R. Lewis, Jr.
William M. Lewis, Jr.
Jessica T. Mathews
Zanny Minton Beddoes
Olara A. Otunnu
W. Taylor Reveley III
J. Stapleton Roy
Shirley M. Tilghman

A CARNEGIE ENDOWMENT BOOK

Confronting the Weakest Link

Aiding Political Parties in New Democracies

Confronting the Weakest Link is the first systematic, independent assessment of the burgeoning field of international aid to political parties. Carothers' masterful, searching account is critical and sobering, yet also sympathetic and constructive.

—LARRY DIAMOND, HOOVER INSTITUTION, STANFORD UNIVERSITY

A timely, original study that illuminates not only international aid for political parties but also the dynamics of political party development generally. Carothers goes well beyond the standard laments and prescriptions about the troubled state of political parties in the world to offer insights and approaches that will stir scholars and provoke practitioners.

—CHRISTOPHER SABATINI, AMERICAS SOCIETY/COUNCIL OF THE AMERICAS

Political parties are the weakest link in many democratic transitions around the world—frequently beset with persistent problems of self-interest, corruption, ideological incoherence, and narrow electoralism. A large and ever-growing number of U.S., European, and multilateral assistance programs seek to help parties become effective prodemocratic actors. But given the depth of the problems, is success possible?

Confronting the Weakest Link is a pathbreaking study of international aid for political parties. Beginning with a penetrating analysis of party shortcomings in developing and postcommunist countries, Thomas Carothers draws on extensive field research to diagnose deficiencies in party aid, assess its overall impact, and offer practical ideas for doing better. This broad-ranging analysis, which spans Latin America, Central and Eastern Europe, the former Soviet Union, Africa, the Middle East, and Asia, sheds invaluable light on a major element of the contemporary challenge of democracy-building, a subject now occupying center stage in the international policy arena.

THOMAS CAROTHERS is vice president for international politics and governance at the Carnegie Endowment for International Peace and founder and director of the Endowment Democracy and Rule of Law Project.

CARNEGIE ENDOWMENT
for International Peace

www.CarnegieEndowment.org

ISBN-13: 978-0-87003-224-0
ISBN-10: 0-87003-224-0

52295 >

9 780870 032240

EAN